*Foundations of
American
Independence
1763-1815*

Foundations of American Independence

1763-1815

J. R. POLE

Fontana/Collins

First published by The Bobbs-Merrill Company, Inc.
in the United States of America 1972
First issued in Fontana 1973
Design: Starr Atkinson

Copyright J. R. Pole, 1973

Printed in Great Britain
For the publishers Wm. Collins Sons & Co Ltd
Collins Clear-Type Press
London and Glasgow

To Joe and Phoebe Pole

Contents

Maps

Acknowledgments

The bulk of this book was written during a fruitful winter at the Center for Advanced Study in the Behavioral Sciences at Stanford, California. I am deeply conscious of my debt of gratitude to the officers of the center, particularly O. Meredith Wilson, Preston S. Cutler, and Jane Kielsmeier, for the opportunities they so liberally conferred on me. I want also to express my thanks to Priscilla Jones for her inestimably useful aid, and, here at Cambridge, to Susan Knight, who typed the manuscript (less one chapter) in twelve days.

Many years of discussion with colleagues have contributed to the judgments in this book, making it difficult to single out particular debts. The manuscript has gained distinctively from the editorial comments of Jack P. Greene, James M. Banner, Jr., and Keith Berwick, and I am particularly grateful to my wife and to David Cairns for comments that have helped to shape and clarify the text. The argument of this book differs from others in some respects, and I must, as is usual, affirm my own responsibility for the interpretations about which my helpers may not have agreed and for which they must be exempted from blame.

This is not intended as a conventional textbook. I have not acquainted the reader with everything he might be expected to know about the period, but have aimed at opening broad lines of interpretation, from which I hope that further reading and even animated discussion will follow. This aim explains much by way of omission and the handling of certain themes. I have expounded what appear to me to be the leading issues; the rest of the work is in the hands of the reader.

J.R.P.

Churchill College,
Cambridge, England

Eastern North America in 1763

Introduction

The Peace of Paris, which in 1763 brought to an end the great wars that had ravaged both Europe and the European possessions in North America, was, among other things, a British victory. It was, moreover, a victory in which Britain's American colonists were keenly conscious of having shared the honors on their continent. The terms of the settlement did not please everyone in Britain; John Wilkes, with the hilarious profanity that was soon to become better known, likened it to the Peace of God, "which passeth all understanding," and, what was more serious, William Pitt was gravely dissatisfied. For the Americans, the satisfaction of the peace quickly gave way to a new and threatening paradox.

From the colonial viewpoint, the greatest immediate gain was the removal of French sovereignty and military power from Canada and the Mississippi Valley. The presence of France had long acted as a restraint on the freedom with which the British colonists could expect to move out into the depths of the continent, and the danger of French expansion made them disagreeably dependent on British protection. These circumstances applied particularly to New England, and it had long been clear to European observers that if the French were ever removed, the New England colonies would be likely to show a greater propensity toward independence in their relations with Britain. The vacancy created by the collapse of France, however, was not merely an invitation to the British colonists; it presented to the British administration an equally compelling invitation to develop a general policy for the American colonies.

Influential spokesmen with a knowledge of the colonies had been demanding new policies. A long series of parliamentary acts had already given indications of British interest in exerting more effective control, which might be advanced if an energetic administration were confronted with a favorable opportunity. With the opening of a possible power vacuum, opportunity became nearly identical with necessity. In this situation, the British began to impose policies on North America about which the colonists were at best only cursorily consulted but which dramatically affected their view of their own prospects for developing the continent and their society. The implementation of these policies began in 1763 with a royal proclamation prohibiting further migration across the line formed by the Appalachian ridge. It continued with laws to raise taxes on imports from the West Indies to North America—the Revenue or "Sugar" Act of 1764—and then, far more general and crucial, to impose a stamp tax (1765) throughout the British colonies. After the Stamp Act had been repealed in 1766, a further round of duties was imposed in 1767. All these taxes, beginning with those levied under the Revenue Act, had been accompanied by far-reaching provisions for their collection.

In organizing a general, colony-wide resistance to these impositions, which they believed to be unconstitutional encroachments on their liberties as British subjects, the colonists discovered among themselves a degree of collective identity whose existence they had hardly suspected. The idea that the inhabitants of these widely separated colonies might share a common identity, more colonial than British and more American than merely colonial, was perhaps not entirely new. It is scarcely likely, however, that the idea would have gained the force required to make a new nation had it not been for the unifying influence of resistance to Britain. Many factors may tend to bring separate peoples together, but nothing unifies so rapidly as a common enemy.

The Americans were a diffused, agricultural, slow-moving people. For the most part, they saw little of central government, paid few taxes, and were accustomed to leaving the control of affairs to a fairly stable, recognized leadership that had proved generally capable and responsible. The later colonial period was not one of homegrown democracy, but it was emphatically an era of political capability. This competent, seasoned leadership soon learned both to confront the British and to instruct and rally the people of the colonies.

The foundations of American independence lay in the structure and quality of American society. In order to build on those foundations, however, Americans had to acquaint themselves with government. If they were not to govern themselves they would soon be governed from abroad, in a manner that promised not to be to their liking. Even before legalistic remonstrances and economic sanctions had finally failed, and fighting had broken out in April 1775, the colonists were obliged to organize a far more systematic and effective government than they had ever experienced before. The Continental Congress took charge of a full range of operations required to raise armies, mobilize the colonies, and conduct a complex foreign diplomacy. It was a further paradox of American efforts at self-defense that in order to resist the encroachments of a distant but powerful governmental machine, they were compelled to bring one of their own into existence.

American society—it was, at the time, more like an assortment of American societies—was thus forced to realize its own identity through the exigencies of political action. Moreover, if anything like a single society was to remain in being, that action had to be sustained on a continental scale. A lapse in energy followed the successful outcome of the War of Independence, but the threat of a real dissolution of the fragile structure of continental government was so serious that new efforts were soon forthcoming. Led by men of continental vision and seasoned abilities, these new efforts brought the Constitution of the United States into being and secured its ratification by a half-informed, and largely skeptical, populace.

America, to an extent undreamed of twenty years earlier, had been unified by these efforts; but unified for what purposes? Under the potent leadership of Alexander Hamilton, the new administration began harnessing the resources of government to give the American economy a new direction. The aim was now to create a society that looked toward a full participation in international commerce and that would eventually develop its own industrial resources; it would be a society moving rapidly in capital development, under the strong guidance of a clearly marked aristocracy of wealth. These aims contravened the vision of innumerable farmers and planters, whose main ambition for American development was that their basically agricultural society should spread gradually into the new West, without any violent

change in government or social structure. Thomas Jefferson
emerged as the unmistakable leader and spokesman of these
conservative agrarian interests, who still believed in local government, and, as far as possible, in weak and limited government.

History, however, would not leave America alone. Early in the
nineteenth century, Europe threatened to resume its ambitions
on the American continent. The great French Revolutionary and
Napoleonic wars raged in Europe and lashed the Atlantic trade
routes. The United States might be neutral, but it could not be
isolated. By 1812, in defense of its newfound independence, the
nation was at war, once again, with Britain. The end of that
war in 1815 left the Americans with the great continent at their
feet.

The unity which I have ascribed to the period of this book owes
its formal character to the peace treaties with which it begins
and ends. The close of the Seven Years' War (the French and
Indian War) in 1763 led to the problems that provide the
substance of this book; the Treaty of Ghent (1815), which concluded the War of 1812 between the United States and Britain,
set the Americans free to immerse themselves in their own continent. In the intervening years, the American people achieved
their independence, established a federal Constitution, and, by
organizing a workable order of politics, secured the social and
economic basis for the development of the continent.

These great events were the results of political action, and
American society in this period can be understood only through
an appreciation of its political manifestations. Yet this lifetime
of ferment had surprisingly little effect on the style and pace of
the lives of farming families scattered over large sections of the
nation. Methods of agriculture had changed only slightly, and
the distribution of wealth remained much as it had been in
earlier generations.

There would have been scant hope of holding such an enormous territory together by the ancient methods of communication; it was the development of steam power that did as much
as any political policy to sustain the hopes of a continental Union.
By that time, however, a new threat had materialized—not from

outside enemies but from internal fissures. The United States had never been a united nation. At its most complete it was a somewhat loosely knit and ambiguous federal republic. The ambiguity was not there by mere oversight or mischance, but represented real and ominous divisions between parts that had never been closely joined and had even threatened to prevent the federal structure from taking shape. As early as 1774, differences between colonies heavily dependent on slavery and colonies north of the Mason-Dixon Line caused difficulties in the Continental Congress; these divisions flared up again both during and after the making of the Constitution in 1787.

Within a few years of the successful termination of the dangers from across the Atlantic, the expansion of slavery led straight to a constitutional crisis, resolved temporarily by the joint admission of the states of Missouri and Maine (1820–1821). For more than a generation, the continent would prove large enough to contain the conflict. But neither space nor constitutional agreements could stall indefinitely the furious onslaught of America's conflicting developments, which led, ineluctably, to a collision over fundamental principles.

Foundations
of
American Independence

1763–1815

1

American Colonists: British Sovereignty

At the time of the Peace of Paris the American colonists were already many peoples. A population map in 1763 colored to show the derivation of the different groups would have startled the eye by the richness of the variety of European and African sources that had given rise, in one or more generations, to this new people. These color patches, however, would have shaded into the dominant color representing the British stocks—English, Welsh, Scottish, and Scotch-Irish. All these national groups differed from one another in religion, in language, in methods by which they cultivated the soils, and in many of the assumptions and manners that governed their social and political conduct. Moreover, the populations from individual countries were sometimes as sharply divided among themselves as they were with other national groups. But a colored map, being static, would have failed to reveal the processes that were slowly transforming them all, eroding their boundaries and changing them, including those of British origin, into an American people, or perhaps—it was early yet to take such views —into a variety of American peoples.

The colonists were by definition subjects of the British crown, which meant that they were members of the British nation, theoretically enjoying a constitutional status fully equal to that of their fellow subjects in Britain. But some were more conscious of this relationship than others, and the differences were significant. In some cases the relationship was claimed with pride, in others it was regarded with skepticism or anxiety. At all levels, colonists who were aware of the British connection were quick to affirm it as the source of their constitutional rights and liberties. Yet the English social system, with the aspirations and values that it implied, tended to be somewhat more admired among the leaders of the southern colonies than among those of the Northeast, particularly New England.

The names of the colonies gave a clue to their historical identities, which were not without bearing on their attitudes toward the mother country. The Indian names of Massachusetts and Connecticut acknowledged no debt to England, although town and county names did immediately reproduce many that had long been familiar to the early settlers, principally from East Anglia. The religious Separatists who had sought in New England a place of safety for a Puritan church had always regarded the Church of England with hostility, and the close affinity between the religious and the political leadership in these colonies had served for more than a century to keep alive a wary suspicion of British political motives. Events in recent wars, such as the colonists' capture in 1745 of the French fort of Louisbourg in Nova Scotia, had stimulated an intense local pride, which was bitterly aggrieved when that prize was restored to France at the Treaty of Aix-la-Chapelle in 1748.

New England's political geography had greatly changed since the first settlements, though even the family farms and highly self-sufficient town governments that were spreading deep into the interior reproduced some aspects of agriculture and local government in England. The domination of the great estates, however, was missing. So, too, was the titled aristocracy and the Church of England. In place of an aristocracy, a prosperous class of farmers and merchants, whose rank in England would have corresponded to that of the gentry, exercised a self-assured but easygoing control. The church recognized, and formally "established," by the colonial governments was that of the Congregationalists. Each town was responsible for the maintenance of its own religious observances, which included the support of a minister, and many towns also paid for the hire of a schoolmaster. These largely independent town congregations were held together in a loose federation that lacked the central authority to be found under the episcopal system—or even, to an extent, under the Presbyterian synods. Thus, in religious matters as in local government—both of which were often conducted in the same meetinghouse—the townsmen had got used to a measure of independence that they believed to be theirs by right as well as by habit.

In the New England provinces, as elsewhere in the colonies, life in the coastal towns was distinctly different from that on the farm-lands of the interior, even though much of that interior was barely more than a hundred miles away in any direction. Boston, with some 15,000 inhabitants by the middle of the century, was the largest of these port towns, which carried on a diversity of trade and other activities that connected them with the farmers, with other colonies by coastal routes, and, by overseas commerce, with England. The shipyards were busy, the harbors were often crowded with masts, and the needs of a town population supported an increasingly sophisticated, and therefore specialized, economy. But specialization had not gone far, and many businessmen not only sold an assortment of goods but carried on several kinds of busi-nesses, among which lending money at interest was often prominent. The dust and rattle of Boston's streets might startle a visiting farmer, but in truth the pace of life left ample time for social visits, for walking round town and falling into conversations along the way, and for the evening society of the tavern, where gossip and news circulated.

New England country towns differed in size but were usually small clusters of houses, with a marketplace, a meetinghouse, and a tavern. The citizenry of the town, however, included the occu-pants of outlying farms, mostly supporting single families; they produced some of their own needs, and the rest could be supplied by trips once or twice a week to the market, where, in season, fruits and vegetables were abundant and fresh. These trips were occasions for indulging in the usual neighborly gossip, and as such were socially eventful. But the tempo of farm life was dictated by the movements of the oxen. Families spent their evenings together —unless a member ventured down to the tavern—and since spermaceti, readily available from the Nantucket whaling fleet, provided candle wax, there was time in the evenings for reading among a country population that could claim an unusually high rate of literacy.

Migrants pressing northward from Massachusetts Bay had al-ready founded the province to which they gave the English name of New Hampshire. Still earlier, Rhode Island (the name recalled the Greek island of Rhodes) had become a refuge from religious persecution, where Roger Williams and his successors steadfastly defended a religious toleration that in due course exposed its inhabitants to the necessity, and hence the advantage, of political tolerance. Connecticut was virtually a republic within the empire; as with Rhode Island, its charter gave it the right to elect its own governor. Both on the coast and in the rich valley of the Connecticut River, the popular spirit of self-reliance was as strong as in Massachusetts.

Southward of New England, the names of provinces celebrated English monarchs or proprietors, and it was not by chance that their inhabitants bore, admittedly in varying degrees, a more affirmative sense of the value of the British connection. Where New England had been founded as—or had almost immediately become—a polity that stood as an alternative to the English establishment, the other colonies in general represented a more positive continuity with their English founders. New England was indeed deeply English; its generic name said as much. Moreover, its population long remained far more exclusively English than those of other colonies. But New England was meant to be an England purged of what its founders believed to be the vices and corruptions of old England. New Englanders, consequently, lived in a state of permanent tension with the mother country. Their very existence and their proclaimed principles represented a kind of challenge, an alternative orthodoxy. They were not so much an expression of English enterprise, or an English investment, as another and in their opinion a morally superior England.

The Dutch, who had originally settled what became New York, retained their pockets of national and religious identity. The town of Albany, around 1750, had some five thousand Dutch-speaking inhabitants who frequented the Dutch Reformed Church. Albany had a bad reputation. "The avarice and selfishness of the inhabitants of *Albany,*" observed the Swedish botanist Peter Kalm, "are very well known throughout all *North America,* by the *English,* by the *French,* and even by the *Dutch,* in the lower part of *New York* province. If a Jew, who understands the art of getting forward perfectly well, should settle amongst them, they would not fail to ruin him. . . . I was here obliged to pay for everything twice, thrice, and four times as dear as in any part of *North America* which I have passed through. . . ."

While Albany, as Kalm's comment implies, was somewhat isolated, Dutch settlements played a full part in the normal economic and political life of the province. The estates of Dutch patroons dominated the Hudson River Valley much as those of the nobility dominated the countryside of Europe. New York, whose great river connected the fertile hinterland with the rising city at its mouth and with the Atlantic Ocean, was perhaps more like an independent European nation than any of the other American provinces. Its politics, however, did not divide clearly along lines of nationality or religion, but reflected the rivalry of great families, primarily that between the Livingstons and the De Lanceys, who depended heavily on the votes of their tenants and dependents at elections. All was not peace in the countryside, and again, in the strife between tenant farmers and landlords, which sometimes reached the proportions of armed revolt against rents and taxes, the social conflict suggested some of the struggles between peasant and lord in Europe.

New York had been named after its original English proprietor, the Duke of York, later to become King James II. New Jersey (originally East Jersey and West Jersey), Pennsylvania, and Maryland were all founded as proprietary provinces, in some measure reflecting the interests and ambitions of their founders. Pennsylvania was much the most complex, and in some ways it remarkably prefigured the characteristics of later American political life. After about 1720, the influx of the Northern Irish of Scottish descent, known as Scotch-Irish, and Germans, who came to be called "Pennsylvania Dutch," a corruption of *Deutsch,* transformed the structure of the population and created the earliest examples of the problems arising from mass immigration. The Quakers, who had always regarded the province as their own by right and by character, adroitly succeeded in winning enough German support to maintain their ascendancy in the colony's representative assembly. In the process they became a political party, which, by a tortured irony of the struggle for power, clashed bitterly with the interests of the province's proprietors, the Penn family. The Penns in turn sought the support not of the Quakers so much as the wealthy Anglicans of Philadelphia and the Presbyterian Scotch-Irish, who had settled the outlying and frontier sectors. The Scotch-

Irish, who were constantly pressing against the Indians, were the most aggressive and turbulent element of a mixed population that did not appear to be mixing well. But it was the Germans who caused Benjamin Franklin to fear that Pennsylvania would "in a few years become a German colony" if their influx were not checked. Peter Collinson, a prominent English Quaker, thought the Germans should be assimilated through English schools and inter-marriage, but Franklin, although he agreed that the Germans ought to be well treated, believed the racial repugnance was too engrained for people of English descent.

> The German Women [he wrote to Collinson] are generally so disagreeable to an English Eye, that it wou'd require great Portions to induce Englishmen to marry them. Nor would the German Ideas of Beauty generally agree with our women; *dick und starcke,* that is, *thick and strong,* always enters into their Description of a pretty Girl.

Franklin had an avowed preference for light skins. He thought there remained a chance "by excluding all Blacks and Tawneys, of increasing the lovely White and Red." That as early as 1755 Franklin had proposed a plan for arranging electoral districts in the manner that would later be called "gerrymandering," in order to keep the German influence under control, suggests the peculiar gift of Pennsylvania politics for anticipating the later problems of American democracy.

In these politics the British connection was of constant importance. By the end of the French and Indian War, the old Quaker party was Quaker only in name and residue; its leaders were the Congregationalist Franklin and the Anglican Joseph Galloway. The party was soon engaged in trying to wrest the territory from the Penns by persuading the crown to resume it as a royal province. This bitter struggle distracted the minds of the leaders from certain underlying realities with which they soon had to contend. The most formidable of these was the rise of discontent among the smaller traders and artisans (or "mechanics") of Philadelphia against the privileges of the wealthy commercial oligarchs who ruled the city. To the discontent among those in the city was allied a resentment amounting to enmity among many small farmers whose economic needs, particularly in facilities for marketing their produce, had long been ignored by the assembly. Augmenting the complaints of the small traders and farmers were those of the Scotch-Irish, who felt that the comfortable Quaker merchants dominating the assembly and professing pacifist ideals had neglected their need for security against the Indians.

Western Pennsylvania's troubles sprang from the different aims and methods of her new population. To the honorable Quaker record of peaceable dealings with the Indians, the Scotch-Irish opposed a violent animosity; Indian attacks occasionally desolated their farms and outposts, leaving trails of mutilated corpses of both sexes and all ages. Since the Scotch-Irish were bent on expansion, enmity was implicit in their relationship with the neighboring tribes. The pacifism and complacency of the assembly leadership, therefore, only infuriated them. In 1763 a group of ruffians massacred a small settlement of friendly Indians who were actually living under official protection at Conestoga Manor. Calling themselves the Paxton Boys, they then marched toward Philadelphia. Worthy Friends took fright and some even began to get the feel of muskets. Assembly leaders met the Paxton marchers at Germantown, and, after much parleying, a statement of grievances took the place of an invasion of the city. The assembly, having recovered its composure, let the issues slide and failed to appease western discontent, which coalesced with the rising indignation of the lower classes of Philadelphia. These groups soon found a voice among radical speakers and pamphleteers in that literate capital; a new radical party would be forged there in the same years in which the imperial crisis was coming to a head—and with dramatic results for the political structure of the province.

By 1760, Philadephia had twenty-two thousand citizens. It was fast becoming a center that would be equipped, when the time came, to be a new and greater capital. By 1775, it had in less than a century become one of the largest cities in the British Empire. Its population, by then forty thousand, was in a high degree industrious, literate, and argumentative, characteristics not always found together. "In this Country," Charles Thomson, a future radical leader, remarked, "almost every man is fond of reading, and seems to have a thirst for knowledge." The city contained seventy-seven bookstores, and Franklin. The merchant rulers lived spaciously enough, moved about in carriages, retired to country houses in the summer, and provoked as much envy as admiration. This resentment was to have grave political repercussions, about which the Philadelphia newspapers offered plenty of evidence. One bitter critic of the social structure asked, in the *Philadelphia Packet* in March 1776:

> Do not mechanicks and farmers constitute ninety-nine out of a hundred of the people of America? If these, by their occupations, are to be excluded from having any share in the choice of their rulers, or forms of government [a great exaggeration, incidentally!] would it not be best to acknowledge the jurisdiction of the British Parliament, which is composed entirely of GENTLEMEN? Is not half the property in the city of Philadelphia owned by men who wear LEATHERN APRONS? Does not the other half belong to men whose fathers or grandfathers wore LEATHERN APRONS?

Few people seem to have been really poor. But many resented the wealth and advantages of the upper classes, especially when these were linked to political privileges that were used in turn to widen the existing distinctions. City life had bred an egalitarian ethos in which even the claim to a form of aristocracy gave rise to politically dangerous resentment.

The three lower Pennsylvania counties began to be referred to as Delaware about 1745, and received a separate charter, while remaining under the Penns, in 1763. The Jerseys, East and West, though divided along a line still marked by Province Line Road, had, by 1763, acquired a single government. The northern counties, which had strong Dutch elements, gravitated toward New York. Those of the south fell under the influence of Philadelphia; Quaker settlements accentuated their affinity with that city. New Jersey's somewhat isolated farmers had no outlets of their own to compare with these two seaports.

Maryland and Virginia, named respectively after Charles I's queen Henrietta Maria and after Queen Elizabeth I, the virgin queen, like the provinces further south, also reflected English influence in their names. That influence represented a development, a fulfillment of English ambitions rather than a retreat from them. Tobacco had early contributed to the rise of these two provinces, for their planters found that they had a market in England and, through the English entrepôt to which their exports were subject, in Europe. But tobacco exhausted the soil, and before the Revolution the big planters had turned over many acres of their tired lands to wheat. This soil depletion had caused migrations and an incipient economic crisis that temporarily shook the confidence of the ruling class of great planters, who were also the magistrates and the lawgivers.

Since the late seventeenth century, Virginia's upper gentry had secured for themselves a reassuring degree of stable political control. They ruled their counties through oligarchic, self-appointed county courts, which did a substantial proportion of local-government work and were entirely free from the perils of elections. They ruled the church through the vestries, and they ruled the province as a whole through the assembly, where the foremost families maintained a quiet hold over the more important committees.

The upper gentry's style of life bore a conscious resemblance to that of the county families of England. The larger planters, who superintended the management of estates that produced for the export market but were mostly self-supporting in food, were heads of extensive families. They were also lords over their slaves. The family consisted of all the immediate dependents of the plantation, itself a sort of village. The slaves were not thought of as members of the family, but they were in every sense the responsibility of the planter, who had to ensure that they were fed and clothed, that their quarters were regulated, and that their work was productive.

Much of the social life of these estates was self-contained. The routine left time for music and dancing, for entertaining and for reading, which in that period was believed to improve the mind. When the wealthier planters entertained they did so grandly, with ostentatious indifference to expense. On the social occasions offered by county fairs, held at least annually, by market days, court days, and fox hunts, they usually mingled with their neighbors with an affability relatively free from ceremonial constraints. They were, however, acutely conscious of questions of social standing. They might have found it difficult to explain the precise criteria that determined such relationships, but on their own estates they enjoyed enough independence to command not only the deference of the tenant farmers and the humility of the free farmhands but the respect of their neighbors as well. In political arrangements they accepted the ordering of the system by which they lived, deferring in turn to men of older and greater estates or of acknowledged superiority in law and business.

The style was costly. Clothes were ordered from tailors in England, books and wines imported, and the wealthier frequently had their sons educated in England. The irritability displayed by these gentlemen in the face of slights on their dignity, real or imagined, was usually based on nothing more than what they deemed due their station in life. They also showed an intense susceptibility to provocation in matters that touched their economic lives and political independence, and this revealed something more than a rational interpretation of the British constitution. The trouble was that—especially after the mid-1750s—they were constantly and humiliatingly in debt, to the merchants who handled their crops and to the British who bought them and supplied their social needs; they could not bear to economize, even though their economic foundations were crumbling. Their proud independence, which they bore so finely in the county court, or when entertaining their friends and neighbors, was flawed by the corrupting state of need.

At the time of the Revolution it was widely whispered that many Virginia planters were determined on separation primarily to throw off the burden of their British debts. The accusation was largely unjustified, but it had enough sting to evoke a disavowal from Washington, who declared that he wanted no support from gentlemen with such motives. But ten years before independence, the death of John Robinson, who had long held the posts of speaker of the Virginia assembly and treasurer of the province, had exposed the extraordinary state to which the gentry had been reduced.

Robinson died in 1766. Rumors about his financial dealings could no longer be concealed, and the administrators of his estate, including Edmund Pendleton, later to be a judge of unquestioned integrity, were obliged to unravel his affairs. As treasurer, Robinson had received the paper currencies that British administrations had authorized during the wars but that were to be withdrawn from circulation in accordance with local and British currency laws. The effect of this unimaginative but orthodox financial policy was to reduce the amount of currency in circulation at a time when the needs of a growing population called for an expansion. Many planters were nearing desperation, and Robinson took advantage of his position to aid his friends—of whom he soon had many. What Robinson did was help the Tidewater planters refloat their affairs by issuing privately the currency that reached him in his official capacity. The extent of the debts that Pendleton's investigations exposed was enormous. The range of the operation, however, and its complexity, somewhat blurred the shock of the scandal. Though Pendleton kept the details from becoming public, many of the colony's first gentlemen and a number of persons of less considerable rank—were involved.

In extenuation of Robinson's conduct it can be argued that by setting himself up as a personal loan office he saved the economy during a crisis in which official policy was completely blind to real economic needs. In all probability he did save some important estates from ruin. Yet when he gave this advantage to some of his friends, he made it all the more necessary for others to avail themselves of the same copious resources. Unfortunately, the time they gained was used not for the reform of their farming methods so much as the extension of their speculations. The Robinson affair helps to explain the predatory ferocity with which the greater planters of the South leaped on the unexploited lands to the west. Some of the most tangled and difficult issues of revolutionary and postwar policy were to arise over the claims of great land speculators, who were often great politicians.

If Robinson had given the upper gentry a breather, he had also shaken the composure of the state. Although the Virginian leadership did not materially alter in its style or policy, it did prove more responsive to pressures that came socially from below and geographically from the west. The composition of committees in the House of Burgesses began to reflect these trends. Elections were more hotly contested, and in certain cases established members had to fight for their seats. Nevertheless, in spite of the tremors, the traditional rulers of Virginia retained a firm enough command of the dominion's politics to steer it into independence. When they divided, over issues like land reform and religious freedom, the opposing sides were dominated by members of the same class—and it is significant that Jefferson's more radical proposals for extending the suffrage failed to gather any wide measure of socially impressive support. Even after the war, with all the changes of fortune, the wartime losses of slaves and property, and the rise of new political figures, the surface of Virginia society was more remarkable for its continuity with the past than for any radical innovations.

The Carolinas, named after King Charles I, and the recently founded colony of Georgia, named after King George II, presented certain contrasts with each other and with Virginia. North Carolina, which lacked a first-rate harbor, had earlier been relatively poor and sparsely populated, although it became the fastest growing colony between the years 1750 and 1776. Still, it remained a colony of small and middling farmers with no important urban centers and without the pretensions of its neighbors. South Carolina had the advantage, in the port of Charleston, of the only important mercantile city of the southern provinces; by 1776, Charleston had a population of some twelve thousand, the biggest concentration of people anywhere south of Philadelphia. Rice, indigo, and slavery had made its planters rich, and riches quickly gained had made many of them arrogant.

In both Carolinas the more substantial men of the Tidewater plantations controlled the provincial assemblies, where they showed little sympathy with the struggles of the poorer settler who had more recently moved into the Piedmont. The people of the South Carolina backcountry petitioned their legislators in 1766 for protection against the rapacious thieves and bandits who had begun to prey on their settlements. Their rulers ignored their demand for law and order, and, in the following year, armed and organized as "Regulators," they took charge of their own defense. The British governor, Lord Charles Greville Montagu, sensing a threat to established power, attempted to suppress these technically lawless activities. It was due to the sympathy of the lieutenant governor, William Bull, a native Carolinian, that these grievances were eventually redressed and a system of courts established.

The situation was different in North Carolina where, by 1768, grievances against unequal tax burdens, against the unfair administration of justice, and against a government in which their voices were largely unheard had driven western settlers into revolt, also under the name "Regulators." Governor William Tryon, who had considerable sympathy for the Regulators, welcomed the outcome of assembly elections in which the dissidents made decisive gains; when the new majority turned its attention to denouncing Britain, however, he dissolved the assembly, after which disorder returned to the west. In the spring of 1771 he at length led a small force that scattered the rebels at Alamance Creek; it was a trifling military action, but lives were lost in the battle and rebel leaders hanged before quiet was imposed on the backcountry. When Carolinian assembly leaders called for resistance to British tyranny a few years later, some former Regulators remembered a tyranny nearer home and gave their support to Great Britain.

All the southern colonies were profoundly rural, and in each the life of the planters and their dependents was in a large measure lonely. In contrast with the northeastern colonies, those of the South were almost destitute of towns, and of the complexities and subtleties that town life bred in its citizens and diffused through the surrounding countryside. Williamsburg, the capital of Virginia in the colonial period, was a mere village of some fifteen hundred people at the time of the Revolution. Its little College of William and Mary was the only institution of its kind in the southern colonies. The small size and quiet life of Virginia's capital city gain significance in comparison with the size of the province—or "dominion"—whose five hundred thousand inhabitants made it, at the outbreak of the War of Independence, the most populous of all the mainland colonies. The one regular event that drew people together was the county court session, a great occasion for meeting, bargaining, speech-making, and drinking. Sporting events, particularly horse racing, also drew people together and gave rise to great contests and heavy wagering; the pulse of life so often languid in the intense and humid heat, and dulled by the intractable loneliness of the countryside, quickened when men and women gathered for argument and play.

Much of the business side of Virginian plantation life was channeled through the Scottish factors, whose center was Norfolk; these indispensable agents of the economy by which the planters lived were as unpopular as the handlers of other men's money and trade usually are. The better-placed plantations lay alongside creeks and inlets where loading and unloading could take place for the estate itself. These conveniences diminished the interest of wealthier owners in promoting the growth of towns to handle trade and business and contributed to the self-sufficiency in which they could dwell at home. Travel by road was often precarious, especially in winter and spring. The style of life or interests of the men whose power and example might have led to economic improvement gave them little incentive to spend money on maintaining roads or other public improvements or in any significant way to transform the scene from one year to another.

The prosperity that gave to southern planters the freedom in which they took such pride, that gave them the leisure for horse racing, cockfighting, and political debate, and that often made them into little lords on their own estates, was based on the life-long labors of Negro slaves. By the middle of the eighteenth century, the distribution of slaves in the colonies had undergone a shift that marked out the prevailing and permanent distinction between what would one day be South and North. This transformation does not appear to have been in sight much before the end of the seventeenth century, when southern plantations still relied on white indentured labor and numerous slaves were recorded in such cities as Philadelphia and New York. But the plantation economy soon became a slave economy as the supply of Negroes, and of mulattoes whom the whites classified as Negroes, multiplied with both importation and propagation. By 1763, in a total colonial population that may have numbered roughly two million, it was estimated that upwards of three hundred thousand were Negroes, almost all of them slaves. Their distribution, however, was uneven. Not only were the heaviest concentrations overwhelmingly in the southern provinces, but in South Carolina, for example, differing estimates for 1766 suggest a white population of some seventy thousand outnumbered by eighty to one hundred thousand Negroes. In Virginia the whites outnumbered the blacks by only about two to one.

The white population itself was increasing rapidly. Even so, the rising proportion of Negroes had begun to cause anxiety, and the Virginia legislature made attempts to arrest the process by forbidding the further importation of Negroes from overseas. These moves encountered the veto of the authorities in London, acting in this case with the personal approval of George III, who strongly objected to attempts to stop the slave trade. Virginia's legislators were not moved by considerations of humanity; whatever their reflections may have been, they entertained no principles that would have prompted them to dismantle the institution of slavery. Their concern was for the future of their own race, which they felt to be threatened. The immediate fear was of a slave revolt, a possibility that the whites could never wholly put out of their minds, however unlikely it might seem at any specific time. They also experienced a vaguer anxiety about the racial composition of a population in which they could one day find themselves permanently outnumbered. Whites regarded blacks as inferiors who were inherently incapable of progressing beyond a limited intellectual or moral point, and this view was a necessary part of the psychological equipment with which they armed themselves to maintain their ascendancy. It enabled them to dismiss, or disregard, the humanity of Negroes, which they constantly encountered. They held the Negroes down by laws based on the assumption of a fundamental and unalterable disparity between the races; oppression began, therefore, by dispensing with the Anglo-American principle of equality before the law. These laws, or codes for the regulation of the blacks, were by their nature repressive and frequently savage. Within these limitations, nonetheless, magistrates often tried to be fair and reasonable.

Negroes and whites exercised on each other a profound and complex influence. Few had experienced the visual surprise and puzzlement presented by the difference of color until confronted with it on the American continent. Both white and black had to absorb it first into their perceptual equipment and thence into their moral and social judgments. When Negroes faced whites they faced a master race to whom, whatever their feelings or opinions, they were obliged to adapt themselves; the need for adaptation undoubtedly affected their personality, especially because it was a lifelong and not a temporary condition. They must often have looked on their masters with hatred and contempt, but usually also with an undertow of fear—feelings tempered in many cases by good nature and good sense on both sides. Both got used to a black-and-white pattern of faces and bodies, and gradually assimilated each other's habits of speech and expression. The geographer Jedidiah Morse, writing in 1789, commented on the influence of Negro speech on the accents of southern whites. A number of common Americanisms, of which "OK" is the most familiar, appear to have been adapted from African languages spoken by slaves.

These were not the only modifications that the different peoples on the continent were exercising on each other. The use of English was another. Although many national groups, such as the Swedes in the middle provinces, the Germans in Pennsylvania, and the Dutch in New York and northern New Jersey, spoke their own languages (the Germans were the only group to publish successful newspapers), the English language dominated all public life. It was the only official language and as such was used in the courts, the assemblies, and the press; its primacy, moreover, carried with it implications of social superiority. Kalm, traveling about 1748, had noticed the declining force of European continental languages; the old people still spoke their mother tongue, but:

> They begin, however, by degrees, to change their manners and opinions; chiefly indeed in the town [of New York] and in its neighbourhood, for most of the young people now speak principally *English,* and go only to the *English* church; and would even take it amiss, if they were called *Dutchmen* and not *Englishmen.*

All the principal public debates were conducted in English, and when these turned on disputes with the British themselves, it was English law, English precedents, and English history that the colonial spokesmen summoned up in their support. The quarrel with Britain brought about the most concerted affirmation of British national identity in the entire history of the American colonies. Britain also supplied the colonists with a kind of social imagery. The court might be three thousand miles away, but they knew themselves to be the king's subjects. Many wealthy people, especially in the southern provinces, sent their sons to the Inns of Court in London for training in the law; many more would probably have done so but for the fear of smallpox, to which Americans seemed susceptible in England. All clergymen of the Anglican Church were obliged to go to London for ordination. Ambitious colonial militia officers aspired to hold king's commissions. The marks of social success in America were such things as monogrammed carriages, clothes made by London tailors in London styles, and, where possible, some familiarity with English society.

Yet through much of the seventeenth and early eighteenth centuries, the British presence had been dimmed by distance and Britain's influence weakened by domestic and European preoccupations. The peoples of the colonies had built up their own institutions in imitation of England's, but with a large measure of practical independence. Their experience was American. In solving their own problems, they had encountered many examples of British obstruction, particularly in the procedure of disallowing colonial laws. They did not, for the most part, question their membership of the empire, but they often had reason to question the wisdom, and fairness, of the British statesmen who controlled its policies. This questioning, which took place against a background of English legal and historical assumptions, was an integral part of the process of self-discovery.

2

The Impact of British Policy

Even by 1763, the empire of which the American colonists were members had not acquired any formal name. The word "empire" was to be adopted by American spokesmen in an attempt to define their relationship to the mother country, a relationship in which they were neither wholly subordinate nor freely independent. The Americans, according to John Dickinson, were "a perfectly free people," not so much subjects of the British Empire as partners within its compass—an idea anticipated by Franklin. British possessions were extensive, ranging from India (administered by the East India Company, not the crown) to the vast semicircle of the Atlantic fringe. On this western arc running from Canada to the West Indian islands, the people were constitutionally inhabitants of a single nation. Britain had other overseas possessions, including Ireland, the small Channel Islands, and Gibraltar. The government of all these possessions differed, but all were under the aegis of Parliament. The king in Parliament exercised lawful sovereignty over the realm of Britain, and no one openly questioned the constitutional principle that parliamentary sovereignty extended over the American colonies.

In practice, the two principal objects of that sovereignty were trade and defense. Alone, the colonies could not have survived in the hostile world of great European powers contending for commercial and strategic advantages. Britain's American colonists, especially in New England, regarded the French threat on the continent with particular dread because the French monarchy combined what they regarded as the two worst ingredients of tyranny: absolute monarchy and the Roman Catholic religion. The southern colonies had long since adopted the English laws that discriminated against Roman Catholics, and New Englanders viewed Catholics with an intolerance bred of religious doctrine and a historical indoctrination of political fear. Without British defense, the colonists would at best have had to resign themselves to being hemmed in without hopes of westward expansion, at worst they might eventually have had to face absorption into the French Empire. Defense and trade were inseparable. To supply, organize, and defend its possessions, Britain needed the New England pines that gave the Royal Navy its masts; it needed naval supplies from the Carolinas; and, above all, it needed the opportunities for economic expansion offered by the market of the rising population in the colonies.

The manufactures and commerce of Britain, like those of the colonies, were owned and conducted by individuals or private companies. But the trade winds of the empire did not blow entirely free from government interference. Ever since the first Navigation Act, in 1651, Parliament had asserted the right to direct trade and control shipping in the interests of the mother country. In the eighteenth century an increasingly lengthy list of articles produced for export in the colonies was designated by acts of Parliament to be shipped only to Britain. These "enumerated" articles, which by 1764 included not only tobacco and the small number of agricultural products listed in the seventeenth century, but rice and molasses, naval stores, beaver skins, other hides and furs, copper ore and iron, potash and pearl ash, lumber, and a variety of spices, were controlled by detailed legislation, the effect of which was to make Britain the primary market and the entrepôt for re-export. Clearly, at every point where agricultural production or manufactures in the colonies had risen above either basic subsistence or the local market, decisions made in London could influence the prospects of future fortune.

The British, like most people, were ready to protect their own interests with a theory. The colonies, it was explained, had been founded and developed in order to serve the wider causes of the kingdom. Deriving their existence from royal charters, they had prospered under the benign influence of British protection for the purpose of increasing the wealth and strength of England—a nation that had been called Great Britain only since the Union with Scotland in 1707. When economic policy was under consideration, it was the interest of the mother country, not of the people of the colonies, that was the object of prime concern. So successfully did British politicians develop this view that they seem to have convinced themselves that the colonies really would never have been founded if the interest of England had not originally called them into existence. By the same reasoning, the founding of native colonial industries that might in time compete with those of Britain was naturally considered injurious to British economic interests; American manufactures, therefore, could operate only under severe limitations. They were not altogether forbidden, but restrictions were placed on the export of their products, even beyond the immediate region of the colony in which they were made. Ironware and beaver hats were the best-known victims of these "restraining acts" of Parliament.

The controls were not an oppressive burden on the colonists. In the first place, no promising American industry was waiting to be born; the restraints were irritants rather than fundamental prohibitions on any major development. Indeed, British industry continued to be the main American source of supply until at least the first quarter of the nineteenth century. But it was intensely galling to a colonial manufacturer to find himself legally barred from selling his product outside his immediate environs by virtue of laws made three thousand miles away and in pursuit of theories of trade and empire that ignored his interests. Kalm's observations provide interesting evidence on colonial annoyance with parliamentary actions:

> These and some other restrictions, occasion the inhabitants of the *English* colonies to grow less tender for their mother country. This coldness is kept up by the many foreigners, such as *Germans, Dutch,* and *French,* settled here, and living among the *English,* who commonly have no particular attachment to *Old England;* add to this likewise, that many people can never be contented with their possessions, though they be ever so great, and will always be desirous of getting more, and of enjoying the pleasure which arises from changing; and their over great liberty, and their luxury, often lead them to licentiousness.
>
> I have been told by *Englishmen,* and not only by such as were born in *America,* but even by such as came from *Europe,* that the *English* colonies in *North-America,* in the space of thirty or fifty years [from about 1748] would be able to form a state by themselves, entirely independent on *Old England.* . . .

The effects of the trade and navigation laws were more complex than those of the restraining acts. Their intention was to protect and promote the shipping and trade of the empire, which meant that American trade and shipping gained a share of the protection. The law decreeing that British goods must be carried in British ships gave a great advantage to American ships, and colonial ship-building, which might have suffered from competition, prospered to such an extent that by the time of the Revolution roughly one-third of all British merchant ships were built in the colonies. The skilled shipwrights of New England and Philadelphia had little to complain of in this aspect of the protective system. The trade laws did not forbid all direct colonial exports to Europe or the Mediterranean, but it was just when American products became economically valuable that the Lords of Trade in England began to take a protective interest in them. The development of this protective-trade system meant that no American province could ever expect to pursue its own economic policy—except in the sense that many merchants illegally visited the Dutch and French islands of the West Indies and frequently balanced their budgets by smuggling, practices that duplicated those of some of the more successful merchants and gentry of the outlying counties in England.

Britain was thus a crucial factor in the American economy. It re-exported, to the advantage of its own merchants, those colonial products that could be sold on the Continent. Because British merchant houses had centuries of experience in European trade, Americans would have found it hard to compete with them if they had been left to shift for themselves. It has often been pointed out that, after the War of Independence, when Americans were at last free to carve out their own channels of commerce, their routes did not differ noticeably from those taken in colonial times. Britain continued as the main source of manufactures, and the Americans continued to export most of their produce to Britain and to rely on many of their established connections with English and Scottish merchant houses. It can be argued, therefore, that the trade acts of the colonial era did not curb or restrain colonial overseas commerce but directed it where the laws of supply and demand would in any case have taken it; and, meanwhile, they gave the colonists the run of the most prosperous and expansive of the great maritime empires. There is an element of truth in the argument. But while the trading regulations appear on the whole to have been negligently supervised, the Acts of Trade had the effect, over an extended period, of building a pronounced bias into the "natural" direction of American commerce, some of which, on purely market grounds, would undoubtedly have gone to the Netherlands. After the completion of American independence, the United States virtually had to absorb British goods because the long and intimate British connection had served to establish a demand for them.

British policy also controlled the supply of the various forms of paper money in the American colonies. No such institution as a Bank of America could be established since the colonies had neither the political nor the economic unity to do so. But British officials looked with extreme disapproval on *any* form of colonial banking. There was room for much division of opinion about the advantages of paper currencies, which, as British and French history showed, had not always been anchored against wild inflation; colonial merchants, especially if they lent money at interest, were often just as conservative in these matters as British administrators. An expanding population, however, engaged in pressing upward its standards of living, needed more fluidity of money than could be found in the types of silver coin—much of it from European countries and gained in the West India trade—that circulated in North America. Exceptions were made in special cases, but the overall policy of Britain in this as in so many other matters was formulated on the basis of firm principles without consultation with Americans and without regard for the needs of colonial life.

Nor was this control a diminishing force in British policy. On the contrary, the end of the French and Indian War gave British administrators an opportunity to extend their grip, and 1764 brought new measures that touched the interests and aroused the anxieties of nearly all colonial merchants. In that year Parliament ordered that issues of paper money, permitted as a matter of necessity during the war, were to be stopped—an action that gradually restricted the currency resources of the colonies.

In that same year, as noted previously, Parliament also passed the Revenue or Sugar Act, which put a tax on imports from the

West Indies. The tax itself was lighter than that of the Molasses Act of 1733, but the significant difference was that the new measure was accompanied by a system of effective enforcement. Americans found themselves confronted with a new set of British customs officials, vice-admiralty courts, and naval officers whose presence was as unfamiliar as their instructions were unwelcome. In 1764 Parliament also agreed to ministerial proposals for an extension of the number of enumerated articles.

All these actions were taken by Parliament. But British administrations also possessed certain powers derived from the royal prerogative, and a year earlier the crown had issued an edict affecting the future of colonial settlement in the West. The Proclamation of 1763 banned all further settlement beyond the Appalachian Mountains, which meant that until it could be rescinded or modified, all colonists who hoped to cross into the Mississippi Valley to make new homes in its inviting and thinly populated lands, and all colonists who meant to profit from speculating in those settlers' hopes, were thwarted by a single stroke from London. To ignore the order might by physically easy, but it was also full of risks, since no land claim could be valid and no protection could be expected.

Colonists could see little to justify this harsh and arbitrary step. Yet the thinking behind it, which had originated in the shrewd brain of the Earl of Shelburne when he was president of the board of trade, was more reasonable than it seemed. The truth was that the frontier was dangerously insecure. The Indian chief Pontiac struck a sudden blow at the fort of Detroit in 1763, and if his plans, which were betrayed at the last minute, had been successful, he would have cleared the Ohio Valley far more quickly and thoroughly than any parchment from London. Ministers in England had reason to concern themselves about the future of relations with the Indians and the legal basis of further advances involving land claims. Shelburne's move was intended primarily to give time to study the problem as a whole; he did not intend to let impatient colonists commit Britain to defend uncharted regions that might be neither militarily nor legally defensible. It was not a rigid policy, and within a few years a new administration did agree to further land cessions, ratified by treaties with the Indians at Forts Hard Labor and Stanwix (1768). From the colonial angle of view, however, the 1763 edict revealed a different and disturbing point. It was now obvious from the proclamation and from the legislation of 1764 that the forces of government in Britain, having swept the French from the field, were moving toward a policy for North America. The French and their Indian allies had threatened colonial security, but the British seemed to threaten colonial liberties.

These liberties were historically as much religious as political. The federated Congregational churches of New England, the Presbyterians of Pennsylvania, and other Protestant sects throughout the colonies were bound to be shocked by the periodic reports that the Anglicans, a minority in their society, were interested in getting a bishop of their own on the American continent. An episcopal see in New England would indeed seem a travesty of history and a mocking comment on the efforts of its founders. Colonial Congregationalists worked in close understanding with English Dissenters in a prolonged series of maneuvers to avert this alarming development. It was not that an Anglican bishop would have any open political power; the implications were social and political almost as much as they were religious. The issue, as seen by the Dissenters, was expressed by the Rhode Island minister the Reverend Ezra Stiles: "It is difficult to lay open and advance with *full force* the *objections* against Prelacy in America, peculiar to this *Age,* and to the present State of the Colonies. Our *peculiar Objections* are much founded in the *Anticipation of Futurity.*"

The opinions of the Anglican clergyman the Reverend Samuel Johnson, president of King's College in New York, help to clarify the political and religious connections that the Dissenters had some reason to fear. In a private letter, he wrote about his native Connecticut: "With regard to our government it is much too popular. The persons in place absolutely depending on the annual election of the people for their posts, popularity and a servile compliance with all their humors and schemes [,] however so extravagant or unreasonable, [considered to be] the greatest virtue." Colonial Protestants were well aware of the fact that a bishop of the Church of England had a seat in the House of Lords. But peers of the realm, though not unknown, were an anomaly in America. The colonial gentry, even when they verged on aristocracy, did not owe their positions to the network of hierarchical connections that constituted the social fabric of England, and a step in this direction must either subvert or challenge them. Colonists, especially in New England and Pennsylvania, instinctively recognized the challenge to their capacity for making a social order of their own whole cloth; a bishop officially planted by the British government, importing the panoply of his office, would carry with him dangerous implications for the future of that order. His mere presence, moreover, would strengthen the hand of Britain. This anxiety was not a figment of imagination. On the contrary, it corresponded to what some of the Anglicans hoped for, as revealed by the recently arrived Scottish clergyman and teacher William Smith in New York. Using arguments furnished by Johnson, Smith wrote in a local paper:

> As to the Political Uses of national Establishments, he must indeed by a very shallow Politician who does not see them. The Statesman has always found it necessary for the Purposes of Government, to raise some one Denomination of religions above the Rest to a certain Degree. This favor'd Denomination, by these Means, becomes as it were the Creature of the Government, which is thus enabled to turn the Balance and keep all in Subjection.

The English Dissenters were keenly aware of the danger to their American brethren. Their efforts to thwart these plans at their source were successful, and no Church of England see was planted on colonial soil. British ministers were not willing to embark on a course that would incite so much dissension at home, and the Anglican Church itself did not maintain any persistent pressure. Nevertheless, the possibility of a new move could not be completely discounted; the issue, partly because it was never officially resolved, reminded politically conscious colonists that the British connection held dangers they might one day have to resist. The difficulty was all the more complicated because Anglican colonists appeared to have as much right to their religious establishment as did the descendants of the Puritans. It was a real grievance that their clergy had to cross the Atlantic to be ordained by the bishop of London, and their efforts to alter this procedure went so far that the house in Cambridge, Massachusetts, of the Anglican clergyman East Apthorp, who was expected to become the first bishop, became popularly known as "the Bishop's Palace." Although many southern Anglicans did not really want to be supervised by a bishop in America, the southern colonies were officially Anglican, which gave the Congregationalists cause to fear that they might one day find themselves outflanked even on the continent in which their forebears had sought refuge.

Against this threat they would wield passionate historical and religious arguments, and they could, and their ministers did, warn their fellow countrymen of all the social and political implications. But they could not prove that it would be illegal. John Adams was later to reflect that the religious question did as much as any other to prepare the minds of Americans for independence. Though this kind of opinion cannot be accurately assessed, he certainly had every opportunity of weighing the other factors that were helping to form an American political mind.

For British governmental ministers, the bishopric question was a side issue. Though it might be brought forward at some propitious moment, it was never worth a storm that would cost them the votes of Dissenters at a general election. The problem of their vast new possessions, however, could not be considered a side issue— and could not be allowed to drift. Experienced men such as Thomas Pownall, a former governor of Massachusetts, had begun to argue in public for a more comprehensive system of colonial administration; the wars had been expensive, the land tax stood at four shillings to the pound, and an administration that depended on the support of country gentlemen was bound to look for some way of lightening its overseas burdens.

The colonists would have had more to fear of a more united or determined British administration. From their outposts they could discern only the outline of the British state; it was like seeing the cliffs of some distant island, massive but indistinct, and betraying no hint of the interior hills and valleys or the marks of habitation. In spite of its victories, Britain suffered from political disunities that made its policies uncertain and hard to predict. The young King George III, who had acceded to the throne in 1760 (he was the grandson of George II), was under the influence of his Scottish tutor, the Earl of Bute, whom he had loyally appointed as his minister; Bute had no other claim to office. The Scots, who were rising to influence in British law and politics, were the objects of intense suspicion and hostility, and Bute could not attract or hold men of ability. The factions that maneuvered or groped for influence and power in Britain were based on personal leadership, on clannish sets of family connections, and on the hopes of preferment, hopes that depended on the play of loyal service and the accurate reading of other men's moves. Men did not go into politics, or seek ministerial power, with a view to implementing specific programs of action, although such programs could well result from changes in office made for other reasons. The great exception was the career of William Pitt, "the Great Commoner," who rose to power in the crisis of war.

It was characteristic of the personal nature of relationships between court and Parliament that the newly enthroned king dropped Pitt in favor of Bute even before the war was won. Bute in due course had to go—George himself grew out of his feelings of dependence on him—and the intensely serious king spent several years trying out combinations of ministers. They all proved unstable and short-lived until he found, in 1769, a man who could combine leadership with loyalty. That man was Lord North, a determined if not particularly efficient administrator, a witty and intelligent debater, and a practical politician who could command a steady following in the House of Commons. Lord North, who could sit in the Commons because he was the son of an earl (that is, not being a peer in his own right, he had no seat in the Lords), became chancellor of the exchequer in 1767, and first lord of the treasury—effectively prime minister—in 1770.

By that time, Britain's relations with her American colonies had undergone so many alarms and vicissitudes that each side had acquired a distorted picture of the other's character and intentions. In 1765 George Grenville, chancellor of the exchequer, had laid a stamp tax on the colonies in order to raise a revenue to defray the costs of their defense. The effect, totally unexpected, was a storm of protest that united the colonies as they had never been united before. In 1766 the young Marquess of Rockingham had held office long enough to jettison the stamp tax in exchange for an act declaratory of full parliamentary powers; he then gave way to a new ministry formed by Pitt, who had belied his sobriquet and accepted a peerage as the Earl of Chatham. Chatham was under some psychological disturbance that rendered him incapable of governing, and during this period his brilliant but wayward chancellor of the exchequer, Charles Townshend, had introduced a new round of taxes. Townshend explained these as being "external" and therefore acceptable in accordance with testimony given to the Commons by Franklin, as one of the colonists' own spokesmen during the Stamp Act crisis. Townshend's new round of taxes, however, produced a new wave of American expostulations and were in due course withdrawn, leaving only a tax on tea. Other quarrels arose out of British demands to quarter troops in the province of New York and the New York legislature's heated objections. While these eruptions of British policy were making their impression on the colonists, another and more immediate impression resulted from the activities of the new batch of British officials. The enforcement of the Sugar Act was no longer the lazy formality that these procedures had been in the distant days of Walpole or Newcastle or Pitt. British customs officers, zealous, avaricious, and often unscrupulous, battened on American merchants and enriched themselves with fees from seizures and prosecutions.

Undoubtedly, these actions could be technically defended within the terms of the laws. Undoubtedly, colonial merchants in Charleston, Philadelphia, New York, Providence, and Boston were guilty of infringements. They interpreted the zeal of the customs men, however, as persecution, and correctly attributed their persistence as much to greed as to duty. The results of these encounters were far more serious than anyone in British administrative circles seems to have understood. Here again the British completely failed to appreciate the implications of what they were doing toward the formation of a colonial public viewpoint. Britain was antagonizing the leaders of American society and the molders of opinion.

British ministers in Parliament and their pamphleteers answered American protests with arguments on law and the constitution. They did not understand that both their policies and their arguments were forcing American colonists to ask themselves where their true interests lay, whether, indeed, they were with a system whose means for inflicting grievances always seemed to be superior to its means for redressing them. Americans were not only unable to check the development of impositions that encroached on their

properties, and hence their liberties, they were unable to anticipate
what the next move might be, even when by the most strenuous and
costly exertions they had obtained a reversal or a mitigation of the
policy in question. While always hoping that the corner had been
turned, that the ministry having seen its error would refrain, as a
matter of principle, from repeating it, the colonial leaders found
themselves forced into being an intellectual armed guard. They
lived in the anticipation of new dangers and the need for new defenses. This state of endemic fear helped to generate a kind of morbid pathology in the minds of American colonists. Many of them
had been brought up to believe that English history revealed a
series of dark conspiracies against popular liberties, and they now
began to perceive that the latest of these conspiracies, bred by
Scottish advisers and King's Friends, was directed against colonial
liberties. Few of them, however, looked to independence as an
avenue of deliverance.

Even after the meetings of provincial and continental congresses
had begun, most colonial leaders hoped for reconciliation rather
than—and in order to avert—revolt. Yet Lord North's administration was incapable of realizing that hope. A handful of British politicians, such as Edmund Burke, Colonel Isaac Barré, and the notorious Wilkes, together with a few political economists, such as
Adam Smith and Dean Josiah Tucker, saw the scale of differences
between Britain and its American colonies and the need for a fresh
concept of the relationship. None of them, though, stood any
chance of impressing these views on either the North ministry or
the House of Commons. What the king and North and the majority
all wanted was firm government. But firm government, based on
inadequate knowledge, could only cause despair to Britain's friends
in the colonies and play into the hands of the small body of determined men whose minds were set on independence.

Although the British attempt to rule the colonies was misjudged,
it was not altogether misconceived. The problems that British ministers fumbled were real problems. Any authority that undertook to
prescribe solutions from a continental standpoint would be obliged
to take account of broadly the same problems, and Britain alone
could prescribe for the continent as a whole under the constitution
as it was then understood. The three great fields of defense, com-

merce, and western expansion, which in turn involved intricate relations with numerous Indian tribes, fell within the purview of the
British government, and the measures taken by the different British
ministries during the 1760s, though often poorly planned, did represent their attempts to act on those problems. One day, somebody
would have to solve them, as the Americans were to learn in due
course.

For the truth that the Americans were to discover for themselves
was that, whatever their objections to British tyranny, the colonies
could not stand alone, and could not stand without government.
They needed an army and they needed a foreign policy. They
would soon need a unified economic policy, at least to cover external trade, and that policy would take on an odd resemblance to
the old British mercantile system. They would need a policy for the
West; and they would need a form of government agreed upon
among themselves. In renouncing British government, and British
sovereignty, they became the heirs to Britain's problems in America.

3

The Inner Crisis
and the
Struggle for Unity

Unity of purpose was not a characteristic of colonial society, or of the politics to which that society gave rise. The colonies were united by their common allegiance to the crown, not by any recognized common interests among themselves. During the French and Indian War, military operations and supplies had been gravely hampered by the unwillingness of the provinces to support each other, even against the threat posed by the common enemy, France, in alliance with powerful Indian tribes in the Mississippi Valley. In 1754, an ambitious plan drawn up at Albany during a joint meeting of colonial governors and other representatives, proposing a form of colonial political union, was coldly received by the several legislatures. In England, Parliament was equal in its lack of enthusiasm, for many feared the long-term consequences of giving the colonies any constitutional means of collective action. Yet the Albany Plan looked to the future: twenty years later, the colonies were to meet, through their representatives, in a continental congress that would provide the outlines for an American government.

At the end of the war in 1763, however, colonists could not easily have been got to admit that their lack of unity was a defect. The lines of authority from each colony ran straight back to London, and any relations between the colonies were merely of an informal or consultative kind. Revivals of religion, inspired by the preaching of George Whitefield and other itinerant ministers, had probably done more than either politics or trade to inform the peoples of different regions about the possibilities of unity. The revivalists, though, were not concerned with politics, which on the whole they regarded as a distraction from the realities of spiritual experience. The vast distances between the colonies were reflected in the vast differences between their interests and ways of life; even their most traveled and experienced men usually knew of other regions only by repute. That a colonist was wealthy or important enough to travel to England, or to send his children there, did not mean that he would have any need to visit other parts of the continent; the colonists' knowledge of one another was probably much less accurate, and more subject to the vagaries of rumor, than their knowledge of Britain.

The Anglo-Americans, of course, with their infusion of other nationalities, were not alone in America, and the continent did not belong exclusively to them. Although France was eliminated as an American power in 1763, it had left a French population under British rule, and might return at some unspecified future date. Spain had acquired the enormous area of French Louisiana in 1762, and in 1763 Britain gained the Floridas to the south of its other colonies. The Indian tribes, potent as either friends or enemies, still controlled immense tracts of land. Faced with rival power, the colonies' lack of unity would reveal itself as a weakness. The defect was not critical so long as the colonies were members of an empire, for as members they were ultimately subject to British control and protection. Without Britain, they would have been in danger from the French and their Indian allies. The immediate result of removing the French threat was to reduce the urgency of the need for British protection—and thus to give the colonists, especially the New Englanders, a keener sense of their own self-sufficiency. However, when Britain itself began to emerge as a threat rather than a protector, the colonists were thrown back on their own resources. In the process they discovered that they possessed more things in common than most of them had suspected. It was British policy that, by touching the nerves of their mutual weaknesses, revealed the existence of underlying unities.

The English Americans not only spoke the same language, that language described closely similar political institutions. In the different colonial societies, economic organization, labor, social assumptions, and religion diverged from one another more distinctively than did their forms of government. Every colony, with minor exceptions, had its governor, a form of appointive council, and an elected assembly; in most, the system of justice was administered through a network of county courts, which also exercised fairly extensive powers of local administration. Even in political matters, the slight differences reflected, and helped to perpetuate, certain structural differences in society. That Connecticut and Rhode Island had charters under which they elected their own governors had always put them somewhat further outside the reach of British discipline than their neighbors. That the Massachusetts assembly elected the governor's council had always reduced the royal governor's control of a body which, in most colonies, represented an instrument of British as much as colonial influence. In the proprietary provinces of Pennsylvania and Maryland, the appointment of governors, councillors, and other officers was a matter for the proprietors, not the British crown. Yet all these arrangements involved marked similarities in formal structure.

All were equally bound by the obligation to abide by the laws of England, and if any assembly felt inclined to disregard this requirement, it was liable to be brought into line by the royal power to disallow its laws. The royal veto, which had sunk into disuse in Britain, was an instrument actively employed in the colonies. Assemblies could attempt to circumvent it, but they could never ignore its existence. English common law was also formally recognized in colonial courts, although it could not be applied with much regularity because the courts possessed too few printed reports or records and colonial judges were seldom men learned in the law. For generations to come, American courts were often to hand down a rough kind of informal, populistic justice that depended more on a shrewd assessment of the case and the parties than on precedent or procedure. Lawyers or judges who did aspire to distinguish themselves would read Sir Edward Coke, whose *Institutes* (1628–1644) constituted the chief treatise on the laws of England before Sir William Blackstone. When Blackstone's *Commentaries on the Laws of England* (1765–1769) began to reach the colonies, they were rapidly absorbed. Professional knowledge, in matters involving parliamentary procedure and principles of law, was always knowledge drawn from England.

The lessons of English history powerfully reinforced what was inculcated through English law and colonial experience. To the colonist, the meaning of the English Civil War and of the Glorious Revolution of 1688–1689, which followed attempts by James II to consolidate the government, had the merit of a vital simplicity: constitutional history, properly understood, dictated a program of action—or at least implied a theory of resistance. The colonial assemblies exercised an authority comparable to that of Parliament. These assemblies, at various times and opportunities, had shown a remarkable similarity in the ways in which they had grasped the powers and liberties that the House of Commons had asserted for itself in the seventeenth century. It would be impossible to comprehend the resistance of Americans to British taxation without appreciating the historical light in which they saw their own constitutional position. They knew that Charles I had tried to govern without a parliament and had subjected England to eleven years of personal rule (1629–1640); they knew that the central issue on which liberty had been pitched in England was that of arbitrary taxation; and they understood the great struggle between king and Parliament in terms of what would later be called the "Whig interpretation." Parliament thus stood for the liberties of the people; the crown stood for an absolutism in which matters were made all the worse by the oppressive power of the Anglican Church.

British policy, after the Peace of Paris, affected most of the colonies, but it did not affect them all in the same ways. Major interests in the southern and central provinces were alarmed by the Proclamation of 1763, which meant less in New England; the Revenue or Sugar Act of 1764 hurt New England and the port towns but did not seriously damage the South. The Stamp Act reached them all. Whatever the consequences of specific acts, all influential colonists were inclined to shape their responses in accordance with a body of doctrine and experience that to a surprisingly large extent they held in common. As new British ministries produced new policies, even the provocations inflicted on the colonists acquired an increasingly similar appearance, and in ways that compulsively reminded them of the similarity of their institutions. These similarities helped to overcome obstacles to the organizing of remonstrances, and eventually resistance, among colonial elements that were temperamentally foreign to each other. Afflicted Boston could and did appeal to her sisters further south on grounds of mutual interest; popular leaders could and did rally people everywhere to the support of a common cause.

When all the distances and differences between the colonies were considered, the British ministers had reason to be surprised at the unity of the reply to their policies—and at the speed with which that reply was concerted. The colonial reaction itself did much to reveal the structure of American society. The significance of the new British measures was quickly made to seem clear and ominous, even though their meaning did not reach the ordinary colonist with the instant force that it struck the upper classes. Different measures affected different groups, but in each case it was an existing, recognized leadership that was the first to grasp what was happening. It was this leadership that reacted to the event, interpreted it to the people, and took the necessary steps toward rallying an opposition.

From a conventional British standpoint, the dominant feature of colonial government, and particularly that of New England, was its popular character. "From what has been said," General Thomas Gage wrote in 1768 to Lord Hillsborough, the responsible minister in London, "your Lordship will conclude, that there is no Government in Boston[;] there is, in Truth, very little at present, and the Constitution of this Province leans so much to the side of Democracy, that the Governor has not the Power alone to remedy the Disorders which happen in it." A year later the governor, Sir Francis Bernard, wrote to Viscount Barrington:

> . . . for these 4 Years past so uniform a System of bringing all Power into the Hands of the People has been prosecuted without Interruption & with such Success, that all that Fear, Reverence, Respect & Awe which before formed a tolerable Balance against the real Power of the People, are annihilated, & the artificial Weights being removed, the royal Scale mounts up & kicks the beam. . . . It would be better that Mass Bay should be a complete Republic like Connecticut than to remain with so few Ingredients of royalty in it as shall be insufficient to maintain the real royal Character.

In Virginia, Richard Henry Lee, who was soon to become an energetic revolutionary, explained in a letter written in 1766 how his colony's constitution differed from the British. In Britain the three simple forms of monarchy, aristocracy, and democracy were

> . . . so finely blended; that the advantages resulting from each species separately, flow jointly from their admirable

union. . . . With us, the legislative power is lodged in a Governor, Council, and House of Burgesses. The two first appointed by the crown, and their places held by the precarious tenure of pleasure only. That security therefore which the constitution derives in Britain from the House of Lords, is here totally wanting, and the just equilibrium totally destroyed by two parts out of three of the Legislature being in the same hands.

Worse still, owing to the prerogative power of the governor to dissolve and summon assemblies, "even the third or democratic part of our legislature Is totally in the power of the Crown!" Virginia had tried four years earlier to remedy this defect by fixing the life of assemblies at seven years, but the crown significantly disallowed the act.

These remarks, from both sides and from two provinces, show something of the way people thought about the balance of forces in a well-ordered government. Lee thought the worst defect in Virginia to be the absence of an independent body comparable to the House of Lords; good government, of the mixed or balanced kind, ought to provide an adequate representation of the people—this was the "democratic" ingredient—along with the presence of a royal governor and a strong, independent element of landed property. If any of these were too strong for the others, the government was unbalanced; and that would be just as true if the strength lay on the side of the "democracy," as royal officials thought it did in New England, as it would if the royal power were strong enough to overwhelm the liberties of the people.

Each province, however, met the British challenge through its leadership, and that political leadership bore a traditional and accepted relationship to the structure of society. Colonial voters took it as part of the order of nature that men of wealth, family, and good character should also represent them in affairs of state. A satirical play about elections, called *The Candidates,* written in Virginia in 1770 (it is one of the earliest extant American comedies), put the position neatly. The retirement of the local great man, Worthy, opens the field to three new rivals, Sir John Toddy, Mr. Strutabout, and Mr. Smallhopes. The fourth candidate, Wou'dbe, is better than the rest but inferior to Worthy. They vie with each other in making promises, mostly about taxes and the price of rum, but in the end the country's need brings Worthy back to his post. The significance of the roles is that Sir John Toddy, Mr. Strutabout, and Mr. Smallhopes make false promises to the electorate; Wou'dbe tells the voters the truth, thus risking his popularity; Worthy, however, does not campaign at all. He has only to let it be known that he is willing to serve; his election is then assured because his standing with the people is in exact conformity with his social position.

It was not always quite so simple as that. Ambitious men treated elections as a test of their social standing; they were expected to disclaim any desire for election and to allow their names to go forward only on the insistence of their friends; a great deal of personal prestige was staked on these elections, and exertions could be strenuous. In the southern provinces the candidates sometimes floated into office on a tide of rum; northern traditions, except perhaps in New York, were more austere. But in any case the results produced a genuine reflection of the ordering of society, in which a conventional deference for rank and superior style of life was spiced with a right to criticize that did not suffer from lack of use.

It was this elected colonial leadership that directed the opening phases of the American Revolution. Its task was twofold. Members of assemblies, lawyers, and men of letters had both to draft remonstrances to Parliament and to explain the dangers of parliamentary actions to their constituents. It suddenly became vitally necessary to consolidate a following that would back them in their arguments and would take unheard of risks to demonstrate the unity of the colonial cause.

These tasks presented the colonial leaders with a severe test of their caliber. The representatives who repeatedly took up the cause of opposition to Britain, leading eventually to armed resistance, and who managed through it all to maintain a semblance of order and government in their severely strained society, demonstrated a quality that their British contemporaries had little expected and resentfully failed to appreciate.

The outcome of the Revolution has made it too easy to overlook the risk that was taken before its success was known. At the same time, the stability of American institutions and the passage from a colonial to an independent political order can readily appear as though they were matters of course. Yet it is reasonable to doubt whether the colonists of any other European power in that period could have accomplished as much, while attaining so high a level of control, at so tolerable a price. The price is not to be underestimated, however. Civil order broke down at times in several provinces, and soldiers and civilians endured intense sufferings. Nevertheless, the civil order that emerged from the ordeal was notably consistent with the public professions of the defenders of American liberties against Parliament and crown. Neither wartime government nor the subsequent crises of peace led, for any appreciable length of time, to either military dictatorship on the one hand or to chaos and banditry on the other. Nor did the United States collapse into a new congeries of warring nations—not, at least, for another long lifetime.

The British measures that followed the close of the French and Indian War did not fall on immature American leaders. Colonial assemblymen had gained considerable experience in a series of struggles with British governors that had left the assemblies with powers closely approximating those of the House of Commons. Moreover, within their own domains colonial assemblies had developed an expertise that was both political, in the wider sense, and parliamentary; standing committees ordinarily handled the various kinds of petitions and other matters that reached the assembly. Partly because of their grounding in English history, and partly because of their legislative experience, these blunt, shrewd, seasoned men were extraordinarily swift to detect the distant menace. The Revenue Act posed no obvious threat to the colonial standard of living; it made the Molasses Act perpetual but it reduced the duty, while adding import levies on an assortment of products. The procedure for enforcement included new vice-admiralty courts with authority over all the colonies; the new courts were granted powers that effectively reduced those of colonial juries, who had tended to be lenient toward people in trouble with the navigation and trade laws. These new institutions, together with the customs-clearance procedures, were bound to give Britain a firmer control, but it would hardly be true to say that many of the colonists felt themselves to be personally involved. The seaport merchants were closer to these events and their implications than the farmers of the interior; Boston was the first to define an anti-parliamentary position toward which other sectors of colonial leadership would later gravitate.

The Boston town meeting took up the challenge posed by the Revenue Act. Apparently guided by Samuel Adams, the meeting voted instructions to its representatives in the provincial legislature, called the General Court, which included a statement of its constitutional position:

> . . . If our Trade may be taxed why not our Lands? Why not the produce of our Lands and every Thing we possess and make use of? This we apprehend annihilates our Charter Right to govern and tax ourselves. —It strikes at our British Privileges which as we have never forfeited them we hold in common with our Fellow Subjects who are Natives of Great Britain.

This statement became the basis of efforts by the Massachusetts assembly to get other colonial legislatures to cooperate in seeking parliamentary repeal of the act. Its reasoning was adopted by the Massachusetts House of Representatives when it learned from its agent in London that Grenville was considering the imposition of a stamp tax in the American colonies.

The Massachusetts protest against the Revenue Act was soon swallowed up in the surge of controversy over the Stamp Act. Nonetheless, the positions taken by the Boston town meeting contained the outline of arguments that were to be substantiated in future years by American spokesmen laboring to explain both to themselves and others the full moral and legal ground of their opposition. The Boston statement referred to "our charter right to govern and tax ourselves." Taxation, of course, results from a legislative act; and when the Boston leaders spoke in the same sentence of the right "to govern . . . ourselves" they made a connection that was probably not in the mind of Grenville and his colleagues in Britain. The British administration wanted to govern the colonies only in the broad sense in which the colonies were part of an empire over which they had a general responsibility. This responsibility was something most American thinkers continued to admit for several more years. The trouble was that as American protests and countermeasures became more energetic and effective, they drew from the British side more stringent governmental controls—which the Americans had wanted to avoid and the British had not intended to impose.

No doubt the power to govern was implicit in the power to tax. As the Americans were soon to discover for themselves, there can be no effective power to govern without taxation, and no effective taxation without government. The Stamp Act of 1765 brought these issues to a head in a blaze of light—much of it provided by the flames of burning effigies of stamp distributors and of homes and property destroyed by mobs. The violence and suddenness of the popular reaction were completely unexpected. Not that Grenville, for his part, had acted without notice; he had sounded the colonial agents in London—perhaps insincerely, but at any rate without success—on ways in which the colonies might be induced to tax themselves. Nor could he be blamed for his failure to anticipate the storm; several distinguished Americans, including Richard Henry Lee and Franklin (then in London trying to transform Pennsylvania into a royal province), so misjudged the situation that once convinced the act would go into force they satisfied themselves with working to secure jobs as distributors for themselves and their friends. A stamp tax was one of the many taxes that the British people bore as a matter of course; its extension to the colonies did not strike them as an imposition.

The Stamp Act levied a fee on the paper used in nearly every type of transaction—court documents, deeds, conveyances, records of shipments of goods at ports, contracts; on newspapers and other public prints (except books); and on all advertisements in newspapers. The range of these impositions, rather than the logic of the constitutional argument, explains the severity of the reaction. What Grenville had done was to touch each nerve center in American life at which either economic or intellectual activity was registered. It was precisely because his policy had touched Americans at these critical points, where activity would bring in a valuable revenue, that Grenville had also touched them where they were most susceptible to protest. The lawyers might not be loved by their neighbors, but certainly they were by profession articulate. Editors, who printed their own papers, provided the lifeline by which news of protest traveled abroad; papers frequently copied items from each other and told of events in distant colonies with which local readers had no other contact and little sense of community.

The economic logic of Grenville's policy defeated him. The colonies were aroused through their own natural leadership, which felt itself to be the prime target of attack. The legislature of Massachusetts had awakened early to the need to organize, and in 1764 established a committee of correspondence to exchange views with the assemblies of other colonies, thus initiating a method that colonists developed and refined as one of the most effective instruments of control and resistance in future crises. It was on an initiative from Massachusetts that delegations from nine of the colonial legislatures met in New York City in October 1765 and adopted addresses and petitions to the king and to both houses of Parliament. These declarations reviewed the constitutional grounds on which Americans, as British subjects, objected to being taxed save by their own representatives; they went on to assert the right to trial by jury, in opposition to the vice-admiralty courts, and to condemn the effects of the recently imposed import taxes, which were causing an intolerable shortage of specie. These addresses were moderate in tone and legitimate in style. They were, in fact, much more restrained than some of the declarations that had already been adopted by colonial legislatures. Virginia, impelled by the rhetorical fire of the young Patrick Henry, had been more outspoken (though Henry's fiercest resolutions were rejected by legislators who feared that they might be treasonable); New York and Massachusetts had also taken strong ground. By contrast, the Stamp Act Congress in New York seemed a tame affair; composed of cautious men, it created comparatively little stir. Its wider significance lay in the precedent it set, however. For the first time, the lawfully elected assemblies of several colonies had signified a common interest, and had hinted what lines of action the colonies might take in the future.

In one of the few pro-American speeches heard in these years in the House of Commons, Barré had referred to the Americans as "these sons of liberty." The phrase was taken up with enthusiasm. Groups identifying themselves as Sons of Liberty acted at first in secret, but soon emerged into open agitation in New York, Boston, and other cities. In New York they were led by young lawyers, in

Boston by small-business men and skilled craftsmen, with a much larger body of small traders and skilled and unskilled workers willing to follow their command. The activity of the Sons of Liberty was persistent, menacing, and well directed. They harassed public officials whose duties in any way connected them with the stamps. They raised mobs to burn effigies and jeopardize property, wrote letters to the papers, conducted surveys, and threatened professional and business men who seemed disposed to comply with the law. In Boston they obtained the resignation of the appointed stamp distributor, Andrew Oliver, after writing him this letter:

Hanover Square, Dec. 16, 1765

Sir,

The respectable Inhabitants of the Town of Boston, observe your Answer to an anonymous Letter published in Messi'rs Edes and Gill's News-Paper of Today, which we don't think satisfactory; therefore desire that you would, To-morrow, appear under Liberty Tree, at 12 o'Clock, to make a public Resignation. Your Noncompliance, Sir, will incur the Displeasure of *The True-born Sons of Liberty*. N.B. Provided you comply with the above, you shall be treated with the greatest Politeness and Humanity. If not. . . . . !

That night a mob intruded into Oliver's house, though apparently without doing great damage. The next day Oliver duly gave his resignation at the appointed time and place, having failed to get the Sons of Liberty to accept it at the courthouse. He stated, cryptically, "I shall always think myself very happy when it shall be in my power to serve this people."

It soon became impossible to use or even obtain the stamps from one end of the continent to the other, and in some places the courts began to open without them. Merchants in New York and Philadelphia, and soon afterward in Boston, agreed to cease importing British goods. The boycott was endorsed only after much deliberation, since halfhearted compliance could easily have given rise to a distinct competitive advantage, and the merchants of different cities were not accustomed to working in harmony.

This tremendous and highly organized outburst of sustained agitation had a strikingly effective impact on its immediate objectives, but its deeper consequences carried far beyond the original design.

The first result was one of astonishing success. A new British administration, under Rockingham, found itself caught between the need to assert its authority and the pressure of London and other British merchants, on whom it depended for support, who wanted an end to the colonial ban on the goods they carried. Rockingham induced the House of Commons to vote the repeal of the Stamp Act by introducing at the same time a bill to reaffirm the rights of Parliament. This Declaratory Act, which passed the Commons just before the Act of Repeal in 1766, did more than save the pride of a defeated parliament; it established as a matter of constitutional law that Parliament had the full power to govern the colonies "in all cases whatsoever," and this presented to the more reflective colonial thinkers a problem that was not to be resolved by the withdrawal of one piece of obnoxious legislation.

The consequences of the uproar were not confined to the field of relations between the colonies and the mother country, however. New sources of power had been unearthed in colonial politics, and mobs that rioted against the servants of British policy now turned their attention to more domestic matters. In New York, control of the Sons of Liberty passed out of the hands of lawyers and into those of mechanics and small traders with far more radical interests. They were to prove an explosive force in city and provincial politics; their influence carried forward into the Revolution as they insistently pressed the great landowners, lawyers, and richer merchants to shift to more radical anti-British positions and, in home politics, to make concessions to the political representation of the lower classes.

Thus, opposition to the Stamp Act had far-reaching significance. Masses of ordinary people, who had never ventured into the fields of high political policy, had suddenly discovered a power to influence events as well as to give vent to their personal jealousies and dislikes without fear of retribution. Never before had the assemblies found it so necessary to consolidate the people behind them in a common policy. On the contrary, the tradition of colonial politics had always been to confer on assemblies a privacy of debate and procedure that went far toward sealing them off from any direct responsibility to the electors. Once elected, the representatives formed a sort of private legislative club, with firm powers of discipline over any ordinary person who might have the effrontery to challenge them. The Stamp Act crisis made great inroads on this legislative privacy. In Massachusetts the assembly voted to erect public galleries so that citizens could attend debates; members went home to report their acts in defense of American liberties and returned reinforced with fiery resolutions, often dictated by themselves and endorsed by their town meetings. A ferment of discussion, incessant letters and essays in the newspapers, the publication of a spate of pamphlets all helped to bring the colonists together into a quite new and, in a sense, revolutionary condition of political activity. Isolated outbreaks had occurred in past generations when an aroused electorate had exercised its powers over a legislature that had for some reason got out of touch with the people. But never before had the people been excited into a general awareness of continuing political responsibility. It was the beginnings of a new politics—a politics of participation.

The crisis imposed a severe strain on colonial loyalties, made all the more painful because the British connection was the pride of those who best understood the nature of colonial rights and liberties. It was precisely from their status as British subjects that they derived these liberties. British law enacted and defended the rights that could be traced to the fundamental or natural laws to which all men and governments were subject.

The moral anguish was particularly striking in the case of James Otis, a Massachusetts lawyer and representative whose father had a bitter rivalry with Chief Justice Thomas Hutchinson. Otis's pamphlets against the Revenue and Stamp acts were probably the most popular of the early protests. Otis made short work of the spurious ministerial claim that the American colonies were "virtually" represented in Parliament, observing tersely that the unenfranchised people of such British towns as Sheffield and Manchester, whose position was being compared with that of the Americans, ought to be given the vote. But in spite of the vigor of his arguments, Otis pinned his case to some extremely dubious historical reasoning about opinions rendered by Coke a century and a half earlier, making connections that were almost entirely irrelevant to the colonial cause. He also emphasized the unbreakable character of parliamentary authority. Parliament, Otis held, was violating the laws of its own existence, and he hoped by making this point clear to place Parliament under a moral compulsion to alter its course. Members of Parliament, however, did not see the matter in the same light, and before long, Otis's arguments became unpopular and an embarrassment to the further articulation of a colonial case. Yet the animosity against Otis did not dispose of the constitutional difficulty. American assemblies had always accepted a certain measure of parliamentary control. Most of it had regulated trade, but some of it had pertained to internal institutions such as the establishment of an intercolonial post office, which was of obvious benefit to the colonies. British regulation of colonial currency was another aspect of internal control; its benefits were questionable, but the policy had not been challenged on constitutional grounds.

Thinkers other than Otis continued to engage themselves in trying to extricate colonial rights from the densely grown hedges of parliamentary authority. A fresh challenge arose with the taxes imposed by Townshend in 1767. The Townshend duties made a distinction between internal taxes, which the colonies had unanimously opposed, and so-called external taxes (levied only at ports of entry and not on internal transactions) which some colonial expositors, including Franklin, appeared to admit as legally tolerable. The Townshend Acts also prompted a Philadelphia lawyer, John Dickinson, to develop a much more advanced view of the political autonomy of the colonies, and his *Letters from a Farmer in Pennsylvania to the Inhabitants of the British Colonies* (1767–1768), which expounded the case with a cool and persuasive rationality, at once became extremely popular. Dickinson denied the power of Parliament to lay on the colonies any tax whatever. He acknowledged the legitimacy of the restraining acts, and he did not repudiate the superintending sovereignty of Parliament. But he held that this sovereignty was lawfully confined to those aspects of empire that no other power could regulate. Parliament had threatened to suspend the assembly of New York to force compliance by that province with an army quartering act. Dickinson pointed particularly to the dangers in the parliamentary assumption of this power, which he called a violation of the liberties of all the provinces. Yet, hoping for a return of Britain's "old good humour," he counseled Americans to speak their complaints at once in "the language of affliction and veneration." But if that failed, he advocated economic sanctions against Britain.

This thinking mixed boldness with prudence. It did not, however, resolve the constitutional difficulties that would persist if Parliament continued to exercise its imperial sovereignty in ways that encroached on the rights reserved to the colonies. Any extension of regulations on trade and finance would now produce still closer scrutiny of those rights. Townshend's duties were repealed, in 1770, not because of Dickinson's powers of reasoning, but because colonial merchants, under renewed pressures from committees of correspondence that were set up by the assemblies or sprang up spontaneously, imposed a ban on the importation of British goods. Once again, the boycott caused repercussions in England.

The nonimportation agreements that went somewhat falteringly into effect in 1769 were the result of two years of negotiation between the colonies. In 1768, in defiance of Governor Bernard, the Massachusetts assembly sent a circular letter to the other assemblies proposing joint action. Joint action, however, required prolonged and patient efforts to overcome all the difficulties of coordination, of mutual distrust, and of legitimate economic misgivings. There were times when it seemed unlikely that the colonists would ever succeed in presenting a united front against British ministers. When at last nonimportation was consummated, its scale was vastly more extensive and its implications more ominous than any previous retaliatory effort. By this time Britain had sent troops to keep order in Boston, and it was this move more than the duties themselves that sharpened the colonial reaction.

The administration of Lord North, who came to power in 1770, could have rescinded the duties without much loss or inconvenience. The policy had been a pet of Townshend's, on which no great ends were staked, and North had no desire to begin his administration by keeping alive an unnecessary quarrel. In April 1770 the duties were withdrawn—all except the trifling tax on tea, which was retained as a symbol of a power that Parliament had not relinquished. The reaction of the colonial merchants was an enormous relief. At last it seemed honestly reasonable to hope that after the disorders and recriminations of the last few years the peoples of Britain and its overseas colonies might rediscover their normal relationship. They had much to gain by trading with each other in harmony and peace, and most of the more responsible colonists certainly believed at this time that they had much to lose by persistent feuds with the mother country. Only a few were set on turning every occasion of discord into another constitutional crisis.

The most dangerous clash occurred, appropriately, in Boston the month before the duties were withdrawn. The British garrison there was a permanent aggravation to the more militant elements, and a target of hostility for the local rowdies. In March 1770, a small British detachment, provoked by catcalls and missiles, fired into a mob and killed five people, one a Negro. An engraving by Paul Revere subsequently converted the mob into gentlemen wearing wigs and three-cornered hats, and lost sight of the Negro. The soldiers were put on trial for murder, but were defended by John Adams and acquitted by the jury. While the "Boston Massacre" inflamed people and was not forgotten, no one desired a repetition, and most of the people of Massachusetts, both in the seaports and in the interior, seemed relieved when the atmosphere grew calmer after repeal of the Townshend Acts.

Although the province of New York, confronted by the threat of having its assembly dissolved, had buckled under to parliamentary dictation over the quartering act, and although General Gage, the British commander in Boston, was getting reinforcements, there seemed to be no serious prospect of disruption. The enforcement of the trade laws and the depredations of British customs officers caused continual irritation and occasional outbursts of fury among merchants and the maritime populations. But these actions, though they might make enemies for Britain, could not make a war. Stronger reasons, on both sides, would be needed for that. In the meantime, colonists experienced an interval of relative repose.

Lord North had some reason to congratulate himself for the comparative serenity that had descended on Anglo-American relations. His most acute anxieties had, on the face of it, nothing to do with America but with the misfortunes of the East India Company, a private company of such importance that it had some of the hallmarks of a public corporation. A few years earlier, members of the Rockingham administration had privately bought shares in the company in order to give themselves votes at its meetings. The British investment was huge, but the financial status of the company was wobbly and the collapse of a speculative boom in its shares in 1772 not only weakened its resources but brought with it a general economic setback that even affected the market for Virginia tobacco. The company had imported more tea than the English and American markets could absorb, but the North administration tried to relieve it of its difficulties by granting it a competitive advantage in the American colonies. In agreeing to a company request for a loan, the administration accepted a new proposal: the company would be empowered to market the tea entirely through its own agents in the colonies, thus not only cutting out the expenses, and profits, of the local merchants but offering price competition with the smuggled tea that came in from the Dutch island of St. Eustatius.

The tea was still subject to the unrepealed Townshend duty, which North decided, despite opposition from the Rockingham party, must be retained as a last reminder of the principle of parliamentary sovereignty. Why should the colonists, who had been consuming large quantities of taxed tea ever since the end of the nonimportation movement, as well as a number of other taxed products including molasses, rum, and sugar, have any special objections to the mere retention of the existing tax on tea? The principle of monopoly was new, but as some of the more important American merchants busied themselves with securing privileges as company agents, the matter of principle seemed moot.

This collusion between the great merchants, such as the Whartons of Philadelphia, and the British Parliament, which had obviously put consideration of the East India Company above the American colonists—a fine comment, incidentally, on the theory of "virtual representation"—played straight into the hands of the radical politicians. In Philadelphia the new radical party, composed of small traders, artisans, and politically advanced publicists, seized the issue to gain the initiative in the politics of the city and the province; they warned the people that if the tea monopoly went through unopposed there was no limit to the articles over which it could be extended. Yet the great and unifying issue was that of taxation. In all seaport cities the old leaders of resistance thundered against the revival of the tyranny of taxation without representation, and merchants who revealed little concern over the question of monopoly were moved to believe that the tea tax proved the worst about British government.

The strictly economic issues were of secondary importance. With the cargoes of tea on their way to America, radical leaders realized that once they had been unloaded the tea would be consumed and the point of the protest lost. In Boston, where four tea ships were due, the committee of correspondence kept up relentless excitement in the populace and equally relentless pressure on the shipowners. Armed guards were set to prevent unloading of the cargoes when the ships lay at anchor. Anyone who helped to unload them would be treated "as Wretches unworthy to live and will be made the first victims of our just Resentment," declared a public notice, ominously signed "THE PEOPLE." On the night of 16 December, after a stormy meeting had broken up in the afternoon, the tea was destroyed. Bands of men, dressed up as Mohawk Indians and armed with hatchets, boarded the tea ships and tipped their cargoes into Boston Harbor while a large crowd looked on with approval. By this one act of defiance they had solved the problem of what to do with the tea, after failing to get it sent back to England—and they had dramatized the issue to the whole continent.

They had also dramatized it to the British, whose reaction could be easily anticipated. Private property valued at nearly £10,000 had been destroyed—a fact that also disturbed a number of American merchants, who needed no instruction on the value of property. In default of any offer of compensation from Massachusetts, the North administration swung over to a policy of discipline. Its feelings were generally shared. Massachusetts had proved a source of constant insubordination and seemed bent on proving that it lay outside the bounds of parliamentary rule. Few in public life doubted that the only proper course was to bring the unruly province to submission. Those who did doubt the wisdom of the administration's measures had no practical alternative policy to propose; moreover, they belonged to a permanent opposition faction that the administration had found it safe to ignore.

Lord North, firmly backed by King George III, by large majorities in both houses of Parliament, and the mass of educated opinion, now proceeded to prove a point that the American radicals had long maintained. Advanced thinkers in the colonies, beginning with the ratiocinations demanded by the Revenue and Stamp acts, had moved toward the conclusion that parliamentary sovereignty was fundamentally incompatible with American liberties. Those colonial publicists who, for personal or geographical reasons, felt disenchanted with the spell of the British connection went further and concluded that their liberty could be made safe only in a state of complete independence. It was natural that colonial dissidents should work through existing local institutions. These institutions, the town meetings of New England and the assemblies of all the provinces, were the actual embodiment of colonial liberties. The North administration saw the point and busied itself with the preparation of laws that would go to the root of the trouble. In the spring of 1774 Parliament passed a group of bills that became known collectively in America as the Intolerable or Coercive Acts. The Massachusetts Government Act, by which Parliament assumed the power to amend a royal charter, made the annually elected council into a body appointed by the governor, increased the governor's other powers of appointment, and curtailed the town meeting; the Administration of Justice Act empowered the governor to transfer British subjects accused in the province of acts done in the course of duty to Britain for trial; a new Quartering Act imposed more troublesome regulations; and the Boston Port Bill closed the harbor until compensation had been paid both for the lost tea and for earlier damage by mobs. Even such a friend of the Americans as Barré believed that the Port Act was a just measure in view of the damage that had been done. Debate was prolonged, but few members of Parliament were disposed to question the principles of the Declaratory Act of 1766, and no less a sympathizer than Burke, after castigating the ministry, ended by voting with the majority.

The punishment meted out to Boston was extremely harsh, and it caused enough suffering to demonstrate that, for the moment, the fate of the colonies really did rest in Britain. The stringency of British policy, however, could not have better assisted the cause of American radicals. Whatever might be their attitudes on domestic issues, they were solidifying in resistance to Britain. Everywhere they appealed for help to the stricken city of Boston, whose people, they claimed, were deprived of their livelihood in the pure cause of American liberties. Although there were merchants and lawyers in New York and Philadelphia who suspected that the Bostonians had got what they deserved, it was impossible to stand against the tide of sympathy or resist the demands for relief.

At this juncture the British administration further outraged its colonial subjects by passing a piece of enlightened legislation for its recently acquired Canadian dominions. The Quebec Act of 1774 recognized the Roman Catholic religion for the Canadian French, and at once aroused Protestant New England's primitive fears of Rome. But the act struck a more sinister blow: it annexed the vast region lying northwest of the Ohio River to the government of Upper Canada, thus depriving prospective settlers of their hopes for self-government. The Quebec Act was immediately classed as one of the Coercive Acts and was assumed to be inspired by repressive motives.

It was in this quickening situation that the more radical elements in domestic politics, representative of artisans, small traders, and tenant and small farmers, were able to gain the initiative. These political groups did not spring out of thin air, nor were their primary interests directed against Britain. They had come into existence in the changed political atmosphere that was brought about mainly by the Stamp Act crisis, a crisis that had encouraged the politically inarticulate to believe they had a voice and deserved attention. The lower classes had much to complain of in the running of economic affairs in the cities. They were frequently deprived of the opportunities for fair competition through ordinances passed by unrepresentative city councils; they were the first to feel the pinch of hardship and unemployment; and they could never obtain redress through the existing systems of government. The greatest mercantile cities of America—Boston and Philadelphia —were badly under-represented in the provincial legislatures; moreover, property qualifications for the suffrage placed the poorer man in a position of chronic political insecurity. Voting qualifications were enforced with varying degrees of rigidity, and they were fairly often evaded. Also, the amounts of property they specified, which generally represented a small freehold or rented farm in the country or the ownership of a small business or workshop in town, did allow for inclusion on the election rolls of a high proportion of the employed population. But the regulations also left many townsmen in a vulnerable position, for economic depression could at any time throw them into debt and deprive them of the requisite property just when their demands for effective political action were likely to be most urgent. In Boston, with its famous "leveling" tendencies and highly demonstrative lower classes, the best estimates show that more than 40 per cent of the adult male population failed to meet the colonial property qualifications. This figure, relatively high for the period, was due to the fact that the city had a class of day laborers, mariners, and paupers not usually found in the countryside.

These urban discontents were buttressed by those registered in the country. In Pennsylvania, the farmers west of the three wealthy counties of Philadelphia (politically separate from the city), Bucks, and Chester had already begun to ship their market produce down to Baltimore because of the difficulties of reaching and selling through Philadelphia. The western counties shared with the city population a desire for fuller representation in the assembly. Up-valley farmers in New York, exasperated by their rent problems, were again showing signs of resentment against the great-family domination of their province.

In most of the provinces the older leadership kept the strands of power together by demonstrating their defiance of Britain while making concessions on broader representation and greater participation to the lower classes in the cities and the farmers in the interior. To argue that internal issues dominated these struggles for power to so great an extent that the imperial question was merely a lever seized by one or more parties for their own advantage would be a distorted simplification of a complex but extremely critical situation. Without doubt, such determined agitators as Samuel Adams and Charles Thomson, his capable Philadelphia counterpart, made the best of their opportunities. But British policies confronted American leaders with a narrowing margin of choice. As an act of provocation the Boston Tea Party was a stroke of genius: king and Parliament reacted with predictable severity, confronting Americans of all shades of temperament and opinion with the question of whether, in the last resort, they could count on Britain to respect any of the rights that they had always claimed as their own.

The problem led to renewed examination of the constitutional basis of these legal and traditional claims. As early as 1770, James Wilson, Scottish-born lawyer of Philadelphia, had embarked on an intellectual inquiry into parliamentary power that led him, against his own expectations, to conclude that Parliament had no constitutional power over the colonies at all. Each colony, in effect, was an independent sovereignty under the crown. He suppressed these opinions when the Townshend tariffs were repealed, in the hope that the question would disappear without the assistance of further pamphlet controversy. In 1774, however, the year of the Coercive Acts, Jefferson, in a survey of the history of the troubles, reached similar conclusions. The practical problem, apart from the fact that no British administration seemed likely to accept these views, was that the king was at one with his ministers. For, if parliamentary control were really to be removed in favor of a direct royal prerogative, the political result would be to give back to the king a great deal of power and patronage that had been won by Parliament since the days of the Stuarts. From a British constitutional standpoint, it would have been a solution full of the dangerous possibilities of a further access of royal power. Even the more radical British Whigs faltered when Americans revealed themselves as extremists.

The problems that faced America when her people defied the source of their existence and their laws lay far beyond the competence of individual provinces. After the passage of the Intolerable Acts, the need for concerted action was beyond dispute. Committees of correspondence, acting for provincial assemblies or congresses elected through the existing procedures, brought about a new intercolonial meeting. Once again the vital precedent was that of the Stamp Act crisis, but this time the meeting was far more representative than before. In September 1774 the first Continental Congress assembled in Carpenters' Hall in Philadelphia.

4

Government,
Foreign Relations,
and War

The troubles—domestic and international—with which the colonists had to contend as the Continental Congress convened were enormous, but the domestic ones came first. All lawful power in the colonies rested in the assemblies and in the systems of local government below them. The assemblies, however, could always be dissolved by royal or proprietary governors. The governor could refuse to issue writs for elections or he could move the place of meeting, thereby raising constant obstacles to effective action. The colonists needed their own representative bodies, based on the same electoral authority but independent of royal power. In each colony a provincial convention was elected to rival the colonial assembly, and it was often filled with many of the same representatives.

These developments, which by 1774 had become general throughout the colonies, stemmed in each instance from the experiences of the previous few years. As early as 1773, Virginia's assembly, foreseeing the need, had issued a call for legislative committees to keep in touch with each other across colonial frontiers; it was this move that heralded permanent intercolonial cooperation. Franklin, hearing the news, had written to Thomas Cushing of Massachusetts: "It is natural to suppose as you do, that, if the Oppressions continue, a Congress may grow out of that Correspondence." He also saw the anxiety of the British ministry. "But if the Colonies agree to hold a Congress, I do not see how it can be prevented."

The "oppressions" had appeared at their worst in New England and in the ports of other colonies. As long ago as 1768, British customs officers had seized the merchant vessel *Liberty*, belonging to John Hancock, one of the colonies' richest merchants; a year later militant Rhode Islanders destroyed the ship by fire. The state of coastal guerrilla war continued, reaching a dangerous level in 1772 when the British naval vessel *Gaspee,* on the lookout for smugglers, ran aground in a chase, was boarded by colonists, and burned in Narragansett Bay.

These provocations along the coast left many of the inland farmers unmoved. In Massachusetts they had always been suspicious of the leadership of Boston, had shown displeasure over the riots of 1765, and had proved obstinately difficult to arouse. Samuel Adams and his militant associates worked ceaselessly to bring home the issues to their own countrymen, and until the Boston Tea Party, they were far more fully engaged in trying to create a dependable mood of opposition than in remonstrating with the British. In the autumn of 1772, however, the ministry further revealed its hand when it ordered that the salaries of five superior court justices were to be paid out of customs revenues, making them independent of local support.

Samuel Adams addressed the populace in a typical piece of propaganda in the local press:

> To what a State of Infamy, Wretchedness, and Misery shall we be reduc'd if our Judges shall be prevail'd upon to be thus degraded into *Hirelings,* and the *Body of the People* shall suffer their free Constitution to be overturn'd and ruin'd. Merciful GOD! Inspire Thy People with Wisdom and Fortitude. . . . Let not the iron Hand of Tyranny ravish our Laws and seize the Badge of Freedom, nor avow'd Corruption and the murderous Rage of lawless Power be ever seen on the sacred Seat of Justice!

As for action, Adams urged: "Let associations and combinations be everywhere set up to consult and recover our just rights."

"Associations and combinations" did spring forth throughout the colonies. The Boston Committee of Correspondence, formed late in 1772, operated as a nucleus for a province-wide organization. Governor Hutchinson became the focal point for a bitter opposition, and his removal was soon the first aim of this early embodiment of an American "Patriot" party. Hutchinson, a man of great ability and courage, exerted considerable influence, and had long stood between the more ardent Boston leaders and their objectives in the assembly. On 20 January 1769, Hutchinson had observed in a letter to England:

> I never think of the measures necessary for the peace and good order of the Colonies without pain. There must be an abridgement of what is called English liberty. I relieve myself by considering that in a remove from the state of nature to the most perfect state of Government there must be a great restraint of natural liberty. I doubt if it is possible to project a System of Government in which a Colony 3000 miles distant from the Parent State shall enjoy all the liberties of the Parent State. . . .

The disclosure—through Franklin—of letters to British officials in which Hutchinson expressed this need to abridge liberty irreparably damaged his standing. In 1773 the assembly majority demanded his removal, and Samuel Adams, who understood the uses of propaganda, used the word "Tory" to vilify the few legislators who stood with Hutchinson.

In New England the ministers of the Congregational churches, still extremely sensitive to the "bishopric" question, formed a potent agency of anti-British opinion. Preaching every Sunday, they probably reached an even wider public than the press—and New Englanders were extraordinarily attentive readers of their burgeoning newspapers. All the same, local committees of correspondence had no lawful foundations and met with much recalcitrance and hostility. It was not until after the Boston Tea Party, and especially after passage of the Intolerable Acts, that the course of events gave them the decisive advantage in their struggle to enforce opposition policies on local populations. After the meeting of the first Continental Congress, in September 1774, they stood on a new foundation of authority; they then became the instruments for carrying out the domestic policies sponsored by provincial congresses, and by the Continental Congress itself.

The delegations selected by the provincial assemblies for the Congress in Philadelphia were characteristic of the more dynamic branch of the leadership that the colonies had produced in recent years. It was still possible, however, to be deeply committed to the assertion of American rights, and to be prepared for sweeping new measures of economic pressure, while fully believing and fervently hoping that these means could yet secure a permanent reconciliation with Britain. It was the result rather than the intention of the Congress's internal policies that caused the local organizations throughout the colonies to be made of revolutionary material. But that result could hardly have been avoided if Congress's minimal intentions were to have any effect.

To exert pressure on Britain, as had been done over the Stamp Act and the Townshend tariffs, it was first necessary to gain agreement among the colonies. Restraint on trade caused hardships, and cohesion had been difficult to maintain on the earlier occasions. Once the Congress reached agreement on the extensive plans for boycotting British trade and produce, it had to rely on the local committees to enforce these patriotic but disagreeable acts of self-abnegation on merchants and consumers. The Congress handed down these powers in a resolution on the Continental Association, agreed to and signed on 20 October 1774, which declared the intentions of the colonial delegations and gave the committees the powers they would need. The first article read:

> That . . . we will not import, into British America, from Great-Britain or Ireland, any goods, wares, or merchandise whatsoever, or from any other place, any such goods, wares, or merchandise, as shall have been exported from Great Britain or Ireland. . . .

Merchants were told to send no more orders to Great Britain, and the delegates agreed to encourage domestic produce:

> We will use our utmost endeavours to improve the breed of sheep and increase their number to the greatest extent. . . . We will, in our several stations, encourage frugality, economy, and industry, and promote agriculture, arts, and the manufactures of this country, especially that of wool; and will discountenance and discourage every species of extravagance and dissipation, especially all horse-racing, and all kinds of gaming, cock-fighting, exhibitions of shews, plays, and other expensive diversions and entertainments; and on the death of any relation or friend, none of us . . . will go into any further mourning dress than a black crape or ribbon on the arm or hat for gentlemen, and black ribbon and necklace for ladies; and we will discontinue the giving of gloves and scarves at funerals.

These items reveal something of the ordinary social habits of the times. They also reveal a much deeper theme, for the impulse toward revolution, of which these were some of the portents, was also an impulse toward a purification of some of the vices that these earnest descendants of earlier Puritans wanted to expunge from colonial society. The colonies seemed to be catching the taint of Old World self-indulgence; men who believed British tyranny to be a product of British corruption had a particularly compelling argument in their drive for purification of the manners and morals of their compatriots. The association resolution further authorized the choosing of "a committee . . . in every county, city, and town, by those who are qualified to vote for representatives in the legislature, whose business it shall be attentatively to observe the conduct of all persons touching this association."

Persons violating the rules were subject to the discipline of the local association committee. When there was reason to suspect that a trader was selling imported goods, or that a private citizen was consuming them, the committee would publish their names, threaten them with boycotts and violence, and sometimes drive them out of the town. Covering a victim with tar and feathers, one of the most popular modes of enforcement, was also the most frightful. Victims included not only those who were trying to beat their neighbors or competitors, but also people who denied that the association committees, or the provincial or continental congresses, had any lawful authority to tell them what they might or might not do.

While these local groups pursued their ceaseless activities all over the country, the delegations in Philadelphia were obliged to grapple with some of the most intractable problems involved in any form of continental organization. On their first day, before they could proceed to make any decision, they had to agree on how to vote, thus finding themselves faced with the basic question of sovereignty. Immediately behind it lay the greater question of nationality: were the delegates to regard themselves as nationally independent of each other, or were they in the process of forming a new nation? In principle, many would have preferred to construct the Congress on a proportional system by which each colony would be assigned a certain number of votes according to its property and population. It is significant of the social and political assumptions not only of the delegates in Philadelphia but of the committees they represented that property and population were considered in the same context. Property was widely distributed through the colonies, but very few people·with an influential voice in public affairs could have been found to argue that individuals, rather than property, ought to be considered the measure of a political system. When under-represented counties petitioned their assemblies for a larger voice in provincial affairs, they invariably stated their tax payments, usually before mentioning their populations, as the reason for seeking increased representation. The priority of property was not a mere side issue of the rhetoric about taxation and representation; it was a fundamental ingredient of the social order and thence, by direct connection, of the political system. What the delegates at Philadelphia would have wished to do was to tie property into the system by which voting power was tabulated, giving to each colony a proportion due to its "weight," to use an expression that occurred in these discussions.

The great difficulty was that the actual distribution of property was unknown. Nor did any reliable census exist. Plans to take a census of population had caused much resistance, both in the colonies and in Britain, on biblical grounds: King David had violated a divine decree when he numbered the Israelites, which was believed to have caused the visitation of a plague. The risk had soon to be run, but the immediate problem indicated the disharmony among the colonies. John Adams explained the issue in a speech on the first day:

> This is a Question of great Importance. —If we vote by Colonies, this Method will be liable to great Inequality and Injustice, for 5 small Colonies, with 100,000 People in each may outvote 4 large ones, each of which has 500,000 Inhabitants. . . . Is the Weight of a Colony to be ascertained by the Number of Inhabitants, merely—or by the Amount of their Trade, the Quantity of their Exports and Imports, or by a compound Ratio of both. This will lead us into such a Field of Controversy as will greatly perplex us. Besides I question whether it is possible to ascertain, at this Time, the Numbers of our People or the Value of our Trade. It

will not do in such a Case to take each other's Words. It ought to be ascertained by authentic Evidence, from Records.

For the time being, an unsatisfactory makeshift was adopted. Each colony was to vote as a single unit, making the smallest equal to the greatest. Meanwhile, taxes would be proportioned on the basis of population, about which more was known than about property. The rationale for this agreement was significant. Everyone knew disparities of property existed between and within colonies; but it was also acknowledged that on the whole the distribution of property throughout the populations of the colonies was sufficiently widespread and consistent to allow the procedure to work without serious distortions. It was not a system that satisfied many delegates as a permanent solution, and it gave concern to those from the larger colonies, who feared a disproportionate influence by the smaller ones. Patrick Henry made a powerful bid to disregard the old boundaries, a course that would have advanced the national as opposed to the provincial nature of the Congress—and of the peoples of the colonies; it would also have given an advantage to the larger states, including Virginia:

> Government is dissolved. Fleets and Armies and the present State of Things shew that Government is dissolved. —Where are your Land Marks? your boundaries of Colonies? We are in a State of Nature, Sir. . . . The Distinctions between Virginians, Pennsylvanians, New Yorkers and New Englanders, are no more. I am not a Virginian, but an American.

These questions were to recur, in various forms, throughout the life of the continental system, and they were to play a profound part in the debates that went into the making of the new federal Constitution in 1787; they involved the fundamental relationship of the individual to the states (as the colonies were soon to be deemed) and of the states to the continental government.

Although the Continental Congress was not a cross section of colonial society, it was in certain important ways representative. The leadership that constituted the several delegations was consistent with that of the assemblies and provincial congresses. Divisions that came to light within the Congress, therefore, reflected divisions among substantial elements in American society. This is not to say that these were the only levels on which social antagonism could produce political divisions; resentful tenant farmers, unemployed mariners, artisans, and small traders smarting under city oligarchies, as well as some former Regulators of the Carolina backcountry, could well feel that the men of means who had been appointed to meet in Philadelphia were closer to being their enemies than their representatives. The great political obstacle in the way of these widespread but dispersed dissident groups was their lack not only of central organization but of any central aim. It was troublesome enough to devise a continental congress; a continental opposition would have been impossible. Indeed, it would have been irrelevant, because discontent was directed against oppressions or impositions at the local level, not the continental. Such intercolonial or internal differences as surfaced at Philadelphia were bound to be those that involved substantial interests, and the views already held by men of political influence.

Regional differences were apparent from the beginning. The new nonconsumption plans threatened to divide the delegation from South Carolina against the rest—until the rest gave way. Slavery emerged soon afterward as a disruptive issue of broader proportions and graver implications. The question of authority over western lands, and of policy for their disposal, isolated the states with claims to these lands from those that had none. It also brought clashes between different speculative interests. Questions of economic policy revealed jealousies between landed and mercantile interests. But before the delegates could begin to resolve any of these issues, it was necessary to decide what policy to pursue toward Britain and what forms of colonial organization to establish in place of the obviously unsatisfactory arrangements of the past.

The experience of recent years made clear that if the American colonies wanted to have a sound alternative to the parliamentary sovereignty that had so plainly proved incompatible with their liberties, they would have to start by achieving a much greater degree of coordination than they had ever been willing to contemplate. For a short period the conservatives in the Congress held an initiative; they had come to Philadelphia hoping to find an

effective means of uniting the colonies in order to demand a
redress of grievances from Britain—and thereby restore the harmony of the empire. Joseph Galloway, until recently one of Franklin's party allies in Pennsylvania politics, offered a simple and
reasonable plan of union. It would give the colonies a separate legislative assembly of their own; legislation for the colonies could be
introduced either in the American assembly or in Parliament, but
it would not be valid until approved by both bodies. A president
general appointed by the king would preside over the colonial
legislature, whose members were to be selected by the thirteen
colonial assemblies. When this plan was presented, the Congress
had just adopted the fiery Suffolk Resolves, drawn up by Joseph
Warren, a Suffolk County, Massachusetts, physician, and brought
to Philadelphia by the indefatigable Revere. In Galloway's view
these resolves "contained a complete declaration of war against
Great Britain." They declared that the rights of Massachusetts
were based on nature, the British constitution, and its charter,
and that George III was sovereign by "compact." The Intolerable
Acts were a gross infraction of American rights; Americans need
not obey them, and should cease trade with Great Britain and ignore the courts.

The adoption of the Suffolk resolutions placed the Congress
firmly behind Massachusetts. It did not eliminate, however, all
possibility of a policy of conciliation. Genuine separatists, led by
Samuel Adams (John may have been a little behind him in ad-
vocating outright independence, still hoping for reconciliation
through bold resistance), well knew that Galloway's plan put their
objectives in danger; if it were adopted, and if Parliament agreed
to it, American independence would be far more remote as a result. The reasonableness of the Galloway plan lay in the fact that
it offered a chance of gaining the expressed purposes of the Congress, and the more militant elements had to fight hard to get it
defeated—which they did by the narrowest margin. They even
succeeded in expunging it from the records when the journals were
later published. It cannot, of course, be known how the plan
would have been received by Parliament, but the episode reflects
the other great division in American society: the division between
those who wanted to press on to independence, and those who

wanted to establish a new system in the colonies expressly in order to retain the British connection. Before dissolving, on 26 October, the Continental Congress ordained elections to a second congress, to meet on 10 May 1775, if their grievances should not have been redressed in the interval.

Delegates to the second Congress, John Adams found, were still suspicious, as many had been in the first, of the intentions of Massachusetts. "America," he wrote to his wife, "is a great, unwieldy Body. Its Progress must be slow. It is like a large Fleet sailing under Convoy. The fleetest Sailors must wait for the dullest and slowest." Yet reconciliation was becoming a more unlikely solution. Fighting had broken out at Concord and Lexington on 19 April when local farmers were called out to resist a British column moving from Boston to seize the armory at Concord. The news fired many of the delegates at Philadelphia with the determination to defend their claims by force of arms. A somewhat spurious compromise offer from Lord North, which arrived with the news of Lexington and Concord, was rejected, and preparations for defense were pressed with a new vigor. Resistance meant an army, and an army needed a commander. The Congress appointed the distinguished Virginia militia colonel George Washington, whose courage at the time of General Edward Braddock's defeat twenty years earlier had been reported in England, to command the army that it called into existence. Washington wasted no time. He made his way to Boston to join his forces, taking command on Cambridge Common on 3 July, shortly after the inconclusive action at Breed's Hill (which has been inaccurately ascribed to Bunker Hill) on 17 June. During the autumn and winter, Washington consolidated his position and hemmed in the British forces. The British commander, General Sir William Howe, found himself unable to maneuver, and on 17 March 1776 he evacuated Boston by sea, taking with him more than a thousand inhabitants who preferred to live under British protection.

The initiative was clearly on the side of those aiming for a break with Britain. Even so, the possibility remained that Britain might still come forward with offers of which the conservatives could take advantage. As events seemed to declare that the Congress and the British were opposing sides in a war that could lead only to independence or submission, some influential advocates of American rights began to grow nervous of the consequences. The most important of these was Dickinson, to whom John Adams once referred as "a certain great reputation and piddling genius." Dickinson's intellectual grasp of the grounds on which the colonies could claim their independence was not matched by that dash of impetuousness that leadership needs in moments of crisis. Nevertheless, Dickinson's standing was so high that he was made chairman of a committee to draft articles under which the colonies were to enter into a permanent confederation; even after opposing the Declaration of Independence, Dickinson continued to be a man of power and reputation both in Congress and in Delaware, the state to which he had moved.

Dickinson and other conservatives in Congress who hoped for a rapprochement were not, however, to prevail. On 6 July 1775 the Congress promulgated a "Declaration of the Causes and Necessity of Taking up Arms" which rehearsed the history of the quarrel with Britain and accused the British of an "unprovoked assault on the inhabitants" of Massachusetts Bay. "Hostilities, thus commenced by the *British* troops, have been since prosecuted by them without regard to faith or reputation."

The fourteen months between April 1775 and the Declaration of Independence in July 1776 were extraordinarily crowded with events. Yet in retrospect, it is what the Congress did not do that seems harder to understand than what it did. For the Congress waited a further year after Lexington, during which its forces scored notable successes in New England and South Carolina, before taking the leap into independence. In the interval, New England was effectively cleared of British troops while the rest of British America made immediate preparations for war. Each colony mobilized its militia, and the Congress raised an army that would be able to cross colonial boundaries as the strategy of the war, and the movements of the British, might demand. Girding itself for a prolonged struggle, the Congress also took steps to encourage the manufacture of American goods, to authorize and issue American currencies without British permission, to organize its internal structure for purposes of establishing an intercolonial government, and to initiate a foreign policy. In August 1775 the Congress was sufficiently confident of its gains and prowess to send an expedition to Canada.

This daring and badly calculated venture was in part a response to the Quebec Act, a measure the colonists had grouped with the Intolerable Acts. In the belief that the Canadians, like themselves, were thirsting for liberty, the Congress dispatched an expedition which, it was hoped, would join forces with a great uprising of British Canadians. The British Canadians did not rise, the congressional force proved dismally unequal to its military tasks, and before the end of 1775 the enterprise had collapsed.

This failure was a setback for the separatists. The Congress remained deeply and anxiously divided, and evidence of military incompetence could hardly encourage the cautious to believe that a war could be won. The prolonged delay in making progress toward independence can be partly explained by the problem of mobilizing, throughout the colonies, a public opinion that would not only support the provincial congresses as legitimate governments, but would also fully accept the risks. There had been nothing automatic about the adoption of the association endorsed by the first Continental Congress. Though Maryland, Virginia, and South Carolina put it into effect with a sense of urgency, in New York only three of the thirteen counties acted on it and seven of them ignored it completely. This caution and hesitation persisted throughout 1775 and early 1776. The permanent presence of the British in New York City, after they had driven Washington southward, secured the port for British use and gave the British armies a strategically important base. It also protected the spirit of moderation among many merchants and farmers who had been ready to proclaim Whig sentiments during the ascendancy of the Sons of Liberty.

Yet in certain important respects events did conspire to assist the separatists, and it was an irony that was consistent with the character of dealings between Britain and her colonies over the previous twelve years that British policy was the driving force behind these events. Samuel Adams clearly saw how American reactions could turn British policies to the advantage of those who believed in independence. "We cannot make events," he remarked; "our business is wisely to improve them." And again: "Mankind are governed more by their feelings than by reason," adding that "events which excite those feelings will produce wonderful effects." A series of events had already done so. In December 1775, Parliament passed a new measure, the American Prohibitory Act. It was a virtual declaration of war. The Boston Port Act was repealed and in its place a complete prohibition was imposed on all American commerce. American ships were made subject to seizure by the Royal Navy, and commissioners were to be authorized to receive the submission of the American colonies, until which time the act was to continue in force. The king and his administration thought the Prohibitory Act would bring the rebellious colonists to their knees, but Charles Fox, who had some sympathy for the colonists' cause, was more to the point when he advised Parliament that it ought to be called "a bill for carrying more effectively into execution the resolves of the Congress."

If at that point the British had been capable of making anything resembling a correct military appraisal, and had sent an army of 200,000, as Gage had earlier demanded, instead of 20,000, and if they had shown any ability to muster the resources of the widely scattered but far-reaching support that existed in the American population, they might have won the war. But they now compounded their earlier mistakes. They had already underestimated the Americans, both in showing contempt for their courage and caliber and in failing to grasp the implications of a war against the people. Now they gave the American moderates no room to maneuver. The tougher the British line, the less chance the conservative leadership had to win an appeal for a reasonable reconciliation.

For years—ever since the Stamp Act—the most persuasive of American spokesmen had been arguing for the legitimacy of colonial claims under the constitution on the basis that the constitution afforded them all the legitimate protection of which loyal subjects could stand in need. In the process, the Americans had been forced to refine their concept of their own relationship to Britain under the constitution. The mere existence of an American Congress implied that if redress were not obtainable when all the colonies spoke in concert, then redress would have to be sought by other means. The idea that the Congress might see its duty as that of mere submission, of a renunciation of all the claims it had ever made, contradicted the cumulative logic of recent American experience. British intransigence narrowed American choices; but many colonists still hoped for a reprieve, failing to see how little ground was left to them. The light they needed, however, was provided by a single flash: in January 1776 a pamphlet called *Common Sense* appeared.

Thomas Paine, a self-taught East Anglian corset maker, had lived in the colonies only two years, but had soon made himself known in Philadelphia political circles. He was in no sense an original philosophical thinker, but he possessed an electrifying power of talking neither up nor down but straight to ordinary readers in language that formulated and set free their thoughts—or the thoughts they had not quite dared to think. The greatness of *Common Sense* as a work of propaganda was in both its language and its timing. It liberated people from outworn loyalties at a moment of doubt and tension by addressing them in a style unfettered by the customary rhetorical elaborations and legalistic refinements. To hear the king described as "the royal brute of England" came as a joyous shock to the common people. Paine was no orator, and Patrick Henry no writer. But the two men had something in common. They were the most urgent and articulate spokesmen of a class and a generation that had been obliged in the past to petition their elders and to get a hearing only through the advocacy of their superiors.

Common Sense sold 120,000 copies and went rapidly through twenty-five editions in distant parts of the colonies. By contrast, Wilson's learned and intellectually important treatise *Considerations on the Nature and Extent of the Legislative Authority of the British Parliament* and Thomas Jefferson's *A Summary View of the Rights of British America* had one edition each. No one can ever measure the influence of a pamphlet or a speech on the mood of its readers or hearers. Yet great risks are seldom taken without emotion, and no one, whatever his sentiments, was inclined to deny the impact either of Henry or of Paine.

In Philadelphia itself the conservatives retained considerable influence. The old Quaker leadership had ceased to dominate politics. Its former authority had become diffused among the merchant gentry, of whom an increasing number were Anglicans and not inclined to push their quarrel with Britain to extremes. These elements, who still controlled the assembly, were keenly aware that the imperial issue was directly linked to that of domestic power. The choice before them was awkward, for concessions to the radicals might mean an anti-British majority and rigid rejection of radical demands might lead to an electoral defeat—or, worse, rebellion. In March 1776, the assembly at last agreed to demands for some extension of representation, and succeeded, for the time being, in keeping control, as late as May, the Philadelphia city elections returned a conservative majority. In the interval, however, the Adamses and other separatists in Congress were working in close conjunction with the Pennsylvania radicals, for they were well aware of the strategic importance of that central province, which would one day have some reason to call itself "the Keystone State."

The spring elections of 1776 to legislatures throughout the colonies gave many of the delegations to the reconvened Continental Congress a mandate for independence. Those of Virginia were particularly important, because people of other colonies, New England especially, were inclined to regard the Virginia gentry as great aristrocrats of naturally conservative disposition. The Virginia elections were exciting, with many voters in a mood to question some of their older allegiances; several longtime representatives lost their seats, and even such an influential leader as George Mason had to fight to win. It was well that he did, for he soon became the strongest hand in drafting Virginia's new constitution. The Virginia results were a vote for independence, and it was appropriate that the resolution to that end should be moved in the Congress by Richard Henry Lee.

The Congress adopted Lee's resolution on 2 July, having previously appointed a small committee to draft a declaration. The drafting was entrusted to Jefferson because of his recognized felicity of style, a recognition that was not to be disappointed. By the time the Declaration of Independence was adopted by the Congress on 2 July, however, it had been through more than one draft, and represented a compromise between the views of different interests that had been brought together more in defense against a common attack than in advancement of inherent compatibilities. Much the most important issue on which Jefferson himself was forced to compromise was that of slavery, and particularly of the slave trade, of which he wrote a denunciation into his first draft. Undoubtedly, Jefferson could have raised widespread support for his views from the provinces further north, but other members of the Congress, sitting as a committee of the whole house, insisted that the danger, at this critical stage, of a nasty split with the colonies further south should be avoided, and Jefferson's condemnation of slavery was duly expunged.

The Declaration of Independence, promulgated on 4 July 1776, was recognized at the time for what it was to be—one of the fundamental documents of modern history. It consisted mainly of a list of grievances against George III dating from 1763; the choice was significant, for it implied that the colonies were satisfied with the relationship that existed at that date and would, in principle, have been ready to re-establish it. All of the exactions, restraints, and prohibitions, including the withholding of representation from some of the interior counties, which successive British administrations had imposed on the colonies, were laid to the charge of the king, as were the depredations of British troops since the fighting had begun. The implicit political theory behind this formulation was that the colonial peoples were equal to the British people, acknowledging the common sovereignty of the British crown but not of the British Parliament. The renunciation was, therefore, a renunciation of allegiance to the crown alone; obligations to Parliament were rejected by omission. The Declaration relied on the Whig theory of contract that had served the Convention Parliament: James II was deemed to have broken his contract with the English people and by that act to have relinquished the throne, which was then declared vacant. This was a step to which the Continental Congress did not proceed, however, and no negotiations were undertaken to induce any of the existing royal houses of Europe to supply a monarch for the United States.

In its philosophical overtones, the preamble invoked the natural laws under which that contract was supposed to have been made. Until recently, colonial remonstrations to Parliament and petitions to the king had assumed the sufficiency of the constitution, which was generally believed to have been the institutional means that the English people had adopted for embodying the natural rights of men in their own political affairs. The most salient of these rights was that of property, and the entire point of American arguments had been their consistency with prevailing English theory on property rights. Now that the colonies took it on themselves to reject British protection, however, Jefferson roundly declared that the laws to which the Americans appealed were those of "Nature and nature's God," not those established under the British constitution. The affirmation that "all men are created equal" flashed like a beacon from the Declaration to illuminate the paths of countless campaigners for liberty in later generations; but its most practical immediate application was that the Americans, as a people, were equal to the British and entitled under the laws of nature to the protection of the same rights. It also clearly carried a more individual resonance, amplified by the brilliant invocation of the right to "life, liberty, and the pursuit of happiness." One of the social and economic, and, moreover, of the psychological consequences of the American Revolution was to be the release of a considerable degree of individualism, which could always draw ideological support from this celebrated phrase.

The Declaration was duly signed and proclaimed. It bears signatures of men who joined the Congress later than 4 July, and the inference must be that the parchment was deliberately retained for the addition of incoming members. It thus became a sort of loyalty oath. The signers, after all, were taking an extraordinary risk, for if they lost the war they could scarcely hope to exonerate themselves from charges of treason. It was right, therefore, that every delegate who participated in the activities of the Congress should take his full share of the responsibility.

Dickinson, cautious to the last, refused to leap over the brink into the gulf of independence. He was not the only man of influence who had been drawn reluctantly to the brink; even Wilson postponed his decision as long as possible. Yet the Congress as a whole knew that it could not now step back. If after all its remonstrances it had failed to take the final step, it would soon have started to lose its credibility throughout the country. Britain, with a fleet and an army, was preparing to bring down the Congress, whose authority it did not reckon one of the laws of nature; a failure of nerve would soon have communicated itself to the people. Beyond this immediate and domestic consideration lay the question of foreign support. If the Americans were to win they would need the aid of France. But would the French monarchy join forces with the Americans merely to enable them to gain a redress of their grievances, thereby restoring the empire and making it stronger than ever? To seek French aid itself meant a commitment to independence.

Independence once declared, Congress turned to foreign affairs; it set up a committee and entered into negotiations with the French court. The prospects for a military alliance with France arose from the fact that the French had never accepted their defeat in Canada as final. For more than a century, the presence of France in North America had acted as a restraint on the people of New England, who could never divest themselves of the need for British protection; by the same token, the collapse of France had released New England from this threat. France, therefore, had waited for what seemed a probable, if not an inevitable, quarrel between those restive northern colonies and their distant parent. Yet the problem for France was not simple; any European power that interfered in a neighbor's colonial war incurred considerable responsibilities, and the French monarchy could not be expected to intervene until it had reason to believe not only that the Americans would fight but that they could win.

France, consequently, could not openly acknowledge its assistance to the new republic until the air became much clearer than it was in 1776, but it agreed to help the Americans through loans and clandestine shipments of arms. Not until after the American victory at the Battle of Saratoga in 1777 was the court of Louis XVI at last willing to enter into a formal alliance. Two treaties were then concluded between the Congress and France, one economic and the other military. The two countries became commercial partners, offering each other most-favored-nation benefits; and they became military allies, bound to pursue the war jointly, with neither partner permitted to conclude a separate peace. France then worked to make the war general, and persuaded the Spanish monarchy to enter on its side. Spain, anxious to regain

Gibraltar, was willing to go to war against Britain, but as the possessor of a vast, ramshackle American empire would not condone a colonial rebellion and refused to ally itself with the Congress. The longer the war went on, the more widespread it became, with Britain's old enemies seizing their opportunity for revenge and the reclamation of lost possessions. Before the end of the War of American Independence, most of Europe had been drawn in either against Britain or in a state of armed neutrality against British sea power.

For the Congress, the other most urgent political task lay on the domestic side of its responsibilities. The legal basis for the existing association between the states had yet to be provided, and a committee under Dickinson's chairmanship was given the job of drafting the Articles of Confederation. The Dickinson draft, which was presented in July 1776, proposed to confer on Congress the powers over war, foreign policy, commerce, and the disposal of western lands, which had devolved upon it from Great Britain. The states would retain jurisdiction over their internal affairs, which included a far greater degree of autonomy than was usually enjoyed by the provinces of European states. Nevertheless, the central assumption of the Articles was that a mantle of sovereignty had been handed over by Britain—or rather, snatched by the United States—and that only the Congress could shoulder the responsibilities that went with it.

The Dickinson draft accepted the earlier decision that voting in the Congress should be by states, not by population. Delegates from the larger states, notably Massachusetts, Pennsylvania, and Virginia, had never been satisfied with this plan; they wanted voting to be in proportion to population. Delegates from the "landless" states—those whose western boundaries precluded claims for their own enlargement—were determined to prevent the landed states from gobbling up the West in their own interests; to this extent, they were anxious to see the Congress strengthened. Accordingly, they were enraged by an amendment to Dickinson's draft by which Virginia and the other landed states removed the power over the West from those conferred on the Congress, and added a provision to protect their claims by affirming that no state might be deprived of its territory without its consent. This amendment might still have left room for legal discussion of whether or not such claims were valid, but a further month of debate led only to a general postponement.

When debate on the proposed Articles was resumed in 1777, a new wave of objections was raised, primarily by Thomas Burke of North Carolina. States that regarded themselves as being weak, either because of small populations, exposed positions, or poverty, were beginning to express fears about their future in a confederation dominated, as they imagined, by the wealthy and populous. The Dickinson draft went back to committee, reappearing later in a form that left the states with sovereign power over their own policies. In short, the Congress, endowed with authority over foreign affairs and with such other powers as were essential for waging war, would continue to function as little more than a league of independent states. It was given no power to tax; it could lay requisitions on the states, but state governments were only morally, not physically, obliged to raise them. It was given no power over internal commerce; though it might conclude treaties with foreign nations, no clear certainty existed that it would have the power to enforce these treaties within the boundaries of the individual states. Since the United States consisted entirely of individual states, these limitations substantially weakened its standing with world powers. On major issues, a vote of nine states was required for action, and the Articles, being in effect a treaty among equals, could be altered or amended only by the unanimous vote of all thirteen subscribing states.

These provisions left the western lands in control of the states that claimed them, a condition that failed to satisfy some of the most influential speculators who lived outside those states. Governor Thomas Johnson of Maryland, being one of them, championed the opposition of his state, which refused to ratify the Articles until the landed states surrendered their claims to Congress. So intense was this opposition that the draft remained unratified until 1781. The greater part of the war was fought by a Congress whose constitutional authority was in a state of suspension.

That such a Congress did manage the direction of a prolonged war is all the more remarkable. Its authority could be sustained, in the long run, only because it represented the varied communities scattered over the land, because it had appointed a commander whose powers of leadership engaged the loyalties of men of all regions, and because the determination of the Americans convinced the French government that they could win. Continental America had no natural or historical context into which to fit its united efforts. It shaped itself in the hour of crisis through its combined leadership in the Congress, and through the exertions of its leaders and enthusiasts in every town and county.

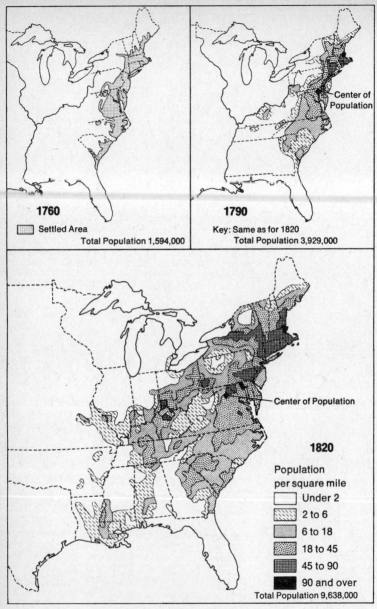

1760

Settled Area

Total Population 1,594,000

1790

Center of Population

Key: Same as for 1820

Total Population 3,929,000

Center of Population

1820

Population
per square mile

Under 2

2 to 6

6 to 18

18 to 45

45 to 90

90 and over

Total Population 9,638,000

Population: 1760, 1790, and 1820

5

The People and Their State Constitutions

When the Americans took up arms against the king they undoubtedly made themselves into rebels, but the history and the rhetorical style of their argument strongly disposed them to think of themselves as rebels in a lawful cause. The contract theory of government was not a mere dialectical convenience; they had been bred in it. They believed that it was they themselves who were the true Whigs, and that in the strictest constitutional sense it was the British government that had broken the bounds of the constitution. This concern for legality made it urgently necessary for the political leaders to satisfy themselves and their constituents that they were acting within the law as they subscribed to it. It also helps to explain why the provincial conventions, which seized power from the old colonial assemblies, set about creating new state constitutions so early in their independent proceedings.

These conventions were not legal bodies. Neither were the committees of correspondence that sprang up under their protection. But a basis of legal continuity was laid by the use of existing election laws for the choice of members to the new conventions. The excited state of the populace brought out more voters than usual, and as it is not likely that the details of the laws were closely observed, the provincial congresses were at least as representative as the assemblies had been. In principle, however, the rule of law was a psychological necessity for men who had staked their entire claims on nothing less. It was also a social and political necessity in a period that offered every temptation to lawlessness and disorder. In some places the courts ceased to sit, to the great satisfaction of debtors and criminals, and the social consequences of the suspension of civil order were forcibly brought home to no less a patriot than John Adams by an encounter that he recorded in his *Autobiography* in the late summer of 1775. A man whom he had often defended, and sometimes prosecuted, in the courts, whom he described as "a common Horse Jockey," saluted him with this expression of gratitude: "Oh! Mr. Adams what great Things have you and your Colleagues done for Us! We can never be gratefull enough to you. There are no Courts of Justice now in this Province, and I hope there never will be another!" Adams made no reply to the man.

> Is this the Object for which I have been contending? . . . Are these the Sentiments of such People? And how many of them are there in the Country? Half the Nation for what I know: for half the Nation are Debtors if not more. . . . If the Power of the Country should get into such hands, and there is great danger that it will, to what purpose have we sacrificed our Time, health and every Thing else? Surely We must guard against this Spirit and these Principles or We shall repent of all our Conduct. . . .

Such were Adams's reflections, until he recollected the good sense and integrity of the great body of the people, and the goodness of providence. Yet the incident confirmed his more conservative instincts. These were soon reflected in a pamphlet, circulated as *Thoughts on Government,* which was read by a number of men who were influential in the making of their state constitutions; and in 1779 he drafted a constitution that the Massachusetts constitutional convention used as the basis for its work.

John Adams's complicated, proud, and intensely serious intellect is of unusual interest to the student of his age. In addition to the influence he exerted over the formulation of early state constitutions, he continued to reflect and to comment on American politics for the rest of his life, prompted by European critics of America and by domestic critics of himself. At times he saw the people of his own country as constituting a single undivided social order; but he was by nature to be drawn back into misgivings about the special interests of social classes, which he regarded as ungovernably driven to act against those of the whole. To check the independence of an aristocracy, which he believed was bound to grow as American civilization advanced, he wanted to confine their representatives to a separate legislative chamber, and to install a strong executive with a power of veto; but to check the riotous spoliations of the unpropertied masses, he firmly insisted on a strict property qualification for the suffrage. In *Thoughts on Government* he advocated a landed suffrage; in a letter, he wrote, "Depend upon it, Sir, it is dangerous to alter the qualifications of voters; . . . . every man who has not a farthing, will demand an equal voice with any other, in all acts of state. It tends to confound and destroy all distinctions, and prostrate all ranks to one common level."

With all the colonies in a revolutionary ferment, it is not surprising that the men who had brought them to that pitch, but who were for the most part the products of a social order in which individuals of rank and eminence were placed in positions of and accorded the respect due leadership, should have felt some anxiety about the domestic consequences of their defiant behavior. Adams had remarked that, for all he knew, half of the people were debtors. In many of the colonies, economic grievances had given rise to disorders, and in some cases these disorders had been funneled into the movement against Britain. In Pennsylvania the radicals seized power and gave the new state an extremely liberal constitution, with the effect of dividing rather than uniting the people; the constitution, which went further than any other contemporary instrument of government in removing the economic basis from political power, was safeguarded against its enemies by a loyalty oath that disfranchised those who would not vow to support it. The result was a growth of extraordinarily virulent party strife, which involved the state constitution itself in the complex of issues turning on questions of economic policy and personal animosities. The Pennsylvania radicals gave their state a single-chamber legislature (strongly resembling the charter form of government given by Penn in 1701) and a taxpayers' suffrage; they could not control the operations on which the economic well-being of the state depended, however, and their authority suffered because some of their leading opponents—notably Robert Morris—had enormous influence in the Continental Congress, which, of course, also sat in Philadelphia. He and his allies organized themselves as the Republican party in opposition to that of the radicals, who became the Constitutional party. After a long period of changing fortunes, the Pennsylvania Republicans achieved the ultimate success, in 1790, of instituting a state constitutional convention, which replaced the unicameral system with a more orthodox bicameral legislature answering to the ideas of social order in which the Republicans had always at heart believed.

Other states, with a considerable range of variations from one to another, generally conformed from the beginning to a more conventional system, dominated by bicameral legislatures that claimed for themselves most of the effective law-making and appointive powers of the state. This legislative structure reflected something more significant than a mere penchant for derivative constitutional forms. Educated Americans had been brought up in the belief that a balance of the elements of government gave the best insurance of liberty. They also believed that British government had degenerated because it had lost this balance, not because there was anything wrong with the principle; America might not have widely separated social orders, such as were represented in Britain by the two houses of Parliament, but people were well aware that differences of rank existed and might increase with the growth of the country. The differences, perceived by American leaders as being consistent with what they already knew about the theory of balanced government, were not between nobles and people but between property and persons; this was a distinction that soon emerged as the accredited explanation of the elements of American government. Government, it was explained, operated separately on the basis of two elements, that of property and that of persons, for which reason they ought to be separately represented in different legislative chambers. A conservative pamphlet, *The Essex Result,* so called because it "resulted" from a conference held in Essex County, Massachusetts, in 1778, tersely stated the reasons why property should have additional legislative influence to ensure genuine equality:

> If each member, without regard to his property, has equal influence in legislation, with any other, it follows, that some members enjoy greater benefits and powers in legislation than others, when these benefits and powers are compared with the rights parted with to purchase them. For the property-holder parts with the controul over his person, as well as he who hath no property, and the former also parts with the controul over his property, of which the latter is destitute. Therefore to constitute a perfect law in a free state, affecting the persons and property of the members, it is

> necessary that the law be for the good of the whole, which
> is to be determined by a majority of the members, and that
> majority should include those, who possess a major part of
> the property in the state.

This argument enabled the new constitution makers to keep to
familiar forms without proclaiming the existence of a dangerously
divisive separation between social classes; at the same time it
enabled them to entrust the protection of property to the upper
chamber.

This precaution seemed to be a matter of some urgency. In New
York the mechanics had assumed an increasingly powerful role in
forcing the province toward independence, while the lawyers and
patroons hesitated, debated the outcome, and then took their places
at the head of the movement as much to contain it as to lead it. In
western Massachusetts the county of Berkshire virtually seceded
from the state, closing all the courts and refusing to accept the
authority of the legislature; at the same time, the Boston mob did
not portend security for the considerable accumulations of local
merchant property. In the South disturbances in the western sections of the Carolinas were a matter of recent memory. The colonial leaders had shaken off the authority of Britain, and they had
firmly deposited the entire frame of government on the foundation
of representation. Once the threat of arbitrary tyranny had been
defeated—before, indeed, the war had been won—the rival threat
of a degeneration into civil and factional strife had to be confronted, and the state constitutions of the revolutionary period were
the best that colonial leaders could do by way of answer to that
threat.

On the whole they were remarkably successful. Their success
could be accounted for by the ability of the provincial congresses
to respond to the varied interests within the states, combined with
the firmness with which the leadership undertook the task of leading. For example, George Mason of Virginia, a great planter and
slave owner, having come near to losing his election, soon discovered that the Virginia convention was made up of what he
called a "hetrogeneous mass of jarring elements" who propounded
an assortment of wild and discordant schemes; but Mason, though
he very much disliked public office, was a man of learning and ac-

customed to command, and he established an authority that others were ready to concede to him, taking a decisive hand in the shaping of the new state constitution.

The constitutions went some way toward remedying grievances felt under the old regime. Where the suffrage had been restricted by such qualifications as freehold land or property valued in sterling, it was eased by the introduction of lighter alternatives. In New Jersey the new £50 qualification was expressed in terms of "lawful money," which meant any form of currency the state chose to put into circulation. (The inflation that immediately followed had the effect of wiping out the remaining restrictions, since the qualification was not raised to keep pace with the decline in the value of money.) In Virginia the freehold qualification was retained, but the amount of land was dropped from 100 acres to 50, a step the Virginia legislature had taken twice in recent years only to have its intentions frustrated by royal disallowance because the acts, by limiting assemblies to seven years, had infringed the royal prerogative. In general, it may be said that the suffrage in the new America was open to small farmers, artisans, small traders, and, probably, to some laborers who looked after their savings. It was an important point of theory that every man was free to earn the right to vote; the corollary was that those who were too idle or too irresponsible to earn it could not be safely entrusted with the power to influence the making of laws on the property of those who formed the solid part of the community.

These principles were applied in detail in Massachusetts, where constitution-making took a form that was actually more democratic than the constitution that emerged. The General Court in 1777 proposed a constitution, which the towns the next year rejected, in large part because many leading townsmen believed it was not for the legislative body to draw up a constitution for the people. So in the winter of 1779–1780 a convention, elected by universal male suffrage, met to undertake the task. The qualifications for voting for convention delegates were not only more liberal than existed under the laws, they were broader than those subsequently embodied in the new constitution; for this election, the people acted as the constituent power of the state. The draft constitution was circulated through the towns, debated and voted on at the town meetings, and then returned to and ratified by the convention, which had to make certain arithmetical adjustments in order to assure itself that a two-thirds majority had in fact approved the constitution.

The new constitution was a popular embodiment of prevalent Whig and, by implication, Protestant assumptions. A prefatory declaration of rights announced the principle of the separation of powers, asserted the equality of individuals as the foundation of political rights, and proceeded to enumerate the points in which the citizens of Massachusetts were to be protected against the encroachments of government. Politically, the constitution showed that it was possible on Whig principles for a system of government to be popular without being fully democratic. The property qualifications for the suffrage were, in fact, raised slightly from the colonial standard. They extended to perhaps three-quarters or even four-fifths of the adult males under the existing distribution of wealth.

In practice these distinctions soon came to be largely ignored. The new House of Representatives was open to the ordinary farmer and man of independent business, providing he owned £100 in freehold or £200 in personal property. Towns were to be represented by local men, qualified by a year's residence in the town. The Senate, by contrast, was to be a different kind of body, representing the state as a whole and incorporating the special interests of property. Its constituencies corresponded to the existing counties, but members were to be apportioned according to taxes paid by the counties, not, as with the towns, according to numbers. Moreover, the residential qualification was five years as an inhabitant not of the county itself but of the state. Senators were required to own £300 in freehold or £600 in personal property. Thus, a county could be represented in the Senate by a man of substance from any part of the state. These provisions were intended to bring into existence a genuine upper house, filled with men reflecting not only the statewide interests of an economic and social elite, whose presence was expected to be a permanent feature of public life, but also the thinking contained in *The Essex Result*.

The governor was to be assisted in his executive duties by a council of nine, selected from the Senate by a joint ballot of both houses.

Samuel Adams, a long-standing agitator and radical, wrote the *Address* that the convention circulated to explain the constitution. Soon afterward he explained his views to the Marquis de Chastellux, one of those members of the French upper classes who took a friendly interest in the American cause. Adams told Chastellux that in his opinion every taxpayer should vote, to which the visitor replied that this might be safe while property was evenly distributed, but that the advance of wealth would bring inequality, causing a contradiction between the democratic form of government and the tendency of society toward a division along class lines. Adams recognized this danger and said, "We are not what we are to become." He defended the Massachusetts constitution as having a "purely democratic" base, but added that what government needed was "the enlightened will of the people," not their passions. The new constitution, therefore, armed the governor and his council with a negative or veto power like that of the crown in England; the Senate and House of Representatives were given the power to override them on second consideration. The governor, with his council, probably supported by members of the senate, thus functioned as a moderator over the assembly, which was "purely democratic" because it represented the sovereignty of the people. Chastellux was struck by the fact that Adams, who had in the past done more than most men to arouse the passions of the people, now used all his influence to keep an army in existence and to maintain a mixed government. Even the description of the assembly as "purely democratic," of course, marked out the difference between the thinking of Adams's generation and that of later times, since the property qualification, if enforced, would not only exclude a possible 25 per cent of the adult males but might exclude still more as time went on.

The more controversial sections of the constitution, however, pertained to religion. Many townsmen objected to the provision for taxation in support of the Congregational Church, or, indeed, for any church to which they did not personally subscribe. Worse still, the qualifications for the executive failed to ordain that the governor must be a Protestant, giving rise to the implausible fear that the electors might be deceived into voting for a Roman Catholic. More towns objected on account of the omission of this precaution than on any substantive clause in the constitution.

Undaunted by these protests, the convention delegates declared that the required two-thirds majority had confirmed their draft, and the constitution became effective in 1780. It has often been amended but never completely revised and superseded, and it is still in operation as the Constitution of the Commonwealth of Massachusetts.

Nearly all the state constitutions differentiated in some way between the interests of the people at large, as represented in the lower house, and those of property, or of the owners of property, as represented in the upper house. In some states a higher property qualification was required for voters for the Senate, in others a higher property qualification for its members; and most states required the governor to be a man of considerable wealth, although they did not endow him with much political power. Virginia did not introduce these economic distinctions, but placed the two houses on the same franchise. This liberality may have been partly due to the influence of Jefferson and his supporters, who had fought unsuccessfully for a still more extensive franchise; but it was also probably due to the sheer self-confidence of the upper gentry, who correctly believed that their grip on the state was secure. Jefferson himself, in his *Notes on the State of Virginia* (drafted in 1781), was severely critical of the distribution of political power in his state. His analysis showed that nineteen thousand electors living "below the falls" enjoyed a representation that gave them control of half the Senate and only four short of half the House of Delegates; the remaining thirty thousand voters in effect received their laws from these nineteen thousand. The analysis was not entirely accurate but its emphasis was, and it was increasingly validated as population drifted west without any alteration in the distribution of seats. Only gradually did the unenfranchised and under-represented sectors of the Virginian population gain enough political strength to force the state's complacent leadership toward constitutional reform. It was not until 1829–1830 that a new convention was held, and even then the representative basis of the constitution remained unbalanced and incomplete.

In general these state constitutions, with the important exception of Massachusetts, were the creations not of specially called conventions but of the existing provincial convention or legislature. In other words, the legislative body that was engaged in making laws and appointing committees to run the affairs of the newly independent state also considered itself fully equal to the responsibility of drafting a constitution to replace the old charter. It was in keeping with the constitutional claims of the times that the two states that did not draw up new constitutions, Connecticut and Rhode Island, were the two that had enjoyed a charter right to elect their own governors; we have been contending, they said in effect, for the sanctity of our charter rights, and on them we stand. Elsewhere, the revolutionary assemblies and conventions felt confident that their claim to represent the people in vindication of their rights against the crown carried with it an equally strong claim to draft a constitution to secure those rights. The idea that a constitution was a body of permanent laws, superior to and separate from statute laws, was already implicit in some of the propaganda of the late colonial period, but had not been clearly worked into a set of institutional forms. The need was not urgent. The new assemblies did not doubt their own authority, and a call for special constitutional elections might have raised doubts about it. Massachusetts, a state with a strong history of constitutional and moral debate, was the exception, and it is worth noting that by the time the question came up there, the war had long since moved south; Massachusetts might not have indulged in the luxury of its prolonged constitutional proceedings if British armies had been close by.

This revolutionary period was to have a profound, if gradual, influence over the character of American political institutions, for which two developments were of particular significance. One of these was the affirmation, first made in Massachusetts, that the people, being the source of sovereignty, ought to give their express consent to the form of government under which they were to live. No other state constitution was ratified by the voters during the War of Independence, though this step was taken in 1784 in New

Hampshire. The affirmation was repeated at the higher level of federal government when the Constitution of 1787 was turned over for debate and ratification by conventions called in the several states. These proceedings went far to establish that, in American constitutional discourse, the concept of "consent" was to mean a positive act rather than the passive acceptance of authority that had hitherto satisfied the consciences of the Whig practitioners of politics in Britain and America.

The second development had a more concrete bearing on political life. Long before the rise of distinctively Whig political thinking, English lawyers had declared that decisions made in Parliament represented the will of the whole kingdom, and in a legalistic sense the English constitution recognized the principle of majority rule. That parliamentary decisions represented the will of the majority was, however, little more than a legal fiction, until validated by piecemeal extensions of the suffrage that were not complete until the twentieth century. In the American colonies, the practice of basing the assemblies on constituencies containing roughly equal numbers of voters gained a firmer footing, but was never established as a matter of principle. On the contrary, municipal corporations and counties of varying size were able to claim their representation as much on the basis of property as population. In New England, each corporate town, as part of its corporate rights, could claim an equality of representation not with towns of the same numbers but with all the other corporate towns; Boston was the only exception, but by numerical standards Boston, which was regarded with great jealousy by many towns, was heavily under-represented.

Nearly all the greatest accumulations of wealth were in the seaport towns and on the Tidewater plantations. By virtue of the distribution of the labor forces, which supported the distribution of wealth, it was natural that the wealthier areas should have the larger populations. The merchants and lawyers who had traditionally run the affairs of their province might be threatened with a dissolution of their power if the increasingly numerous western counties or corporations were given representation based on mere existence rather than population. Their best way of retaining control was through the majority principle—implemented by proportional, or numerical, representation—under which equal numbers of individual voters were represented in each district. When this step was adopted in Massachusetts, in 1775, the Boston delegation in the assembly rose at once from four to twelve; even at that it was probably too low. The same principle applied, with the usual local variations, in other mercantile states. The critical force working toward the proportional system was exerted by the combination of artisan or laboring populations with the dominant men of business, who controlled the great concentrations of wealth. These businessmen knew all about running assemblies, keeping the keys to the main committees in their own pockets, and consulting each other between and during sessions. The southern states, where city populations were small and the mass of the labor force was made up of slaves, moved more slowly toward numerical representation, but they too responded in time to the shifting distribution of population and property.

This combination was of the greatest importance. It would not have been possible in a society chronically afflicted with political divisions cutting along lines of economic class. Under an essentially deferential order, however, the combination of numbers and property under the patronage of the mercantile and landed leadership sufficed to keep political power in the hands of that leadership. Once introduced, of course, the majority principle could not be reversed. However, other interests—slavery, for example—did continue to find legal representation, and the state senates firmly embodied that of property; at a slightly later date the Senate of the United States was to preserve the identity of the individual states, regardless of their size. Thus, the majority principle entered into American politics with a somewhat ambiguous authority. Nevertheless, as state election laws were gradually reformed to allow direct election of state senators by the voters, and as the same step was taken for presidential electors, it became more and more obvious that the majority principle was the dominant principle—the only one allowing a rationally measurable basis to the age-old claim that men were equal, and that all were to have equal weight in consenting to the laws.

The new constitutions were the political foundations of American independence. On their strength would depend the liberty, and

perhaps the survival, of the new Republic. It was in the nature of
the American situation that they reflected the social structure from
which they emanated and for which they provided a future framework of government. The suffrage laws manifested only a part,
though an integral part, of the overall shape of this government;
the wide base of an extended suffrage supported a narrowing
pyramid of power. Several states made professions of Christianity,
or of its Protestant genus, a prerequisite of eligibility for office; in
Virginia, Roman Catholics were not officially permitted to vote
until 1784. The property qualifications for members of the assembly were generally stiffer than for the suffrage, allowing the election
of farmers and independent businessmen or of artisans who owned
their own workshops, but certainly not of farm laborers or unskilled town workers. The adult sons of farmers and businessmen
who had not yet acquired independent property were also excluded from office. The qualifications for membership in the state
senates were more rigid still, making that body as nearly as possible a reflection of whatever pretensions to aristocracy the men of
substantial property might claim in America.

Assemblies were tied to the social structure by one strong strand
in which nearly all American republicans implicitly believed:
annual elections. From English history, Americans derived the
conviction that frequent elections were the foundation of politica'
liberty, while long-lived assemblies were liable to grow lazy, tyrannical, and corrupt. They dated the decline of the British Parliament from the Septennial Act of 1716, which extended the life of
parliaments between general elections from three years to seven.
What mattered to American republicans was not so much that the
common people should have equal access to seats in the legislature
—for experienced men of learning and of public life were not
convinced that the ordinary voter could be trusted with such
weighty matters—but rather that the legislators should be brought
back into repeated contact with the people. It was of vital importance that members of a legislature should never develop
separate interests from those of their constituents but should come
home to mingle with the people, thereby losing all sense of separate
identity as lawmakers.

Having been secured to their electorates through annual elections, the assemblies were singularly free from other forms of constraint. It is true that the declarations of rights that introduced several of the new state constitutions usually contained an affirmation of the principle of the separation of powers. "In the government of this Commonwealth," stated Article XXX of the Declaration of Rights of Massachusetts, "the Legislative Department shall never exercise the Executive and Judicial powers, or either of them; the Executive shall never exercise the Legislative and Judicial powers, or either of them; the Judicial shall never exercise the Legislative or Executive powers, or either of them: To the end that it may be a government of laws and not of men." This historic formulation—which no doubt was influenced by similar statements promulgated in Pennsylvania and Virginia, and which appears not to have come from John Adams, who was more convinced of the importance of mixed government than of the separation of the different departments of government from each other—must be credited with great subsequent importance. The future federal Constitution would also owe much to the institutional thinking to which these declarations were openly dedicated. In the state governments, however, these declarations on the separation of powers remained more as dedications than as policies.

A closer scrutiny of state governments would have revealed that nearly all the effective powers—legislative, judicial, and executive—were gathered into the assemblies themselves. The governorship was retained with certain important wartime powers, and with appointment prerogatives that were not to be dismissed as trivial. But the powers of the governor were vestigial when compared with those of the assembly; in some states the governor was even appointed by the assembly. The governor, usually required to be a man of great wealth and long residence in the state, was advised in some states by a council of prominent men. In others he stood alone. In either instance, since the constitutions specified the duration of assemblies and the frequency of elections, he lost all the power over the assemblies that was implied by that of the royal governors to dissolve an assembly and issue writs for new elections. In many states, the lower house in joint session with the senate gained the power to make most of the senior appointments in the other branches of government, including the judicial. Senior military commands also became legislative appointments.

This was not what would later be meant by the separation of powers. It did mean that when these appointees had been installed they were expected to go about their duties free from interference from the executive and judicial branches, but the fact of legislative appointment and the prospect of reappointment were expected to exert some influence on their conduct. On the whole, the outstanding characteristic of these new state governments was their continuity with the British principle of parliamentary sovereignty, which Blackstone had propounded in his *Commentaries,* a work that was to exert more influence on American law than any other for several generations.

Not only during the life of the Articles of Confederation but for many years afterward, the state constitutions continued to embody the character and represent the interests of the American people more closely than did the continental forms of government. In Europe, government, with its continuous monarchies and inaccessible aristocracies, acted as a lid placed over the pot in which the common people lived; in America the only way to apply the image would be to view the lid as an intrinsic part of the pot. Nothing could compel Americans to take an interest in politics; many had left such matters to their social superiors in the past and many more would ignore politics in the future. But politics would not ignore them. Americans could seldom be entirely free of the consequences of political action. To be ignorant is not one of the more effective ways of exercising control, and the advance of settlements, the growing complexities of economic life, and the needs of old and new communities for solvency, defense, and education would create the substance of politics. Those who concerned themselves with the issues of society were, of course, the more likely to control their outcome. And it was in state government, and to a greater degree in local government, that people could make their own mark. The struggles that so quickly followed under the Confederation revealed the extent and the limits of state governments as instruments of public opinion and policy.

The Revolution was too great an event to leave the foundations of American society unshaken or the traditional layer of leadership undisturbed. Both the war itself and the acuteness of the social and economic problems produced conditions of stress that exposed the weaknesses of some men and the strengths of others. The composition of state governments in turn began to reflect the upheavals in society, not least of which was the removal of unprecedentedly large numbers of people to recently settled regions in the western counties. During and after the war, elections to the lower houses of state legislatures produced surprising changes in their social and economic composition: a greater proportion of men with comparatively modest backgrounds. In this process, men of great wealth or traditional family leadership lost some of their grip.

An analysis of the legislatures of six states ranging from south to north—South Carolina, Virginia, Maryland, New Jersey, New York, and New Hampshire—has shown a remarkable similarity of trends. The proportion of the really wealthy legislators dropped from 46 per cent to 22 per cent after the end of the war; legislative members from prominent families declined from 40 per cent to 16. In Virginia, with its strong tradition of planter leadership, the trend was less pronounced; nonetheless, between 1773 and 1785 the great land and slave owners holding seats in the lower house dropped from 60 per cent to 50, the percentage of ordinary farmers rose from 13 to 26, and men of the intermediate range doubled their share of seats. The new counties in Virginia simply did not possess anything like as much property as the old, so that their admission necessarily introduced a number of representatives who were both less wealthy and less well-known. Yet the overall trend toward assemblies of men of more modest means and background was less accentuated in Virginia, partly because more representatives were still land owners and slave owners of some substance. The decline in the median of ownership, from 1,800 acres to about 1,100 acres, and from forty slaves to twenty, which is enough to mark a shift of emphasis, should not obscure the fact that Virginia counties were continuing to select men with the attributes of wealth and the recognized if somewhat diminished traits of leadership. These changes did not produce a social revolution in Virginia. On the test issue of paper money, the state remained conservative throughout the critical phase in the postwar years.

As a phenomenon, much more marked in many other states than in Virginia, the movement of men from broader social sources into public life followed in part from structural alterations in the new constitutions. Assemblies became larger and the new governmental systems created a host of new offices. In the past, public office had been related to social position; in some cases, it was, in effect, an attribute of social position. This connection between social status and political eligibility took a long time to sever, but the burgeoning of offices that had to be filled did begin to open the field of public life to a much wider range of ambitious men. Office-seeking rapidly became a substitute for older forms of personal advancement in status as well as in income.

After ratification of the federal Constitution, the public official slowly came to play a part in American life that was different both from the role of the European functionary or, later, civil servant and from what the founders of the American Republic would have expected. The American situation manifested itself in a way that was explained, in 1828, by Edward Everett, the Massachusetts politician and orator, who attributed the analysis to the English statesman George Canning. The condition that he described, in a letter to Postmaster General John McLean, had been developing for many years, and in some of the states his remarks would have held good a generation earlier.

> In this country . . . office is more important, than in England. In England . . . hereditary family politics are of vast consideration. . . . Besides this, mere Rank is of vast consequence there, and fills the utmost ambition of many persons in a large class in Society. Here it is unknown. Prodigious accumulations of fortune exist there, conferring of themselves very extensive influence and power, and making mere office a small thing with its possessors. The outgrown naval and military establishments open a career, in which ambitions find scope for their talents. In place of all these, we have nothing, to which the ambitious can aspire, but office: I say nothing, because all the private walks of life are as wide open in England as here, and afford, in that country, as well as in this, occupation for much in the active talent of the Community. But office here is family,

rank, hereditary fortune, in short everything, out of the range of private life. This links its possession with innate principles of our nation; and truly incredible are the efforts men are willing to make, the humiliations they will endure, to get it.

In the years immediately following the inception of revolutionary state constitutions, social developments of this scale were not yet in prospect. Many of the ablest and most deeply committed makers of the new system would have been dismayed to learn that they were inaugurating a political order in which the scramble for office would displace the more dignified concept of the burden of public service. But this new order resulted from their work—and from that of the drafters of the federal Constitution—and it gave American public life one of its distinctive characteristics.

As the states' constitutions absorbed new social forces, the alteration in their political balance also produced changes in political geography. In some states, notably South Carolina, Pennsylvania, and New York, the state capital was removed from its seaboard fastness to an interior spot, a gesture toward the people of the newer sections. (In Virginia, however, the move from Williamsburg to Richmond was convenient to the leadership.) These changes were more than merely symbolic, for access to the legislature, the state courts, and their records were matters of concrete significance. The moves broke up the pattern of seaboard habits that had been intimately connected with seaboard control. The one great state that did not yield to this trend, Massachusetts, where the capital remained in Boston, also produced a recurrence of merchant control and obduracy in the face of economic distress, eventually resulting in a breakdown of confidence and a minor rebellion.

Through these constitutional structures, the state governments both represented and at the same time restrained the pressures within the social order. These pressures and the consequent disturbances to political tranquillity differed sharply from state to state. In New York the supple and pervasive political organization, which Governor George Clinton elaborated into something resembling a one-party system, managed both to represent and to contain some of the most urgent forces of the age. Clinton's party superseded the old politics of the great families, and resisted the efforts of newer aristocratic formations around the family of General Philip Schuyler, Alexander Hamilton's father-in-law. But the legislative initiatives that Clinton permitted himself were mostly of a kind that echoed the interests of a merchant, lawyer, professional, and business order rather than the needs of tenants and artisans, though numerous small farmers supported him against the great landlords. Clinton's party organization embodied a control that for the most part remained patrician in style while it took the trouble to pick up the sounds of discontent and to respond to them when, as in the need for paper money, action was expedient.

The state governments were soon to become the principal agencies of economic change. The growth of the Union—a name that applied only after the adoption of the Constitution—did not mean that the central government overshadowed or replaced that of the states; as the Union grew in size and wealth, the state governments became more deeply engaged in providing the legal framework for the development of an economy of energetic capitalist enterprise. The chartering of banks, of private corporations to construct turnpikes, bridges, ferries, foundries, and mills, and the creation of systems of company law all fell primarily within the purview of state governments. More than a generation would pass before Chief Justice Marshall challenged their pre-emption of the field.

One of the effects of the Revolution—one of the ways in which the events of the era were revolutionary—was the compulsion of Americans to relate their aims to the agency of government—and to its authority. It was their government now, and that fact assisted another great discovery. The Americans of the several former colonies had characteristics in common that could, under government, become national characteristics. But the process was not transcendental or inevitable. The people were closer to and more concerned about their own state governments than about the remote and often ineffective Continental Congress, and their primary loyalties toward government remained state loyalties. The state would long continue to exert an emphatic claim on their affections.

The Economy: 1763–1815

Cattle
Cotton
Fishing
Furs & Skins
Grain
Indigo
Iron Works
Lumber & Timber
Rice
Rum
Shipbuilding
Staves
Tobacco
Trading Center
Whaling

6

The Economics of War and Independence

American independence started from a strong economic foundation. The complaints against British policy in the years before the Revolution were far from being those of a declining or impoverished people; they were the remonstrances of an expanding, productive population that was already capable of entrusting its goods to an international market, that was pressing into unexplored lands across the first barrier of mountains, and that wanted to enjoy the rewards of its own enterprise.

This enterprise had taken various forms. It involved trial and failure in the cultivation of certain crops in addition to experimentation with others; it also involved the learning of special skills as well as the development of a general capacity for economic management. Crops that could not be grown in Europe were a particularly important American asset, but they had often tempted men ambitious for overnight gains to reach out not only beyond their means but beyond reasonable hopes of return. The range of American manufactures might be limited, but it showed promise of enlarging when market and investments joined together to give the necessary encouragement.

No one sector of the economy was self-sufficient in the late colonial period, but when Americans pooled their resources, the activities of the different regions, carried on with some degree of rational specialization, worked in the direction of an efficient division of labor. The differences between the regions had emerged most clearly in the form of difficulties over agreements to implement a continental boycott of British goods. The delegates to successive intercolonial meetings and Continental Congresses were among those best placed to view the continent as a whole; that perspective was a strong influence in converting them from provincials into Americans.

Agriculture, which continued to dominate American life for

generations after the Revolution, determined the quality of life throughout most of the settled regions. "The great Business of the Continent is Agriculture," said Franklin in 1786, in "The Internal State of America."

> For one Artisan, or Merchant, I suppose, we have at least 100 Farmers, by far the greatest part Cultivators of their own fertile Lands, from whence many of them draw, not only the Food necessary for their Subsistence, but the Materials of their Clothing, so as to have little Occasion for foreign Supplies; while they have a Surplus of Productions to dispose of, whereby Wealth is gradually accumulated.

The southern colonies had learned to concentrate on the raising of a minimum number of staple crops, for which they could rely on a vigorous demand in Europe. The large fortunes of Virginia and Maryland accrued from the growing of tobacco, those of South Carolina and Georgia (so far as any fortunes in Georgia were large), from rice, primarily, and later from indigo. But southern agriculture was not standing still either in the types of crops or in the regions in which they were grown. The shortsighted methods of Tidewater planters had so ravaged the land that those who could afford to move were rapidly sowing the fresh soils of the Piedmont; in some cases whole estates were abandoned, in others a family that had long lived beyond the means made available by London creditors was reduced to scratching the surface for its existence.

Farming methods were more often than not extravagant of land, partly because the land seemed endless and partly in order to conserve the resources of labor. Washington, himself a conservative manager, gave an accurate account of farming methods and the reasons behind them in a letter written in 1791 to Arthur Young, the famous English agricultural reformer:

> An English farmer must entertain a contemptible opinion of our husbandry, or a horrid idea of our lands, when he shall be informed that not more than 8 or 10 bushels of Wheat is the yield of an Acre; but this low produce may be ascribed, and principally too, to a cause . . . that the aim of the farmers in this Country (if they can be called farmers) is not to make the most they can from the land, which is, or has been cheap, but the most of the labour, which is dear; the consequence of which has been, much ground has been

scratched over and none cultivated or improved as it ought to have been; Whereas a farmer in England, where land is dear and labour cheap, finds it his interest to improve and cultivate highly, that he may reap large crops from a small quantity of ground.

The more enterprising managers salvaged themselves by converting to other crops, wheat and corn being the most successful. But the Tidewater planters occupied a less dominant position in the cultivation of these crops than they had as tobacco producers, for many smaller farmers, most of them of Scotch-Irish or German stock, were filling up the countryside where the land rose toward the mountains and were growing cereals. The combined efforts of these older and newer farmers suggested a trend of considerable significance: Virginia and Maryland, as they had begun to do shortly before the War of Independence, were surpassing the middle and northeastern colonies as exporters. Livestock farming also proved a profitable enterprise, and their exports of barreled beef and pork were catching up with those of their northern neighbors. Further south, the Carolinas and Georgia were also turning into rivals of the middle and northeastern colonies as exporters of corn, beef, and pork; they even challenged New England in the export of pickled fish. After all, just as much sea lapped the shores of the South as the North, and New Englanders did not enjoy their dominance as a right given by natural law. New Englanders did, however, retain their near monopoly of the export of dried fish, which was to give Massachusetts its emblem of the sacred cod, and was of such importance as to be a significant factor in John Adams's conduct during the peace negotiations with Britain.

The westward pressure of southern populations eventually changed the emphasis of their economy at the expense of their fishing and shipping. Charleston remained the only southern seaport of any consequence until the acquisition of New Orleans in the early nineteenth century. The swiftness with which fortunes sprang from the inland soils proved a far more intense and lasting attraction. Much of the virgin land being forest, the process of clearing produced a substantial trade in lumber, in which the South also began to encroach on New England.

The middle and New England regions, by contrast, did not yield any strikingly new economic developments. Even during the war, when trade with Britain had been severed, cereals and flour, beef and pork, timber and dried fish continued to find their markets at home and in Europe. New England also specialized in manufacturing molasses into rum, and suffered correspondingly by the curtailment of supplies from the West Indies. When the British government, in 1783, stunned the Americans by closing the British West Indies to their shipping, a postwar step that confirmed the fact that the American mainland was no longer a part of the British imperial system, the blow was severely felt by New England's merchants and manufacturers; the loss of this commerce might be considered an early indication of the impending decline in the power and influence of Massachusetts. But that was a very gradual process. Massachusetts continued for some time to lead New England and to rival Philadelphia as a great center of shipbuilding, a class of skilled manufacturing that was carried on in most of the country's seaports. The craftsmanship was of a high order, and many British merchants were happy to equip themselves with American-built ships, whose cost was competitive because the proximity of timber and the low overheads tended to offset the good wages commanded by American artisans. Before the War of Independence, American shipyards sold some fifty ships a year to Britain, and of the total American production—389 ships in the year 1769—New England contributed more than 60 per cent.

The war closed these sales to Britain just as it closed commerce, but it introduced new stimulants and unexplored opportunities. American merchants took advantage of the fact that privateering became public policy, encouraged by the states and by Congress. This form of enterprise offered a quick return and helped to create new fortunes. American merchantmen, released from the confines of British mercantilist policy, were free for the first time to probe trade routes with other nations. After Congress had given its blessing to unrestricted foreign trade, in April 1776, they developed a prosperous trade with France, the Netherlands, and Spain. These countries supplied many American needs, while the Netherlands, which, not being at war, continued to import British products, was able to re-export some of these manufactures to the American market that had always depended on Britain.

Privateering and wartime commerce were best conducted in fast ships, and American ship designers began to show an enterprise equal to the pace of events. Brigs and schooners were widened, giving them greater cargo capacity, and lengthened, allowing them to cut through the water with a speed that would outdistance their more conventional rivals. In Baltimore, which had barely started its later rise as a commercial center, shipbuilders began to cover the bottoms with copper sheeting. These improvements were to give American shipbuilders a strong position when the end of the war reopened the traditional passages to the British Isles. The rising overseas commerce of the new nation suffered new setbacks in the postwar years, however, and construction was depressed until after the adoption of the new federal Constitution. The next revival, which began in 1789, was abetted by a tradition of enterprise, ingenuity, and technical skill.

Americans, no less than the British, were heirs to the doctrines of mercantilist economics, which had always maintained that the volume of available world trade was inherently limited. This entirely antiquated opinion, which had been formulated in the seventeenth century, was no longer rigidly held; but the rules and restrictions that it had fostered kept the expansion of trade within the boundaries of the several trading empires, each of which represented, in theory, a closed system in animated rivalry with all the others. The prosperity of British America did not spring unassisted from its soil or ports; it came on a rising tide of world trade, and so long as the colonists remained British subjects they had the advantage of a connection with the most vigorous of these economic systems. Yet as Adam Smith showed in *The Wealth of Nations* (1776), the theory itself was defective. More was to be gained by the rivalry of free trade than by that of exclusion. Smith's ideas impressed the younger William Pitt, who tried to formulate them into British policy when he became prime minister in December 1783. There is little reason, though, to think that they had much influence on the same generation of Americans. Nevertheless, the disruption of British restrictions gave the Americans unprecedented opportunities for expansion. The merchants did not expect their ships or commerce to be able to compete without aid in the world's markets, and the state governments, which alone had the legal power to do so, soon began to pass laws for the protection of their own shipping. The first act of the first Congress to meet under the federal Constitution was the Tariff Act of 1789, which included protective clauses for American shipping.

The war stimulated the demand for home-produced crops and goods, but it also curtailed the demand for other items by restricting luxuries, such as tea (which some regarded as an unpatriotic beverage, though the palates of others were unaffected by this judgment; after all, tea could be imported from the Dutch islands), and concentrating on military needs. The merchant towns along the coast and at certain river ports throve on the new trade that opened up with Europe when American merchants found themselves liberated from their old dependence on British houses. It is difficult to attribute to the war itself all the expansion that took place during the period, however. The continental armies obviously constituted a special center of demand for foods, clothing, and military supplies, but the numbers of troops involved were hardly large enough to affect the course of economic development. In any case, they were often deployed in limited areas. New England saw practically no actual fighting after the initial campaign, and large sections of the South were quiet through most of the war. The British armies, with their base in New York and their frequent movements about the country, were also a market for the crops and merchandise of adjacent areas; as a source of demand, they had an economic effect beyond the immediate localities. But military demands, American or British, could also take the form of a severe strain on the domestic consumer. Washington himself complained bitterly of the avarice of farmers and merchants who held back, in expectation of increased prices, supplies needed by his army. Patriotism and profits might rejoice in the same ends, but they did not necessarily arrive there by the same routes.

British policies had channeled the directions of the American economy, and the war imposed new pressures and distortions. Even so, the natural impulse of the economy was buoyant. Whatever may be argued for the protective advantages of the British navigation laws in earlier times, the Americans seized their independence at a time when they were ready to support it by the energy and intelligence of their own economic efforts.

To foster these efforts they had at their disposal a number of social, business, and institutional devices. Family networks, business partnerships, a brisk trade from port to port along the coasts, and the exchange of information and credit among merchants in different cities were all interconnected and all contributed to stimulate and serve the demands of a growing population. But the most important agent in the expansion of the American economy was that of government. Americans had in the past been lightly governed, but government had provided services that were available in moments of necessity, more often civic or military than economic. The state governments now stood closer to the people than the former assemblies, for the wartime crisis heightened the intimacy between rulers and ruled. The structure of the Continental Congress left most of the control over economic affairs and the general course of civil policy to the states themselves, so that the state governments emerged with an extraordinary measure of independent authority.

The legal power to act, with the object of regulating economic developments, did not prove fully equal to the needs. Inflation, in particular, kept getting out of hand. The responsibility for control, nevertheless, devolved on the states, and a large share of their labors both during and after the war was directed to economic problems. None was more urgent than that of the supply of money, a fact that had also been recognized in Britain, where permission to emit specified quantities of new paper currency, though not strictly as legal tender, was given by an act of Parliament in 1773. The new state governments alone had the power to raise taxes; and they availed themselves of their independence to issue their own currencies, which initially took the form of bills of credit, backed only by their promise to redeem the pledge printed on the face of the bills from the proceeds of future taxes. These bills were legal tender. Refusal to accept them in payment of debts became an offense, though a difficult one to punish when any sizable proportion of the public lacked confidence in their value. The states also issued treasury notes, which bore an annually payable interest and were not circulated as legal tender beyond certain specified types of transaction.

The Congress, which lacked any direct power to raise taxes, was under even greater pressure to relieve its financial burdens by similar methods. Here, precisely, was the crux of the problem. Americans had made much of their dislike of taxation without representation; now it began to appear that they had an almost equal dislike of taxation by their own representatives. This was a point that the representatives themselves were obliged to bear in mind, if they took an interest in the continuation in their legislative careers. Accordingly, taxation remained the least used of the possible expedients for raising public money. The Congress made its first emission of bills of credit for the purchase of military supplies and the payment of soldiers in June 1775, in the amount of $2 million—the dollar being valued by the Spanish milled dollar, or "piece of eight," which was worth 4s. 6d. in sterling. (Monetary values continued to be expressed in pounds more often than in dollars for several years, and it was not until an American mint was established under Hamilton that the United States dollar gained ascendancy and the mixture of other coins and currencies disappeared into legend.) But Congress had less power than the states to back its currency with real wealth. The promise of redemption implied that funds would be raised by taxation, but Congress could not tax and it had little power to enforce its requisitions on the states. Although members of Congress, being appointed by their own state legislatures, did not owe their position to direct elections, they were hobbled by the intense reluctance of state legislatures to embark on effective policies of taxation. As a result, congressmen were left with no choice but the expedient of multiplying and diversifying the paper currency for which they made themselves responsible.

The problem of sustaining a paper currency was essentially one of social psychology, which does not mean, however, that ordinary people's doubts about the soundness of the medium arose from irrational causes. Not all psychology is the psychology of the irrational, and the first and most realistic cause for uncertainty was that it was by no means a foregone conclusion that the Continental Congress could win the war. To be sure, there were other reasons for doubt. The paper was not backed by deposits of gold or silver nor even by promises of land, and the outcome of any future tax collections was obviously debatable when the present Congress seemed so intent on avoiding the imposition of taxes. Continental paper soon began the steep but easy descent into the inferno of inflation.

The Congress, meanwhile, had to pay for the war, and could only fall back on the issuance of more paper currency. Army quartermasters and commissaries issued certificates of debt against supplies received from merchants and farmers; as these certificates, which ran into huge numbers, bore a government promise to repay, they could be passed from hand to hand in payment of private or public debt. Again, however, the question of when the government would repay, and how much, caused recipients to treat army certificates at less than their face value. The Congress also tried to encourage savings by issuing loan certificates, which failed to lure buyers at their original 4 per cent rate of interest; their sale later improved when the rate was raised to 6 per cent. Congress also made the loan certificates more attractive by accepting paper money at its face value in payment for them, and as the paper money depreciated, this procedure added to the actual value of the loans. By the end of the war, loan certificates had become heavily concentrated in the merchant states, particularly Pennsylvania—a circumstance that made them unpopular in the South, whose inhabitants did not relish being taxed to redeem them.

Altogether, thirty-seven emissions of currency were authorized by the Congress between 1775 and 1780, for a total face value of more than $190 million. In December 1776, $1 dollar in coin was worth $1.50 in paper bills; in April 1781, it could only be bought with paper bills worth $146.67. By that time, Congress had determined to cease its emissions, recall its paper moneys, and, on the basis of long-term loans intended to be somewhat more credible, refund them at a ratio of forty to one. This policy was strengthened by the agreement of the states to take their own bills out of circulation. Congress had also raised money in loans from France and the Netherlands, and although these were not a primary means of war finance, they assisted in the work of stabilizing the credit of the government at critical periods. Near the end of the war they were an important factor in helping Robert Morris float the new Bank of North America.

Morris, who was elected by Congress in 1781 to the new post of superintendent of finance, was a partner in the prosperous Philadelphia firm of Willing & Morris, which obtained advantageous congressional contracts at the beginning of the war. His financial operations were as intricate as they were obscure; by the end of the war it would have required an accountant of genius to separate his private from his public arrangements. If Morris did indeed back his personal speculations with public funds, it should also be said that on occasion he used his private interest to add security to public measures. Morris possessed, to an unusual degree, the ability to keep a mass of financial details in a controlled relationship to his central objectives, and the jealousy and not unjustified suspicion with which he was regarded by many of his contemporaries should not be allowed to obscure the fact that his success in the financing of the war was more important than any other civilian contribution to the ultimate American victory.

Morris was intent on founding a permanent financial institution along the lines of the Bank of England. He differed from orthodox American financial opinion in that he had no fear of a public debt, which he regarded as a legitimate source of government income through continuing investment. He was well aware, as was his disciple Hamilton, that when men of substance could be induced to invest in government funds their interest would duly strengthen the political stability of the government. With these aims in view, and using all his immense influence as finance superintendent, he promoted the moves by which the Congress established and chartered the Bank of North America, which began operations in January 1782, as the first specie-based and the first national bank in America.

Morris prudently obtained a charter for the bank from the state of Pennsylvania. Although the bank could not hope to escape the currents of Pennsylvania politics, it had at least the reinsurance of a state charter in case it fell into disfavor with Congress. The bank made substantial loans to the Congress and undoubtedly contributed to its stability in the postwar period of weakness and dissension. Yet that stability itself seemed to many people to benefit only certain commercial and business interests in the Confederation and in the state. The Constitutional party, therefore, revoked its state charter in 1785, but the Republicans, recapturing the legislature in 1787, succeeded in renewing its license. These maneuvers had broad implications, for it was not clear whether Congress could charter an institution to operate within a state that opposed its operations. Morris resolved the problem for himself by retiring from public life to promote his own fortunes in schemes that eventually caused his ruin. His departure, however, did not come before he had laid foundations and set examples that were to have an immeasurable influence on the financial policies of Hamilton under the new Constitution. The creation of a national bank was one of the most formidable of all forces affecting the establishment of national policies, nationally centered private interests, and national loyalties. It would also become a potent force in the Americanization of local interests.

The currency crisis of the revolutionary war years was not only the worst that Americans had yet experienced, but probably involved the most severe decline in monetary values of any period with the exception of the collapse of the Confederate currency toward the end of the Civil War. It caused extreme bitterness and a spate of controversies that were not the less intense for being imbued with keen economic intelligence and a firm sense of moral values. The import of this debate for American society and its subsequent history can best be understood in the light of two different but overlapping considerations, the first economic, the second moral. When John Adams remarked that for all he knew, half the people might be debtors, he did not really mean that they verged on insolvency; after all, men did borrow to undertake new enterprises. Yet the man whose business prospered could find relatively few outlets for his funds. Partnership laws gave little security, and no stock market existed to satisfy eager investors. The private loan usually proved to be the most reliable form of investment. The social range of creditors, therefore, was remarkably wide. As an example, it was not unusual for artisans who found a little surplus in their wallets to offer money at interest, usually to other small or aspiring mechanics or traders. The more prosperous merchants combined several types of business which in later years would be separated into specialized professional activities. Lending money at interest was one of the more important, for without any source of credit there could have been little economic enterprise or expansion.

The depreciation of the currency in which these moneys were denominated struck wide-swinging blows at this army of creditors, small and great. It corroded the savings of former years, and made every debtor into an undeserving beneficiary of public policies. The moral considerations of this crisis turned on the question of just deserts. Generations of ministers had handed down the economic tenets of a Puritan morality, a morality that did not condone borrowing. These tenets entered into the souls of the people and were not dislodged merely because the church had ceased to dictate moral law directly to the town meeting.

Puritan morals still placed an emphasis on saving, on austerity, and, in a measure, on some form of service. But the very people whose work and self-sacrifice and devoted attention to their duties had produced these savings were now being made to suffer. Economists like Pelatiah Webster, who insisted that to issue depreciating paper currencies was to combine bad morals with bad economics, made a point that appealed to both instinct and interest.

When allowance is made for the value of domestic and foreign loans, paper money did provide the sinews of the war and, at considerable cost to individuals, it did prove adequate to the need of the crisis. The outcry against depreciation, which as Benjamin Franklin had once remarked was itself a form of taxation, may in some cases have been exaggerated. Nonetheless, the sense of insecurity produced by this inflation was profound, and carried the most portentous significance for the future. Townspeople on the whole suffered most, and began to look with hostility on the less disadvantaged farmers, whom they also suspected of withholding produce from the markets. Americans were not strangers to social conflict in their midst, but the shock of these years infected many of them with a feeling of suspicion and alienation, of having been defrauded as a reward for their honest labor and services—and defrauded through the connivance of their own governments. The policies of the ensuing years bore the marks of these feelings.

Whatever views of government policy those marks might imply, one of the most unexpected transformations to which Americans accustomed themselves in these years pertained to the amount rather than the direction of government activity. Almost overnight, Americans had to get used to being governed. While policy questions were debated with fervor and often with acrimony, it is perhaps more remarkable that every discussion entailed the more basic question of whether government ought to be taking so large a part in economic and public life. Governmental interference developed logically from the assumption of initial responsibilities, and was soon extended into attempts to control the consequences of the inflation.

The attempts were made where the need was most acute, and several of the northern and middle states instituted price and wage controls. Their legislatures, acting on information provided by committees of investigation, published detailed tables of prices and set the pay rates for almost every kind of work. In 1779 the legislatures of the New England states and New York sent delegates to a convention that reviewed the causes and consequences of inflation and recommended still more elaborate measures. These early efforts at price control proved almost entirely unsuccessful. In later years, even governments equipped with far more detailed systems of enforcement have proved unable to control the effects of inflation. Legislators and publicists were left to inveigh against the lack of patriotism which they saw represented everywhere in the soaring prices, and in some instances they were undoubtedly right. But these years of economic turmoil produced gains as well as losses. Every kind of skilled labor was in demand, shortages promoted domestic manufacturing, and farmers could be sure of good prices, even if they had to accept payment in some form of army certificates.

The need for government did not end with the war. The people had spent nearly ten years making sacrifices, and, understandably, they greeted with enormous relief the reopening of commercial relations with Britain, whose manufactured goods were cheaper, more various, and more numerous than those of America, or of the new nation's allies on the Continent. With remarkable alacrity the American consumer snapped back into his colonial habits of dependence on British sources and an implicit faith in British superiority. The result was that after a short spell of self-indulgence, the supply of hard money suddenly disappeared. The British suppliers required payment in specie; Americans were willing to pay in specie, only to find themselves encountering a new currency crisis, now complicated by having a balance-of-payments dimension. The terms of the Treaty of Paris, which brought the war to a close, included clauses for the payment of debts owed to British merchants by the former colonists; the British, however, were not interested in being paid in any of the currencies that swirled and drifted about the states like autumn leaves.

By the end of 1784, the people of the young Republic faced their first peacetime crisis, and they faced it with deep internecine resentments and inadequate institutional means of making or enforcing economic policy. This public crisis was the multiplication of countless private crises. Hardworking farmers with modest savings, whose families depended on the subsistence of their own farms, were trapped in the price spiral. Larger planters in the South, and the more substantial farmers of other states, despite a somewhat greater financial margin, were frequently in debt to some degree. The agricultural community could not free itself from the effects of the general decline in purchasing power in the towns. In the towns and villages, artisans who had borrowed to promote their businesses, and merchants who had accepted as well as extended credit, also found themselves sucked into the spiral.

In each state the victims experienced their own private misery—a variant of the public problem of debt brought on by a diminished supply of money. The inadequate money supply in turn mirrored the broader problem of America's balance of payments, since its produce could not purchase everything that its people wanted to import. The economic policies adopted in the different states depended, however, not on the acuteness of the crisis, but on the composition and distribution of forces that could be brought to bear on legislative policy. The legal sanction against the debtor, after distraint on his property, was imprisonment; it was not always enforced, but the terror was there to haunt every farmer, artisan, or man of business who knew that he could not meet his creditors if they descended on him in a pack; many of his creditors might be in exactly the same position and require payment for the same reasons. The economically humbler men, however, were usually the least able to influence political policy, and least free to address themselves to the possibility of legislative remedies. Public policy swung around to confront the crisis where the men of substance were themselves directly affected.

In South Carolina, after successive crop failures in 1783, 1784, and 1785, the threatened planters, whose distress was complicated by heavy indebtedness to British merchants, were instrumental in 1785 in convening a special session of the legislature. Two measures were proposed, one of them a new issue of paper currency and the other a virtual stay law on the payment of debts. Charleston merchants had their reservations about both, but were persuaded to give their support when the provisions covering uses of the new money were so drafted as to make it ineligible for the payment of private debts contracted before 1786; after 1786 it could be used to pay duties and taxes owed to the state—with the income then helping to pay interest on the state debt. A boom in South Carolina's exports refloated the planters' economy within the year, and the paper currency became a considerable and sustained success.

The combination of forces that obtained an issue of new paper money in Pennsylvania, the first state to adopt this policy after the war, was of a different order. It consisted of merchants, speculators, and holders of congressional and state debts, who had become impatient for payment, and of representatives of western farmers who were already debt-ridden and deeply feared new impositions. Over intense opposition from Morris and the Bank of North America—which helps to explain the subsequent legislative revocation of the charter—the legislature, dominated once more by the Constitutional party, in March 1785 issued one hundred fifty thousand pounds in bills of credit, one-third of which was set aside to be loaned against farm mortgages while two-thirds was to pay interest on the state and national debt.

In New York a prolonged legislative struggle resulted in 1786 in the passage of an act to provide the issue of two hundred thousand pounds in paper money, most of it to be loanable against real estate. New Jersey, North Carolina, and Rhode Island also took steps to relieve their debtors by similar processes, Rhode Island by a tortuous plan that creditors and men of property everywhere else regarded as notoriously dishonest. Where these remedies were adopted, they afforded a valid measure of relief. They could not in themselves have resolved the wider problems of the American economy, and they did not diminish the long-term need for a stronger central government with far more extensive powers of taxation and of economic legislation. Nonetheless, they did suggest that much had been learned by recent experience, and that state legislators, acting under pressure, could make shrewd estimates of the balance to be struck between flexibility and restraint.

In certain states, however, the dominant forces were those who had learned the opposite lesson from the wartime inflationary policies, and they were determined not to repeat that grim experience. The liberal policies that Jefferson and Madison and their associates had effected in religion, in land and in law reform, did not endow Virginia with an expansionist attitude toward matters of money. Madison himself was strenuously opposed to paper money, regarded Rhode Island's indulgences with abhorrence, and was not impressed with the efforts of other states. More serious consequences of such economic orthodoxy were felt in Massachusetts, where local history suddenly acquired a significance that reached far beyond the boundaries of the Bay State.

The merchants who dominated the Massachusetts legislature represented Boston and the other seaport towns. Rivalry was keen between these places, but it was a rivalry of kindred interests, which were able to show an impressive solidarity in matters affecting those interests as a whole. From an early date in the independent history of the state, the legislative leaders determined on an orthodox financial policy; after the wartime issues of paper money had been withdrawn, the state maintained a singularly rigorous adherence to specie, which showed signs of achieving a reasonable degree of stability until the onset of the depression in 1784. The legislators were sufficiently aware of the difficulties to lighten the burden of taxation, a measure that only created new problems by raising doubts about the state's credit. As a consequence, the state in 1785 imposed the heaviest tax levy in three years. Many farmers who had done comfortably enough during the war to feel satisfaction with the management of the government now found themselves short of cash, and pressure from both the tax collector and private creditors drove them to desperation. The plight of the weaker farmers was often that of an entire community; it was represented graphically in a statement from the town of Palmer asking for the removal of the General Court from Boston and the establishment of a "bank of paper money, . . . Considering the great desperateness of the Inhabitants of this commonwealth (and of the said

Town of Palmer in particular) labours under by reason of the great scarcity of a surculating medeam."

Suits for settlement, distraint, and, in the last resort, imprisonment for debt naturally came before the courts, and the courts became the focal point of a sporadic but determined movement of resistance. Courts played a large part in the lives of so habitually litigious a people. The county courts, moveover, were not merely judicial bodies, they possessed a number of powers of local government, including the power to fix certain assessments that fell outside the jurisdiction of the townships. What helped to fortify the authority of the courts was the fact that the judges, being appointed by the legislature, were beyond the control of the voters. In August 1786 the word passed among the debtor farmers of Worcester County that the sitting of the county court must be stopped at all costs, and a small army of farmers, armed with their own shotguns, descended on the town of Worcester. The movement rallied behind a former revolutionary captain, Daniel Shays, and during several months of disorder and occasional fighting, the government of Massachusetts was unable to enforce its laws through the western and central portions of the state.

Considered as a military event, Shays's Rebellion was a trivial affair that posed no serious threat to the center of government. There was no march on Boston, and when the revolutionary general Benjamin Lincoln took an army out to suppress them, the rebels were soon dispersed. Many escaped to become refugees in other states, and some were tried for treason, sentenced to death, but subsequently pardoned.

Shays's Rebellion was not purely, nor primarily, a military event. The seriousness of its political implications can be appreciated in the light of the state's constitutional history. Only six years earlier, the people of Massachusetts had debated a constitution, and, despite their doubts over two or three points of detail, that constitution had gone into force with the most massive affirmation of popular approval accorded any polity in the contemporary world. If this was not government by the consent of the governed then it would be hard to see how that concept could ever be realized. Yet it was here in this very state that open rebellion had broken out against an American government, and the episode generated a wave of painful doubts as to whether, after all the sacrifices of the war years, the American people would prove equal to the onus of ruling themselves.

These doubts were most active in the minds of the creditors, businessmen, and economic conservatives, who interpreted the currency crises as a dire warning against popular government. In moments of confidence, these men would declare their belief that in America, where property was broadly distributed, there were no extremes of rich and poor, no insuperable divisions of social class. Periods of instability, though, would revive all their instinctive fears of the rise to power of a mass of unpropertied laborers and tenant and debtor farmers, supported no doubt by small traders and artisans. Shays's Rebellion appalled the propertied classes throughout the United States; suddenly they were afraid that the existing powers of government might be totally insufficient to deal with any further economic crises. The Congress actually ordered an armed force to the affected area, under the shallow pretext of security against the Indians, and, although this expedition was not involved in any fighting, its presence gave a clear indication of the extent to which the Confederation was concerned with the insurgency. During the months that Shays's forces were on the move, all state legislatures were deliberating the proposition, which had emanated from Congress following a meeting of several state delegations at Annapolis, that a general convention be held at Philadelphia to find ways of strengthening the Articles of Confederation. The news from Massachusetts undoubtedly spurred some of them into an affirmative response.

If the legislators of Massachusetts had proved themselves more receptive to the condition of their own state and more flexible in action, events on the continental scene might have gone differently. It was ironic that the worst crisis of political confidence should have occurred in the state with the most advanced system of representation. The crisis arose in a direct sense from the rigid and unimaginative financial policies of the state legislature, but in a deeper sense it reflected a failure of information and of representation. Each town was responsible, under the constitution of 1780, for paying for its own representative in the assembly, and it was precisely in times of extreme hardship that the poorer towns were least able to afford the expense. In 1786 the worst afflicted parts of the state were the most weakly represented. Partly as a result, the interior towns, many of them long resentful of governmental dominance by Boston and the seaboard cities, did not trust the General Court to protect their interests. In the management of the assembly, the seaport merchants had every advantage of accessibility to one another, superior information, and the easy habit of experienced authority. The western counties tried to concert their efforts by resorting to the practice of holding county conventions, a tactic that reminded their opponents too much of proceedings before and during the Revolution; such conventions were denounced as illegal and unconstitutional on the one hand, while on the other they were upheld as the people's only means of uniting to tell the legislature of their grievances.

The problem can be understood by reference to the political institution that the insurgents did not have at their disposal—the political party. Parties had sprung into existence in the advanced politics of Pennsylvania, and it was a form of party through which Clinton and his faction ruled New York; the ingredients of party organization also existed in Rhode Island. Elsewhere, however, they were yet unknown, and attempts to develop political parties with the intention of influencing elections were regarded as an interference with the liberty of the voter to make his own choice. Orthodox opinion held that parties were selfish factions directed against the public interest. And it was not long before the organizers of parties in the early years of congressional government encountered difficulties springing from precisely the same attitudes. Only after the suppression of the rebellion did the voters of Massachusetts turn in large numbers to the polls as a means of providing specific remedies. The period of disfranchisement with which the rebels were punished by legislative act was short-lived, and the elections of April 1787 produced a marked overturn in membership of the legislature, together with the reinstatement of John Hancock as governor in place of James Bowdoin, who had failed to anticipate the storm. The new legislature provided a handful of remedies for afflicted debtors, and demonstrated more humanity than did the old. But what really came to the rescue of Massachusetts was the increase in economic activity that began during 1787 and continued under the auspices of the new government of the United States.

The issuance of paper currencies was much the most controversial means used by state governments in the years following the war to bolster the economy, but it did not constitute the only method. The self-imposed restrictions preceding the war had begun to nurture domestic manufactures, a process greatly accelerated by the war itself; the depression gave rise to a positive movement for the protection of American manufactures. All classes involved in the production of goods were concerned. In the manufacturing cities of Philadelphia, Boston, and New York, the owners of workshops, together with their skilled artisans, held meetings from which resolutions demanding import duties and support for domestic producers were sent to their state governments. State legislatures had every reason to respond to these appeals. They were influenced if not led by men with similar interests, and could not be indifferent to the concentrations of votes in the cities, more especially since the majority system now gave these populations a proportionate degree of representation. Merchants dealing in overseas goods were not by nature sympathetic to restrictive legislation, but the state governments accompanied their protective measures with duties that discriminated in favor of American shipping. Many domestic manufactures were given support in the form of import tariffs on foreign products; the tariffs fell heavily on luxuries but included items of daily use in which Americans were struggling to compete for the market. Bounties and tax exemptions were also offered by the states to assist manufacturers. In short, American shipping began to benefit from the kind of protective legislation that it had once received from Britain.

The supply of capital was stimulated by the incorporation of banks. Adhering closely to the precedents laid down by the Bank of North America, the Massachusetts Bank and the Bank of New York had come into existence by 1784. They issued notes in excess of the specie paid in by their stockholders, and the prosperity of the bank's business increased the interest payable to the stockholders while at the same time multiplying the effective circulating medium. Bank notes were not legal tender, but so long as the public retained confidence in the security of the specie deposits, the notes could circulate in such a way as to give a new elasticity to the currency. Borrowers were simply credited with fictitious deposits. The bank was thus beginning its career as a source of capital for expansion, a career that frequently ended in disaster when the loans burgeoned out of all proportion to deposits. Prudent management, of course, could control the extent of credit through phases of business fluctuation. The Bank of the United States, which Hamilton inaugurated, and which opened for business in New York in 1791, had behind it the example of several years of successful operation by various banking institutions.

Most of the enterprise behind these business activities was that of private capital, but state government provided it with protection, support, and official sanction, without which business could never have enjoyed the security that was so essential to its progress. Yet the cover that state governments could offer was indeed pathetically inadequate, as merchants everywhere soon discovered. Since each state was sovereign, each could discriminate in favor of its own manufacturers and shippers and against those of its neighbors. New Jersey and Connecticut were made to feel the oppressive power of the great states of Pennsylvania and New York, upon which they depended for a sizable proportion of their supplies. No superior authority could be invoked to oblige the state governments to comply with a single policy. No superior authority could be invoked to promulgate a policy of protecting all American shipping, an inadequacy that was an obvious disadvantage. The Congress lacked even the power to enforce the collection, within the states, of prewar debts to British merchants for the repayment of which the United States was under obligation by the Treaty of Paris. The economic revival that began toward the end of the 1780s was thus imperiled by political insecurities that could be surmounted only by strengthening the machinery of continental government.

Americans had turned to government as an agency of their own purposes. They did not need to be disciples of the mercantile system to appreciate the fact that in the weakness and vulnerability of their own enterprises, government had the power to protect and support them; the point was that it was now their own government, serving their own purposes, not that of a distant country ruling them for its own ultimate ends. Americans did not fight the War of Independence in order to open an area of free enterprise capitalism of the sort that came to dominate the economy of the nineteenth century. They fought it to take into their own hands the ultimate power of decision; the experience was not without touches of exhilaration. But people seldom unite, or long remain united, about economic policies. In economic matters, more perhaps than in others, differences of method can be quickly transformed into differences of aim. When these were perceived they raised the large question of what sort of a society the United States was to become.

7

Religion and the
Community of the Land

The upheaval of the Revolution spread like a shock wave through all sectors of American society. In a sense the Revolution was the upheaval. Almost every institution, including religion, local government, and the marketplace, was in some way affected, and colonial styles of thought came through the experience shaken, if not radically changed. Not everyone could react to these new currents with equanimity. The onrush of events, which swept so quickly beyond any conventional controls, was doubly menacing to all who believed in an established order—precisely because that order was itself so precarious, so easily jeopardized by the natural and endemic conditions of American life.

When the French were still on the northern and some of the western borders, the threat was explicit and military. The removal of the French did not eliminate the Indian tribes, several of whom were capable of fighting American armies to a standstill and of striking constant terror into outlying settlements. These dangers, however, could not stop the unceasing, restless drift toward the interior. All communities, no matter how well established, how stable, were influenced by this feverish drive toward new lands, a migration that brought instability to land values, wages, prices, and family life. For those who had enough vision to discern such an entity, it also challenged the security and cohesiveness of the American body politic. These geographical movements were not the only events to affect American life. Many people both in new regions and in old and settled ones, whether or not they were touched by the physical disturbances of the times, were thrown intermittently into the grip of religious excitements that had equally telling effects on those whom they enthralled, or deranged.

A state of excitement was in many ways characteristic of the social and psychological atmosphere of the Revolution and its aftermath. The conditions that American publicists preferred to report, and to hold out as most typical of the emerging nation, were of boundless hope and reasonable expectations. Evidence to substantiate these conditions is abundant. After all, the huge masses who migrated across the mountain passes and down the river valleys were confident of finding better lands and richer prospects; the promotional, or what would soon be called "boosting," literature scattered by speculators naturally emphasized the wealth that lay in the West and in the future. Further, the reports of travelers convey an almost tangible sensation of personal liberty in the manners and speech of the innumerable individuals they encountered on roads, in taverns and inns, in meetings public and private. But not all hopes were destined to be fulfilled, and not all messages conveyed by the disturbances of the times were in fact messages of hope.

The most alarming of all were those belonging to what are sometimes described as "the consolations of religion." Ever since the 1730s, the early years of that series of convulsions known as the Great Awakening, the most potent preachers of religious revival had obtained a significant part of their effects by appeals to fear. Jonathan Edwards' famous sermon "Sinners in the Hands of an Angry God," in which his parishioners were invited to liken themselves to a loathsome spider that might be dropped at any moment into the furnace, was the prototype of thousands of attacks on the tranquillity and self-satisfaction of a sinful people.

Edwards saw the chief dangers of his time as deriving from various English influences in theological training and doctrine, and in the ever-present temptations of avarice and worldly acquisition. The doctrinal enemy was vaguely known as Arminianism, officially held in the colonies primarily by the Anglicans; in its latter-day connotation, Arminianism had come to mean a kind of rationalistic questioning of harsh Calvinist absolutes, an implied modification of the Calvinist emphasis on the primacy of spiritual concerns at all times and in all activities. Edwards and his followers perceived that worldliness and material temptations had begun to corrupt Americans, soiling the God-given purity of their earlier vision. This view was not necessarily that of an older generation; the revival of religion was a fresh enthusiasm for old values, exerting an influence on people of all ages. The message of the revived Calvinism was carried in countless sermons, including one by Ebenezer Pemberton, a Presbyterian pastor in New York City:

> And what can all this World afford us beyond a competent supply of our bodily wants, and a suitable provision for the comforts and conveniences of life? And these, if our desires be moderate, and we do not give the reins to an ungovern'd fancy, may be easily provided for. Every thing else is burdensome and unprofitable.

Edward Wigglesworth observed in a sermon of 1733 that New Englanders were churchgoers, sober and industrious; the trouble developed from the consequences of their industry: their "Exorbitant reach after Riches" had come to be "the reigning Temper in Persons of all Ranks in our Land."

The Great Awakening spent its force, but was succeeded by other revivals in different regions. The indomitable itinerant minister Francis Asbury, who after the War of Independence was appointed a Methodist superintendent, or bishop, found marked evidences of an Anglican revival in Virginia over a period that roughly coincided with the years of disputes with Britain, 1763 to 1776. This effusion of religious emotion washed through the colonies in 1763 and 1764, and like nearly all these phenomena it was accompanied by an intense belief that the millennium was at hand. Thirty years later, Calvinists were again "calling the attention of the pious to an expectation of the introduction of this glorious day." The course of events, however, had wrought decided changes in the movement by the end of the century.

The social convulsions that attended the War of Independence could hardly have left the religious order of the colonies untouched. There were clergymen everywhere who feared the onset of war, not primarily because of the rupture with Britain or because of the loss of life and property, but because of the threatened corruption of religious values. The clash of priorities—between man's salvation and man's freedom—is dramatized by an entry in Asbury's journal for August 1775: "On Monday I spoke both morning and evening; but we were interrupted by the clamour of arms, and preparations of war. My business is, to be more intensely devoted to GOD." And rather than exhort the people to take up arms in defense of their liberties, he urged his listeners to take care of their souls. And then in October: "But if it is thought expedient to watch and fight in defence of our bodies and property, how much more expedient is it to watch and fight against sin and Satan, in defence of our souls, which are in danger of eternal damnation!" Often he was near to despair, for the "clamour of arms" confused the land.

The war multiplied the moral dangers from fear and greed, and the ministers who warned their flocks against them proved only too accurate. Together with some of the political leaders, particularly those of New England, they believed that public conduct could still be measured by the civic and personal values found in the religious tenets of Puritans, tenets that continued to survive even though the original religious fervor had long since faded. A certain austerity, together with a commitment to the performance of public duties in connection with government, was characteristic of the values that many persons prominent in the religious and social life of their communities wanted to sustain in American society. Indeed, for many of these leaders the struggle for independence from Britain represented a signal opportunity to assert these values in America, in distinction to their corruption in Britain. These principles, however, did not stand up well under the onslaught of economic opportunity. The only comfort that devout Calvinists could draw from an economy of paper currencies, rising prices, and market shortages caused by deliberate forestalling was that these circumstances provided a true test of the American character; one such minister declared that he was ready to admit

> that the especial design of Heaven, in the present war, is to manifest the real character of the present generation in America; and that in the course of events, every class of men will be tried so far as to manifest the temper of their hearts, either in one way or another.

Calvinists could also draw some satisfaction from the evidence that Americans were like other men in their propensity to sin.

From a Calvinistic position, which was represented, in attenuated forms, by Congregationalists and Presbyterians, there appeared to be a sinister connection between the collapse of moral standards in economic matters and the insidious increase in morally harmful forms of theology. The Reverend John

Murray in a sermon in 1783 made a forceful attack on "the love of money," which,

> by whatever means obtained, rages universally: Extortion is become an avowed practice, that sordid covetousness which is idolatry, rears its front without shame, and defies the beams of noon: Fraud and dishonesty in the way of trade, is considered as expertness in business and passed over with a smile.

These severe strains on the moral integrity of the people, which the Congregational and Presbyterian clergy regarded as falling wholly within the domain of their responsibility, resulted in grave losses to be set against the material gains of liberty and independence. Moreover, the Revolution also unloosed the opportunity for translating political liberty into religious liberty. Reiterated assertions of political liberty on grounds of law and reason carried disturbing implications for those claiming authority in religion.

In the competition between the sects for people's souls, the most violent animosities did have a political basis, and one of the deeper consequences of the revolutionary upheaval was the breaking down of politically imposed religious barriers. Until after the Revolution, the differences of religion were maintained by law. The Congregational churches were established through all the New England states except Rhode Island, which meant that churches were maintained and ministers paid from public funds. In the seventeenth century it had also meant much more, for rival sects were persecuted and forcibly driven out. Later, however, the spread of settlement from the interior, the growing interest of farmers in their connections with the market, and the concomitant decline of early Puritan zeal, which proved difficult to transmit undiluted to later generations, all combined to forge a less intolerant attitude.

The Congregational order was well suited to New England. A loosely knit federal scheme allowed each town to elect its own minister and left to the people of each meetinghouse the full responsibility for complying with the obligation to provide for public worship. The clergy of the orthodox persuasion were usually well-educated men, with a certain proclivity for flattering the established leadership as represented in the legislature by reminding them, in election-day sermons, of the comfortable view expressed in Romans 13 that "the powers that be are ordained of God." This opinion, however, was not seen to extend to the powers of the British government, and in the clash between rival authorities the New England clergy used their pulpits to proclaim the American cause. There were, certainly, exceptions to this course of action, but on the whole it was only the Anglicans of New England who by the very nature of their association found themselves aligned with the British. It was this alignment, and its political implications, that the Congroga tionalists had so urgently feared when they encountered the repeated rumors of plans to establish a Church of England bishopric in Boston.

The Revolution in New England did little to disturb this religious order. It may well have shaken what the ministry regarded as priorities of faith, and contributed to a general weakening of traditional institutions, but it did not unseat the clergy or set it against the will of the populace. In Connecticut, where the old charter was retained, the traditional establishment remained undisturbed; elsewhere, it was reflected in new state constitutions. The clergy continued to occupy a position of impressive authority, and by its presence it reminded the people that even if the laws under which they lived were made by men, they must one day settle their account with God. One attribute of the clergy that added to its influence in New England was the fact that it was large; and a numerous body of men, each with an acknowledged position of moral leadership in his own town, all adhering to a certain code, could never be discounted as a force in politics. According to Jedidiah Morse, whose *American Geography* was published in 1789, the Connecticut clergy, whom he regarded as respectable, had "hitherto preserved a kind of aristocratical balance in the very democratical government of the State; which has happily operated as a check upon the overbearing spirit of republicanism." It continued to operate as a check until as late as 1818, when for the first time the mounting pressures for structural reform in the government forced a reluctant and not excessively democratic leadership into holding a constitutional convention. It was only then that the Congregational Church lost its official connection with the government. In Massachusetts the same step was not taken until 1833.

The situation was different in those southern states where the Revolution probed and divided the loyalties of the established church. The Church of England ministered to the gentry of Virginia and the Carolinas, and the gentry identified themselves socially as members of the church. The clergy exercised its ministry by deputation from the bishop of London; its position as a branch of the English establishment, however, rendered its members vulnerable to attack. This attack gained much of its strength from the fact that the Piedmont and transmontane regions of these states were being rapidly filled by settlers of Scotch-Irish descent who had no connection or sympathy with either England or its church. The shifting balance of population eventually made the position of the church untenable, and its disestablishment occurred soon after the Revolution—or, rather, as a substantive element of the Revolution—throughout the South. The most dramatic of these moves took place in Virginia, where the church was disestablished first.

The peculiar strength of the Virginia disestablishmentarians was in the extraordinary abilities of their leaders. Moreover, these men themselves belonged to the ruling order that was steering the state through the war and would continue to govern it for generations. Jefferson's views on religion and its connection with the state were those of a member of that widespread band of passionately individualistic thinkers whose intellectual sources were in France. In Europe the philosophes of the Enlightenment attacked the dominant abuses of the age: the vast preponderance of privilege and power in both the Roman Catholic Church and the nobility. While in America these abuses were attenuated by space, by the weakness of the disciplinary powers of state, church, and nobility, and perhaps by the gentler pace of life, they were visible, nevertheless, and if they were not curbed they might grow worse. For men of Jefferson and Madison's cast of thought, nothing could be more ominous of the dangers of tyranny over the mind than the connection between church and state. Jefferson was a true religious tolerationist because his inquiring mind was skeptical of all claims to exclusive authority; he believed that God had created the world, but he did not believe that God had given the truth to any single religious persuasion or sect. Jefferson's fight for religious liberty in his own state was thus one of the most passionate and earnestly committed struggles of his life, and he carried it against strongly entrenched and equally passionate defenses.

The cause at hand, which gave Jefferson his opportunity, was that of the Baptists, who petitioned the assembly to be relieved of having to pay taxes for the support of the Anglican Church. But the old order was formidable. Most of the members of the assembly were loyal Anglicans as a matter of course, and they were led in defense of their church by Edmund Pendleton, the distinguished judge who had earlier been entrusted with the accounts of the Robinson estate and who, along with Jefferson and Benjamin Harrison, had represented Virginia at the first Continental Congress. Jefferson and Pendleton, though they had differences of opinion that were not purely intellectual, were personal friends. Jefferson, both in his struggle for religious liberty and in his parallel campaign for the abolition of primogeniture and entail, was striving to bring into existence the conditions for a society whose elements would find their own natural places, freed from traditional order or imposed authority. Pendleton was fighting to retain an order that would always dictate and determine the outlines of the social structure. It took Jefferson three years to win the battle in the assembly, which he did in 1779 when compulsory levies for the support of the Anglican Church were finally abolished. "The religious issue," he afterward wrote, "brought on the severest contests in which I have ever been engaged." The fight to separate church and state, however, was not over, for Patrick Henry now came forward with proposals for the compulsory support of religion, with the proviso that individuals might choose which religion to support. Henry's new attempt to establish a permanent connection between church, or religion, and government was not finally defeated until 1786 (by which time Madison was taking the lead in the assembly). Jefferson always regarded religious liberty in Virginia as one of his greatest triumphs, and caused it to be commemorated, in company with the Declaration of Independence and the founding of the University of Virginia, on his tombstone at Monticello.

Individual states clung to their religious establishments for varying lengths of time, depending on local and historical circumstances. But the American revolt against British authority carried strong undertones of resentment against an ecclesiastical establishment. Church and state were seen to be in infamous collusion against the liberties of the people. Their joint powers subjected all forms of religious dissent to serious social and political disabilities. The movement toward disestablishment received added impetus from the ideas of religious toleration, often based on skepticism, that the French enlightenment transmitted to the foremost American political thinkers. Men as far apart as New England and Virginia in political geography were to some extent students of the same philosophers. Their clear conclusion was that the state should cease forever to interfere with the privacy of the citizen's religious conscience. This conviction was set forth in 1791 in the first amendment to the federal Constitution, which declared that "Congress shall make no law respecting an establishment of religion, or prohibiting the free exercise thereof. . . ."

The battles for religious liberty did not represent any decline in the efforts by ministers of rival sects to stir people's souls. Evangelists are seldom satisfied with the state of belief that they discover, and the numerous American itinerant ministers were repeatedly dismayed by the ignorance and apathy of the masses, particularly in the more remote settlements. The revival meetings conducted by these ministers made many converts, and produced vivid evidences of an intense and dramatic experience. To the ministers these signs caused either exhilaration or anxiety, depending on their own beliefs and judgments. The meetings, which sometimes lasted two or three days, produced a strange condition of collective excitement: men and women would fall, roll about on the ground, or be seized with a dancing fever. These reactions always occurred in crowds, but each crowd was a vast aggregation of private states of frenzy. At times, which tend to be well reported, the collapse of acquired inhibitions led to sexual encounters that seem to have been unhidden, sudden, and strangely impersonal—intense but loveless.

American revivals underwent certain changes of content and character, and those of the early nineteenth century were dominated by a far less educated and a less rigorous theology than those that had occurred previously. Yet similarities exist in the reports of masses of people experiencing and yielding themselves to a sudden, convulsive tearing away of their normal social postures and restraints; and they seem often to have been infused with a fearful belief that the Day of Judgment was upon them. The American revivals appear, by eighteenth-century standards, to have been unusual among those of the Western world both in the extent of the population that took part in them and in the intensity of the experience they invoked. John Lambert, an Englishman traveling in America about 1807, was disturbed by the hysteria he saw at religious meetings. These, he observed, were not the *consolations* of Christianity; the people were lost in a maze of doubt and perplexity and they thought of nothing but everlasting damnation. "In no part of the world, perhaps," he reflected, "is religious fanaticism carried to more extravagant heights than in the United States, by a few artful designing men." The history of religion records many instances of collective hysteria, often induced by charismatic preachers acting on the exposed defenses of the weak and the poor. They occurred during the Crusades, and repeated themselves in northwest Europe from roughly the twelfth century to the sixteenth. All were manifestations of social malaise associated with chiliasm—a belief in the end of the world and the advent of the millennium. It might be fanciful to suggest that the American revivals re-enacted those of the chiliastic movements of the later Middle Ages; but the discernible similarities are not merely incidental. In the earlier American phases especially, revivals occurred both in towns and in the country; the extremes of mass hysteria, however, were apparently reached in frontier or recently settled territories, or in areas not subject to the restraining social and educational influences of the city. Both in the Middle Ages and on the American frontier, frightful warnings of judgment and damnation blasted the imaginations of simple people with few resources and little knowledge or education. Professor Norman Cohn writes of the medieval movements:

> A bird's-eye view suggests that the social situations in which outbreaks of revolutionary chiliasm occurred were in fact remarkably uniform. . . . The areas in which age-old prophecies about the Last Days took on a new, revolutionary meaning and a new, explosive force were the areas of rapid social change—and not simply change but expansion: areas where trade and industry were developing and where the population was rapidly increasing.[1]

The millenarians of those times were not the beneficiaries but the victims of these changes; their lives were cheap, fear-stricken, and insecure. It cannot be said that Americans were threatened with starvation or with the same cluster of dangers. But the intense loneliness of many of the settlements—a condition applying not only to the frontier—the lurking doubts about the Indians, the wildness of a continent that seemed at times to be laden as heavily with dread as with hope, these may have helped to make men and women liable to outbursts of feeling that would have appeared aberrant in a more settled and more formally educated community. They suffered, too, from a very marked shortage of socially organized forms of emotional expression or communal activity. It is also possible that many individuals, mainly in the older communities, saw in the emphasis on salvation an offer of something deeper, more spiritually satisfying than the competitive struggle that, even before the middle of the eighteenth century, had begun to transform the market into a determinant of social position and future aspiration.

Revivalists were constantly striving to counter not only ignorance but indifference. Morse called it "Nothingarianism" and observed that it was rampant in the western settlements of southern states—a statement that may have reflected something of his own New England bias. It could also be observed that religious doctrines were becoming confused and even composite. The Reverend David Rice, founder of Presbyterianism in Ken-

---

1. Norman Cohn, *The Pursuit of the Millennium* (Fair Lawn, N. J., 1957), p. 22.

tucky, noted in a sermon in 1805 that not only was there too much drinking of ardent spirits and too riotous a neglect of the sabbath, but that people who professed themselves Christians did not really understand the basis of the religion. Too many of them expected to see justification by evidence without reference to Scripture, and too many ministers preached sermons that contained an odd mixture of incompatible forms of Christian doctrine. Rice did think, however, that the revivals that had been going on in Kentucky since 1798 were genuine revivals of religion, and not because of numbers, or bodily agitations, or earnestness, for men might be earnestly engaged in false religion; he based his conviction on the quality of revivals that he saw. What impressed him was that he discerned "a compassionate concern for the salvation of precious souls." Rice, a deeply humane man, believed that the revival had been granted in answer to prayer, and for that reason alone it had his blessing.

Despite the activities of the sectarians, morals were becoming more important than doctrines, and people of different sects were coming to regard one another with a benign and informal tolerance. About the same time, the Scottish merchant John Melish remarked that in Pennsylvania, west of Philadelphia, no religious privileges existed and people lived together in Christian charity. Their forbearance did not, of course, mean that the teachings on which ministers laid their emphasis were of a lenient or permissive character, or that the doctrinal element was entirely absent. Many of the people of the interior evidently took to heart the awful warnings they periodically heard about hellfire and eternal torment, which seemed directly pointed at their earthbound lives and self-indulgent pleasures.

That people should be feeling a new freedom to decide for themselves about religion was consistent with the absence of a distinct or intellectually informed doctrinal affirmation—which was also noted by the observant French visitor the Duc de La Rochefoucauld-Liancourt—and with the lively sense of liberation from previous patterns of social identification. When decisions about religion took people to church, they found that the kind of social habit or orthodoxy of association that had so often separated them in the past had lost its binding force, and, moreover, ceased to segregate churches into different social communities. Thus, intermarriage between the sects became a matter of course where it had once been rare. Not only did Lutherans and Quakers marry each other, but Protestants married Catholics with a freedom from restraint that broke with the past. People tended to choose their own religion rather than to follow a traditional pattern laid down by their family or their community, and they took this latitude literally enough to allow their children to choose for themselves, too.

There were, nevertheless, many men of prominence and power in America who perceived with anxiety that the dissolution of politically authorized religion would bring with it a decline in morals and a disintegration of the old order of society. Not everyone had fought the Revolution for the same ends, and Virginia became a testing ground in the conflict over the structure of land rights. Pendleton and the Virginia conservatives earnestly believed that the social principles they had defended in the established church were equally at stake in the question of the disposal of estates, which were affected by the laws of primogeniture and entail. Under the former, the estate of a landowner dying intestate went to the eldest son. Under the rules of entail, which had developed in England in the 1680s and had been copied in Virginia in 1705, estates whose owners had taken certain legal steps to secure them in perpetuity could not be alienated by subsequent heirs; the estate itself acquired a sort of permanent life, over which an owner was merely a temporary trustee. The great estates of England had been aggrandized with the aid of this legal device, though the restriction could, in fact, be as much trouble as it was worth to the active estate manager who wanted some flexibility in his sales and acquisitions of land. To Jefferson the practice and principle of entail were anathema because they were meant to build up great and perpetual estates on which a permanent landed aristocracy would reside. He wanted to reduce the bastions of privileged order in land as he did in religion; the Enlightenment was above all the enemy of privilege. In Europe leaders of the Enlightenment were best able to assault the power of the nobilities by siding, at least temporarily, with the central authorities and the king; but in America the task was to sweep away all legal safeguards for the growth of such nobilities by invoking the power of the people.

Again Jefferson was opposed by his colleague Pendleton, and again the ranks of the conservatives massed against him and Madison. The battle for reform was somewhat facilitated by the doubtful commitments of many landed families, who did not find entailment an economic advantage; and in the matter of primogeniture, Jefferson subsequently maintained that he carried the argument even against a double portion for the eldest son by asking whether younger members of the family were expected to eat half as much. Both Jefferson and his opponents believed they were engaged in a contest that would determine the shape and future of Virginian society, and to some extent they were right, even though other conditions in the life of the state would have worked to loosen the social structure. The settlement of the West, still in progress through migrations from the Tidewater and down the valleys from further north, was bound to bring an alteration in the balance of both religion and the ownership of land; it is doubtful whether the question of either religious establishment or of perpetuity in private estates was as close to the central problems of future political and social control as Pendleton and his friends believed. Owners of private property meanwhile retained an interest in the debt law, which provided that land could not be seized in settlement of debts; this law gives a clue to the prevailing conservatism of the landed order, which was prepared to defend the interests of its members, of all ranks, against those of the merchants and bankers of the cities. The issues of the revolutionary phase of Virginia's politics divided the leadership of the state without changing its social character; for the remainder of Jefferson's long life, and for many years afterward, that leadership's most remarkable feature was not so much its reforming propensities as the stability and the firmness with which its members continued to exercise control in their own interests.

Geographical developments also affected the other states. In South Carolina they were underscored in 1790 by the removal of the capital from Charleston to the new city of Columbia, actually and symbolically in the center of the state. The changing balance of population had made a clear beginning, before the end of the eighteenth century, in the direction of redefining the interests, the religious affinities, and the loyalties of all the southern states. Pennsylvania had no formal religious establishment to sustain, and the influence of the once predominant Quakers had been in slow but extended decline; the removal of the capital to Harrisburg was the geographical manifestation of the same population shift, though it did not constitute a challenge to the cultural predominance of Philadelphia. New York's gesture of the same order took the capital out of the great and rising international seaport and placed it in the obscure village of Albany.

These political moves, of course, ministered to needs and demands different from those of religion, yet there were similarities in the social implications of changes occurring in both politics and religion. In politics, as represented by land laws and by the concentration of authority in the old seaboard capitals, as well as in religion, as dominated by a state-supported church, an old order of society was under stress. That the population was coming increasingly to be made up of groups whose geographical differences also implied certain differences of social background was reflected in the political pressure to move the state capitals; but often these differences of background were also differences of religion.

Some of the groups overlapped and distinctions became blurred. A society in which Protestants and Catholics were beginning to marry each other was one in which inherited differences were losing their rigidity. There existed in the early American nation no machinery, no social police force, capable of regimenting the religious loyalties of the people. The sects were too numerous to be subdued from any societal center. If, for example, Virginia had continued to insist on collecting taxes from Baptists for the support of Anglicans, it seems likely that in a short while the tax collectors would have had a rough time. But the sects were also too numerous to subdue each other, and as they learned to live side by side they also learned a certain measure of respect for the individuality of religious opinion. Their respect did not arise, as it did with Jefferson, from an intellectual skepticism about the more specific claims of religious doctrine; Jefferson was even dubious about those of Christianity, a position that would have horrified many of the people for whose religious liberty he had fought so hard. For most of the sects, religious toleration was simply a fact of life before it was a considered opinion.

Diversity was an inevitable characteristic of religion in America, but diversity by itself did not make tolerance inevitable. Most of the sects were Protestant, and assumed without question that the fundamental character of the country was Protestant no less than it was republican. Among them existed the resources for a violent rejection of Roman Catholics, when the latter became numerous or concentrated. Jews enjoyed a comfortable and spacious place in the life of New York and Philadelphia; but that, too, would change. Where social identity was losing its grip on its former connection with class or "rank," and where the republican ethos made rank difficult to affirm, a sense of social position could easily be rediscovered in connection with religion or national origin. The struggle to establish religious toleration not only as a principle but as a social phenomenon was not yet over. In its graver aspects it had barely begun.

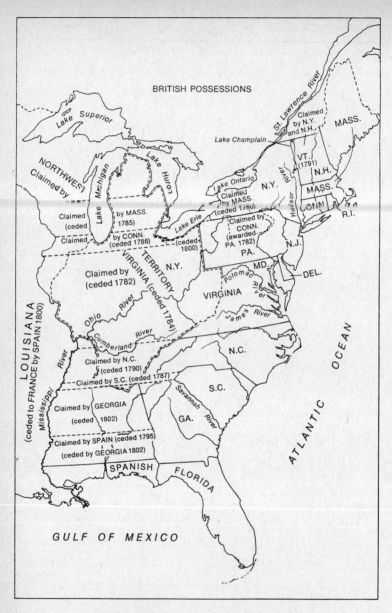

State Claims and Cessions: 1776–1802

8

Migration, Resettlement, and the Community: Did the New Change the Old?

The spiritual upheavals manifested in the religious revivals were fully matched in the material world. The war disturbed many settled habits as it bore down on many settled villages. The deepest disturbance, however, was of the people's own making, for the lifting of British restraints gave the land itself to the Americans, and they laid hold of it with an irresistible energy. "The land was ours before we were the land's," wrote Robert Frost, reflecting, in the twentieth century, on the interplay between the immense, rough, bounteous continent and the American character that it helped to mold and even to create.

Land hunger was as old as any of the forces that drove Europeans to migration, rebellion, and war in the centuries that preceded the adventure into northern and southern America. It had partially accounted for the Norman Conquest of England in 1066; it was the cause of endless peasant revolts and nobles' aggressions; and it continued, well into the nineteenth century, to drive the peoples of overcrowded, famished soils, like those of Ireland, to seek not merely refuge but a new life in the hazy but bright opportunities of America.

Except perhaps for the merchants who put all their capital and profits into commerce, economic ambition in America almost always found its outlet in land speculation. Washington, who began his career as a surveyor, took careful note of the opportunities for purchase and development of the tracts over which he worked on commission, and laid the foundations for a substantial fortune in land in the western part of the Old Dominion. The speculative land companies that came into existence before the Revolution were generally promoted on both sides of the Atlantic. The Grand Ohio Company, to whose plans the British Treasury gave its approval in 1770, was sponsored in England by the Earl of Hertford, by the former colonial governor Thomas Pownall, the merchant Thomas Walpole, and many powerful politicians; in America its backers were Samuel Wharton, the Philadelphia merchant; William Trent, the Indian trader; Governor Thomas Johnson of Maryland; and Franklin, to name only a few. It was Franklin's protracted residence in England that enabled him to act for this company and disposed him for a long time to hope for a reconciliation of the imperial disputes. The Grand Ohio Company aimed to carve a province, to be called Vandalia, out of the Ohio Valley to the west of the existing boundaries of Virginia. After Franklin had been exposed as a colonial partisan and politically discredited in England in 1774, the company soon collapsed, which opened the way to renewed rivalry for the Vandalia territory. As late as the summer of 1775, though fighting had already broken out, the newly formed Wabash Company, under the guidance of Lord Dunmore, governor of Virginia, and Governor Johnson, began to challenge others with claims in that vast area. At about the same time, Judge Richard Henderson and a group of North Carolina speculators, organized as the Transylvania Company, moved to acquire a large tract in what is now Kentucky. Henderson, having in 1775 acquired a dubious title to the land by a form of purchase from its Indian inhabitants, and having sent the frontiersman Daniel Boone and a party of settlers to Boonesboro, in central Kentucky, then tried—unsuccessfully—to confirm his title through a grant from the government of Virginia.

Washington, now commander in chief of the Continental army, had long-standing interests in the Virginia land companies. Such interests had to be promoted through the governor and council, who, until the Declaration of Independence, still held the legal right to make cessions to private purchasers; but independence plainly took the full and final responsibility for land disposition away from the crown or its surrogates and placed it in the hands of the Americans. But which Americans? The question was of urgent importance to the promoters of the rival companies and to everyone with a claim or an interest in the West.

The provincial conventions of those states whose charters endowed them with claims to western territories, which included all of the southern states except Maryland, and New York, Connecticut, and Massachusetts, now averred that these territories had devolved from the crown directly to the states. Their assertion was a logical inference from the fact that each state had previously held its charter directly from the crown, from which each had now declared its sovereign independence; it did not, however, satisfy the inhabitants of the remaining states, which happened through no fault of their own to have firmly drawn western boundaries beyond which no such claims could be made. Men with interests that seemed insecure in the hands of the new state governments also hotly denied the legal claims of those governments over the West. They countered with the assertion that the whole of the western territory had descended to the people of all the states, whose only acknowledged government was the Congress itself. It was, after all, the Continental Congress that had formally declared the independence of the United States.

This debate persisted with intense bitterness through most of the war. When Dickinson's committee offered its draft for the Articles of Confederation, it proposed to give Congress the power both to limit the bounds of states with charter or other claims extending, as they then said, "to the South Sea" (which meant the Pacific) and to dispose of all these lands "for the general benefit of all." However, an upsurge of state-sovereignty arguments, touched off by the threatened transfer of governmental powers at the cost of the states, succeeded in placing restrictions on Congress when the Articles were approved, in November 1777. This did not end the matter, for Maryland's Governor Johnson, who continued to have extensive personal interests in the Ohio Valley, led a move to block ratification of the Articles. The result was that the Congress conducted the war for the next four years without the authority of a formal agreement on a confederacy beyond those already entered into.

The economic exigencies in the background of these maneuvers were almost as pressing as the reasons for the war itself. In both causes, men of daring ambition were fighting for their fortunes, which meant as much to them as their liberties and almost as much as their lives. Their interests, however, differed from state to state. Powerful Virginians and New Yorkers had the advantage of access to government in their own states, which they wanted to keep; but in Maryland, the exhaustion of the soils had forced the planters also to look further west. Maryland planters, and speculators in other states, mostly Pennsylvania, had reason to believe that their influence would be much more effective with the Congress than with an external state legislature in which they had no voice and no power. Meanwhile, a clash between settlers from Virginia and those of Pennsylvania, in the Pittsburgh area, caused animosity between those states and resulted in a Virginian withdrawal. Virginia also had conflicting claims in the Ohio Valley with New York. Other clashes threatened to set state against state in the largely unmapped and untraveled territories about which the only thing generally known was that they held out prospects of enormous wealth.

No doubt the cause of common sense would have dictated that Congress assume the power as the Dickinson draft had proposed. But common sense seldom solves economic conflicts, and more cogent reasons were required before the great states would surrender their claims. Throughout these debates, the war was being waged, and by 1780 it was by no means clear that it was being won. French pressure for ratification of the Articles, and the obduracy of Maryland, began to undermine the tenacity of the landed states, and in February 1780 New York authorized the cession to Congress of its western claims. Congress then became a factor in the issue over western lands because, as the only continental government, it needed funds to pay the army and run the war. An unpaid and bitterly resentful army had long rumbled with threats against the Congress itself. When, in January 1781, the Pennsylvania Line mutinied, there was practically no recourse left but to promise the soldiers land—and to plan to use the land as a source of future income.

Early in 1781, pressed from without by this crisis, and urged from within by Jefferson, whose vision of a West settled by independent yeoman farmers owed nothing to the dreams of the great speculators, Virginia at last agreed to cede its Ohio Valley claims to Congress. Maryland, nonetheless, was still dissatisfied. The cession contained a stipulation that Congress was to reject all previous private land claims in the territory. At this point, the disgruntled Maryland administration was forced by events to ask the French minister for naval help against the British in Chesapeake Bay; he declined to act, however, unless Maryland ratified the Articles. So it was done, and in this somewhat untidy manner the United States acquired its first formal constitution of government.

The Confederacy became heir to the western territories, which by the Peace Treaty of 1783 reached as far as the eastern banks of the Mississippi. The United States at once assumed the role of a colonizing power, whose imperial character was perhaps obscured by the fact that the new nation's additional territories lay overland and not overseas. Americans, who had so long been colonists from the mother country in Britain, now became colonists from their own native country. They spilled and spread out beyond the formal boundaries of their states, lived for a while in remote regions that often involved them in ambiguous loyalties, and were finally reabsorbed into the American nation, which periodically enlarged itself in the process. This process required both organization and legal cover, and the Congress began work, even before the transfer of the Ohio Valley claims, on drafting provisions for government in the West.

The need for revenue, already urgent in 1781, led to a congressional committee report in July 1782 recommending the cession by New York, Virginia, and Connecticut of their western lands to help discharge the public debts incurred by Congress during the war. Discontent over army pay had not been allayed, and in 1783 the officers stationed at Newburgh, New York, became so turbulent that Washington himself felt obliged to intervene; the result was that an incipient mutiny was converted into a petition to Congress requesting land grants in payment of military service.

When Congress met these demands before the end of the war by offering land grants to army officers as a means of discharging its debts, it provided an early example of a procedure that would later become a more general social phenomenon: public land, held by the government in trust for the people, could serve as a release for gathering social pressures that might otherwise explode. The process has often been likened to a safety valve. The analogy, however, as with most mechanical analogies applied to human institutions, is misleading; steam from a safety valve escapes, but the people who moved out into the West were retained within the political system. Their future fortunes and political loyalties would depend in part on the way that system worked for them.

The congressional committee working on plans for the survey and organization of western lands had to consider modes of settlement best suited to the particular needs of people from different parts of the nation. The New England way was generally collective. In the western reaches of the existing New England states, areas for settlement were surveyed and laid out in advance for carefully planned townships, and the local government provided for defense, education, and the support of religion. Southern methods were more individualistic, less controlled, and lacking in the strong sense of community responsibility characteristic of the New England style. Washington approved of the New England methods because he saw them as compact, efficient, better adapted to military defense, and also more difficult for speculators to exploit. Southern states made no provisions for defense, education, or religion, and they allowed individuals to claim any tract of any size within a surveyed area. Jefferson was a member of the first congressional committee on the land question, and his influence was apparent in its proposal. Local government in the West would combine elements from both methods of settlement, and the settlers themselves would administer it; moreover, slavery would be excluded from the territory after 1800. This plan was dropped after Jefferson had departed for Paris to replace Franklin as American minister, and in 1785 Congress adopted an ordinance that included much of the earlier plan's self-government by the settlers but omitted the exclusion of slavery.

By the Land Ordinance of 1785, the Northwest Territory was to be divided into townships of thirty-six square miles each; Congress retained an interest by reserving four of the thirty-six one-square-mile sections in each township, and one-third of any gold, silver, or copper. A lot was to be set aside for a school, and land sales were to be conducted by public auction in each state, at not less than one dollar an acre. Payment for the Northwest land was to be in specie, loan-office certificates reduced to specie value, or certificates of the liquidated debt of the United States. Land sales, however, went slowly. The cash price of at least one dollar an acre was hard to meet in the middle of the 1780s, and the requirement that the purchasers themselves pay for the survey must have discouraged everyone who was poorly equipped to meet such charges. In addition, Congress was competing with both Pennsylvania and the Maine provinces of Massachusetts, which wanted settlers and were prepared to offer greater enticements.

The end of the war had seen the emergence of new speculative interests. These interests, ably led by ambitious New Englanders, had little connection with prewar groups, such as the Grand Ohio Company. These were new entrepreneurs, some of them with quickly made wartime fortunes, many of them dissatisfied former army officers, who were certain that vast fortunes were to be

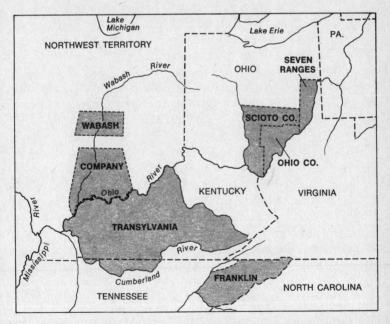

Company Claims and the State of Franklin: 1776–1802

made from the enormous pressure for settlement in the West. For about a year, 1785–1786, it looked as though Connecticut, which claimed a large tract of "Western Reserve" in the Ohio country, might prove to be the one remaining state through which successful western claims could be made. But the Connecticut government was beset with domestic scandals and economic weakness, which helped to establish that the main route to control of the West was clearly going to lie through Congress. Early in 1786 New England army officers took a new initiative; using a procedure similar to that of familiar political associations, General Rufus Putnam of Connecticut and Benjamin Tupper of Massachusetts issued a call to Massachusetts officers and soldiers of the revolutionary army to organize a new Ohio Company. They enlisted the services of the Reverend Manasseh Cutler, a former army chaplain, who soon proved himself to be a lobbyist of extraordinary skill.

Cutler discovered that William Duer, the secretary to the congressional Board of Treasury, was bidding for a million acres on the Scioto River at a nominal price; the two teams—Duer had interested some government cronies in his scheme—agreed to advance their claims in a joint venture. Cutler smoothed the negotiations with Congress by dropping the plan to make Samuel Holden Parsons, one of the Ohio Company's founders, governor of the territory, and offering that post instead to Arthur St. Clair, at that time president of Congress. He also countered what was at first a cool response from Congress by threatening to do business with the state governments that had lands of their own to sell. This maneuver induced a more favorable legislative frame of mind, and soon led to an immense concession in the Ohio Valley: 1.5 million acres went to the Ohio Company, and an option on a further 5 million to the Scioto Company, which, however, failed to develop and patented no land of its own. The price was to be one dollar or more per acre, but the burden of purchase was eased by providing that some of this might be paid in congressional certificates issued to soldiers and officers. As these were then changing hands on the open market at ten cents apiece, huge profits appeared to await the promoters.

The political side of the settlement was embodied in the

famous Northwest Ordinance of 1787. The provisions for government, compared with the 1785 ordinance, amounted to a
sharp decrease in the amount of control and responsibility confided to the settlers themselves. Ultimately, not less than three or
more than five states were to be created, but for temporary purposes the territory would be one district over which a governor, a
secretary, and a court of three judges were to be appointed by Congress. These men were to form an interim government, with power
to adopt whatever laws they chose from among those of the existing states, subject to veto by Congress. Later, the territory would
be divided into two or more districts as Congress deemed expedient. Self-government began when a district, or "proto-state" marked
out in the ordinance, had five thousand inhabitants, at which time
the landowners—not the populace at large—were to hold an
assembly whose first duty would be to nominate ten men, from
whom in turn Congress would appoint five to act as a legislative
council. A district, or territory as it was to be called, would be
qualified for admission to the Union as a state when it had
acquired a population of sixty thousand. The governor, meanwhile, retained a power of veto over territorial legislation.

These provisions indicated Congress's desire to keep early
development of the Northwest Territory under a control that
would provide the strongest safeguards for the interests of
property. The temptations that the popular assemblies in some
states had recently proved unable to resist, particularly in connection with paper money, were much in the minds of the
promoters, who had an immense investment of property at stake;
moreover, both private speculative interests and many members
of Congress entertained doubts about the fitness for self-government of the anticipated populations of the West. Richard Henry
Lee wrote to Washington that it was necessary "for the security
of property among uninformed, and perhaps licentious people,
as the greater part of those who go there are, that a strong toned
government should exist, and the rights of property be clearly
defined." He also commented in another letter that "the form of
government . . . is much more tonic than our democratic forms
on the Atlantic are." Representative institutions were to come in
due course; in the long run there could be no practical alternative.

The provisions of the ordinance were intended to ensure that during their formative years those institutions would be molded by the fundamental influence of property.

This was not the only current view of the purpose of political institutions—or of the controls under which government ought to develop in the new West. During these years, the settlers of Kentucky were trying, through repeated conventions, to wrest self-determination from Virginia, to which their province belonged. The *Journal* of their first convention, held in January 1785, bore a resolution that effectively presented their views:

> Resolved That to grant any Person a larger quantity of Land that he designs Bona Fide to seat himself or his Family on, is a greevance, Because it is subversive of the fundamental Principles of free republican Government to allow any individual, or Company or Body of Men to possess such large tracts of Country in their own right as may at a future day give them an undue influence, and because it opens a door to speculation by which innumerable evils may ensue to the less opolent part of the Inhabitants and therefor ought not to be done in the future disposal of Lands in this District.

Kentucky farmers, however, had few doubts on another, and less democratic, point: they were determined to retain slavery. The zealous efforts of an early antislavery campaign led by David Rice were rejected. In this matter their views differed from those of the framers of the Northwest Ordinance. Under one of the most important provisions of the ordinance, Jefferson's earlier recommendation was adopted and slavery was forever excluded from the Northwest.

The terms of the Ordinance of 1787 were imprecise and permitted the retention of slaves already in the territory. French settlers, in fact, continued to hold slaves in Illinois as late as 1845, when they were finally freed, or excluded, by the state supreme court. Nothing in the climate or soil of the Ohio Valley determined that slaves would not be introduced to raise the crops and work the farms; slaves could be used in many ways and in various regions, and the opinions of valley farmers were by no means united on the merits of the slave restriction contained in the ordinance. The movement for statehood in Ohio was accompanied by a lobby for the introduction of slavery, and as late as 1820, a powerful proslavery group sought to hold a new constitutional convention on the subject in Illinois. But the Northwest Ordinance had determined the foundations for a free society as well as a nonslave economy, and the great Ohio Valley remained free soil. The ordinance was a vivid example of the importance of formative influences on the growth of social institutions, and a decisive instance in which laws made from above controlled the economy and forced a divided society to discover the benefits of freedom.

The achievement was the more striking because the Constitutional Convention at Philadelphia had just completed its labors and the old Continental Congress of the Articles of Confederation was nearing the end of its road. The ordinance was one of its last acts. Yet by this act it exerted an extraordinary power over the future development of America and predetermined much of the political geography and economic basis of the entire Northwest. This influence was ensured when provisions of the Ordinance of 1787 were enacted early in the history of the new Congress under the federal Constitution.

The forms and outlines of the new states, both in the Ohio Valley and in the Southwest, remained unclear until after the making of the new Constitution. During the interim, a state called Franklin experienced a brief life west of North Carolina. For several years, men of great power in the regions that would become Kentucky and Tennessee—Henderson, John Sevier, and William Blount—could dominate their peoples, negotiate with the governments east of the Alleghenies, and maintain ambiguity toward the United States while toying with the temptations offered by Spain, which owned the Louisiana country and controlled the Mississippi Delta. Only gradually, and with the emergence of a new national constitutional power and stronger government, did these regions discover that their interests and loyalties coalesced with those of the government of the United States.

That government continued to exercise a distant surveillance, sometimes protective, sometimes patronizing, and often irksome, over the development of the western territories. It was responsible, in accordance with the Constitution, for guaranteeing a republican form of government to every new state and for disposing of such public lands as remained with the states. The pace and price of settlement were regulated by Congress from 1796 to 1862 through a series of land laws that at different times reflected the divergent interests of squatters, farmers, speculators, and of government itself. Occasionally, and notably in 1841, pre-emption laws gave squatters—the genuine but unauthorized settlers—the advantage of legal recognition. But both government and speculators were essentially opposed to granting this recognition. Squatters could not be expected to provide public revenues to ease the overall burden of federal taxation. Income from land sales fell persistently below expectations, but the purpose could not be ignored and long continued to cause friction over public-land policy. Not until after the beginning of the Civil War did Congress at last, in 1862, pass the Homestead Act that recognized the principle that the land of the continent legitimately belonged to those who were willing to work it.

Government thus played an imposing part not only in military defense—or aggression—against Indians and Mexicans, and in formal supervision, but in the development of institutions. Yet the influence was so largely negative, so restrained, and so neutral in character that during much of the nineteenth century the United States was represented by a central authority far weaker and more indecisive than those of the other great nations whose unity was forged during the same era. The rise of competitive, thrusting, and unscrupulous business enterprises encouraged the myth that the Revolution itself had been made in the interests of private capitalism; and the Jeffersonian philosophy of limited government, whose original principles had nothing in common with such purposes, proved easily adaptable to the ideology of the myth. The truth was much more complicated, but experience proved that the American forms of government did very quickly lend themselves to the service of capitalist enterprise; and it was in keeping with eighteenth-century traditions that both legislatures and courts respected the interests of property as much as, and often more than, those of persons.

The process of developing the western lands might be called reverse socialism (except that socialism was invented more than half a century after the American Revolution). The great aim of European socialists was the nationalization of the economic resources upon which the people depended, and the most fundamental of these was land; in America, the whole of the land beyond the Atlantic states passed into the hands of Congress and thus began political life in a condition of nationalization. But from that point on, the Congress made a policy of dispersing it into private hands, a process over which it managed to retain an ever-diminishing control and from which it raised an uncertain and diminishing income. As the center of gravity of the American population and resources advanced steadily into the West, so the government came to reflect these new interests, and to present itself sometimes as an agent for, sometimes as a broker between, the great geopolitical sections whose growth was the dominant fact in the growth of the country as a whole. Not until the twentieth century was government able to resume and recapture the initiative in the making of public policy. One of its chief obstacles was that American thought about the relationship of government to economic policy had become permeated with a mixture of achieved facts and half-remembered dreams, which could be used, by business interests and political parties, as an almost independent political force.

The nation itself was consciously new, and in a geographical as well as a figurative sense it was bursting with vitality. For the hordes who pushed alone or with families, in wagons, on horseback, or on foot, across the passes into the Mississippi Valley, the scenes, the smells, the feel of the soil, the prospects of life were new. These adventurers, however, were bent on realizing old ambitions, and it is possible to exaggerate the extent to which the creation of new states, with new constitutions and laws, amounted to or represented new ways of thought. The laws of the states that arose to the west of Virginia and North Carolina, in the Ohio Valley, and soon afterward in the Southwest, were distinguished more by their adoption of well-tried eastern principles than by any spirit of innovation. The state constitutions usually discarded or eased the property qualifications for the suffrage and adopted more liberal election laws than those of the era of 1776. Yet this process was no longer novel. The institutions of the western states reflected the development under way in the more complex politics of the older states. It is in no way surprising that the recently arrived Westerners, whose entire investment was to be gained or lost by the work of the first few years, should have spent little time on the subtleties of political reform of institutions that were already broadly representative. The same frame of mind was manifested in the planning of cities, for in the Ohio Valley the urban frontier was a planned rather than a haphazard phenomenon. The master plan for such cities as Cincinnati was that of Philadelphia; the grid system repeated itself again and again in large cities and small towns, modified from place to place, but revealing a basic satisfaction with the notion that the American city had been invented and needed little improvement.

The opening of the West was itself one of the more revolutionary aspects of the Revolution. The movement into the Mississippi Valley was no doubt inevitable, but the sweeping away of a restrictive British government hastened an onrush of staggering proportions. The example of the rich lands of Kentucky affords striking statistics. In 1783, when the war ended, the population was some 12,000, which rose to more than 73,600 at the first national census only seven years later; by 1810 it was well above 400,000. It was not the general direction of this migration, which might be called a fulfillment of previous trends, but its dimension and speed that were revolutionary. As for the pioneers themselves, most of those who were able to afford the costs of the move were men, or the sons of men, with some moderate economic competence in their home states. The agricultural laborer could not equip himself for the trek west, unless he were unmarried and prepared simply to fend for himself; still less could he manage to rent or purchase a new farm. Most settlers, then, were in the process of advancing their fortunes on the basis of a well-laid economic foundation. They were not making a new society nor practicing a new social philosophy. Wherever the laws allowed, those who owned slaves took them along or aimed to acquire them as soon as their means permitted. The movement west also resulted in a further diffusion of economic resources. The land was rich, and the rising cities of the East, together with a growing world market, worked together to bring solid returns on agricultural produce. The opening of the West caused a revolutionary disturbance in American society and in the balance of American political and economic geography; it did not cause a revolution of philosophy or aims.

What innovation took place in the frontier settlements was primarily the result of circumstances that rubbed against familiar institutions and broadened the basis of political life without involving acute clashes of property or ambition. Western communities showed a marked spirit of cooperation in the provision of fundamental needs. Men gathered to help one another construct new cabins, came to one another's aid in emergencies, turned out in bodies for the harvest, and sometimes joined together to resist the tax collector or the central authorities; women met for one another's company, for spinning and weaving, and to soften the strain and toughness of the masculine life that surrounded them. The life both of the frontier and of the early years of the more settled farming areas was little relieved by entertainment, or by the qualities of individual taste. John Reynolds, a child of the new West, who became a judge and eventually a governor of Illinois, recalled that by the time he left home to go to college—itself an extraordinary adventure—he had never seen a carpet, a papered wall, or a Windsor chair. "I think," he once remarked, that "before I was twenty years old, I never lived in a shingled-roof house, or one that had glass windows in it. My father was about the most wealthy farmer in the neighbourhood." His first encounter with the more polished society of Knoxville, Tennessee's seat of government where Reynolds went to college, caused him an anguish of embarrassment. The reminiscences of Levi Beardsley, who was reared in the early years of the century in upstate New York—in Otsego County, which William Cooper, father of James Fenimore, had opened for settlement—reveal a comparable pattern of life: "plain, coarse and primitive." Tea was scarcely known until three or four years after the county had been settled, coffee came several years later. The men used to amuse themselves with contests in wrestling, jumping, and hopping. More exciting entertainment was promised by the public hanging of a schoolmaster who had whipped a girl to death. All the rites had been performed before a big, enthusiastic crowd, and the halter was around the murderer's neck when the sheriff produced a commutation of the death penalty to life imprisonment. The spectators were bitterly disappointed, and the reprieve cost the governor votes in the county.

The crudity of these raw settlements broke down the pretension of social refinement. "We had no aristocracy in those days," commented Beardsley in 1852, ". . . all were workers; and hard labor brought all on a level of equality." This characteristic observation, however, had a double edge. There is no lack of evidence for the toughening familiarity of life under conditions of early settlement; and there is likewise plenty to show that a blunt sense of personal equality carried over into later periods of much more firmly embedded social and institutional life. But Beardsley's comment shows that an aristocracy, or something like it, did, in fact, grow up later, that persons of wealth did come to consider themselves as persons of rank in a society built upon the very foundations that had once "brought all on a level of equality."

These social and economic differentiations were products of the same soil that had nourished the earlier sense of basic equality. When Asbury's ministry took him across the Allegheny Mountains in 1788, he observed: "This country will require much work to make it tolerable. The people are, many of them, of the boldest cast of adventurers, and with some the decencies of civilized society are scarcely regarded, two instances of which I myself witnessed." He does not say what they were, but he goes on to anticipate the rise of an aristocracy of land: "The great landholders who are industrious will soon show the effects of the aristocracy of wealth, by lording it over their poorer neighbours, and by securing to themselves all the offices of profit or honour: on the one hand savage warfare teaches them to be cruel; and on the other, the teaching of Antinomians poisons them with error in doctrine. . . ." These conditions came to be realized more fully in the South and Southwest than in the Ohio Valley, where the Ordinance of 1787 and the influence of New England migrants exerted some restraints on the growth of estates and the power of property. Yet the Northwest was not entirely free from such influences. In many cases, the owner of the tract was a speculator living in the East, who sold or rented farm lots without taking measures to improve them with communications or services. Cooper, who prospected a forty-thousand-acre tract in Otsego County in 1785 and sold all the lots within sixteen days, was keenly aware of the differences that existed between the absent landlord and the one who staked his own fortune on that of his settlers. The landlord, he stated emphatically, must be friendly, must live among his settlers, and must never reserve any of his land; a spirit of cooperation was essential to the success of the enterprise, and he recognized that this would be discouraged if the settlers felt that the best land was being reserved. Cooper gave generous credit, helped to establish maple sugar and potash works, and collected the people to make roads and bridges, attaching importance to the division of labor and the personal example of the landlord. Those landlords who failed, he said, reserved water mills and other advantages for themselves, and did not live on the land. The soundness of Cooper's principles was confirmed in the observations of a later traveler who noted the poverty of settlements where the landlord was a comfortable absentee.

Cooper's people, like those of other frontier regions, endured great hardships before beginning to reap their rewards—which in Otsego County occurred when "herring" were discovered in the local river. Hardship alone, however, was not enough to account for the differences in quality of life between different regions. The masculine games of the areas populated by migrants from New England, New York, and, to a lesser extent, Pennsylvania gave way to spectacles of savage ferocity as the traveler moved further south.

The violence of the South and particularly the southern frontier regions was an old phenomenon. Charles Woodmason, the itinerant Anglican minister, witnessed it in the 1760s, and connected the degenerate morals of the people with the banditry and crime that were practically without check. J. Hector St. John de Crèvecœur, in most respects an enthusiast for Americanization, admitted his horror of the violent and savage behavior along the frontier that he had seen before and during the War of Independence—and Crèvecœur was writing about the edges of the middle provinces. The crowds that collected to watch fights between quarreling individuals were not enthusiasts for fair play; nor was their lust for the infliction of pain and disfigurement restrained by the advance of civilization in other parts of the country.

Men cannot strictly be said to have fought like animals, because animals lack the weapons and the techniques with which the hearties of Kentucky, Virginia, the Carolinas, and occasionally of more sedate areas maimed each other in man-to-man fights. A traveler in Georgia reported fights in which noses were bitten off. The gouging of eyes was practiced by a technique that involved the skilled application of the thumbs; the blinded victim staggered away, hearing the uproarious shouts of the delighted crowd.

These pleasures were almost unknown in the North or Northwest, and it seems significant that they were not imitated by the Negroes, who were perhaps subjected to more severe provocations, and must have indulged in some strange ruminations on the civilization that kept them in chains. Southerners, and not only in frontier districts, also began to play the European game of dueling with pistols, which spread with extraordinary virulence in the South in the early nineteenth century when it was dying out in England and falling into disrepute on the European continent.

Violence manifested an absence of government, most marked in the backcountry but observable wherever migrants from the southern states lived for long stretches without courts, without clergy, and without any visible form of guidance or patronage from a native gentry. Crime records would show that the incidence of ordinary personal crimes, such as petit larceny, was low, that murder was rare, and that where bands engaged in horse stealing, armed robbery, or forging currency, popular feeling demanded countermeasures and severe punishments. The number of convictions for murder was small, and of executions still smaller, by comparison with later decades; but many savage assaults, mutilations, and even murders in the course of fights were simply not recorded as crimes.

The absence of institutions of the older, settled society also

had a relaxing effect on sexual morals. In many frontier sections
no clergyman could be found to perform a marriage, and women
shared with men the advantages of this practical liberation.
Woodmason was shocked to see that many lived together unmarried, while "many hund[reds] do live in Concubinage, swop-
ping their Wives as Cattel, and living in a State of Nature, more
irregularly and unchastely than the Indians." Men and women
swam naked in the rivers, even on Sundays. He could not break
the girls of their habit of dressing lightly in hot weather:

> They draw up their Shift as tight as possible to the Body,
> and pin it close, to shew the roundness of their Breasts, and
> slender Waists (for they are generally finely shaped) and
> draw their Petticoat close to their Hips, to shew the fineness
> of their Limbs—so that they might as well be Puri Natu-
> ralibus—Indeed Nakedness is not censurable or indecent
> here, and they do expose themselves often quite Naked, with-
> out Ceremony—Rubbing themselves and their Hair with
> Bears Oil, and tying it up behind in a Bunch like the Indians
> —being hardly one degree removed from them.

In the hottest weather, Woodmason preached in a gown and
wig before audiences who gathered incredulously to stare at these
strange garments if not to repeat the Lord's Prayer, which many
of them had never heard in their lives. "After the Service," he
reported one sultry day in 1768, "they went out to Revllg,
Drinking, Dancing and Whoring, and most of the Company
were drunk before I quitted the Spott." Similar conditions prevailed in other parts of the southern backcountry, and do not
seem to have changed twenty-five years later when M.L.E.
Moreau de Saint-Méry, an accurate observer in these matters,
reported that sexual promiscuity was rife and that girls would
submit themselves to the caresses of men whom they had seen
that day for the first time and would not see again. The frequency with which the county courts had to deal with cases of
bastardy and the disposal of illegitimate children, especially
those of servant girls, suggests that the advance of the more usual
public institutions did not altogether suppress these bucolic
felicities. A more socially recognized form of sexual play was
that of bundling. A girl could expect little attention on a lonely

farm unless she made herself known, and parents permitted their daughters to advertize by putting a light in the bedroom window; the girl was supposed to remain bodily within a bag or bundle tied to enclose her legs. Bundling was widely practiced in western Pennsylvania, New England and in the South, and was a subject of astonished comment by European travellers. The custom diminished in the early nineteenth century.

The advance of western cities seems to have placed some curb on these pastoral amusements. Earthy as the Westerners were, they eventually came to reveal a growing tolerance in religion. They were also capable of appreciating that the character of a man was not an attribute of inherited rank or unearned privileges. The inhabitants of these new cities began to reassemble some of the older trappings of civilization in their attempts to build an ordered and orderly society. But country life, including the life on well-established southern plantations, continued to be rudimentary so far as learning, religion, and conversation were concerned. The limited class of landed aristocracy, which in public life was an oligarchy controlling the county courts and the assembly, had little to offer the common people by way of style or taste; only in the most elementary sense was it an aristocracy of manners or even of education. Most of the really wealthy southern planters did send their sons to Europe for an education, causing a cleavage between them and the mass of planters, not to mention the poorer families who scratched their living from the soil, and whose children had no schools to attend. The bulk of southern children got what little education they had from their mothers and fathers, and the rest from their senses. Southern assemblies showed little interest in accepting the civic responsibilities that were commonly assumed in the North and that spread as a matter of course with northern migrants to the Northwest. The quality of school education in the North was often meager, but it was much more widely diffused than in the South, and it tended to supply some uniformity of information. Such education as did exist in the South accentuated social divisions.

In spite of these differences, which gave to the leaders of southern society an underlying advantage, a tradition of personal equality persisted. Men might feel themselves to be separated by great differences of fortune and power, but in personal relations they did not stand on ceremony. Whatever their rank—and the word "rank" continued to be used as people faltered for a term to describe these relationships—the men of the frontier, North and South, assumed a right of access to each other. Travelers were astonished at the informality of the courts, where people kept their hats on, smoked, chewed tobacco, talked and joked while the judge was on the bench. John Reynolds recalled that the sheriff of his court would open proceedings, sitting astride a bench, by declaring: "The court is now opened. John is on the bench."

Whatever new social formations might be taking shape in this emergent and turbulent culture, individuality and informality were to remain pervasive characteristics. Individuality, however, was generally mitigated by personal isolation; people in new settlements, and indeed in many established ones, may have been remote from the impact of government, but to survive they had to become a part of the closely knit life of a largely self-sufficient community. The absence of government was a sort of idyllic illusion, produced partly by the simplicity of political needs, partly by the vastness of the continent; it was necessarily impermanent. Yet the habits and ideas associated with slack and distant government entered into the character of America's rapidly growing society, making people impatient of restraints imposed by legislators, especially of those laws borrowed from other sections. Local communities would not indefinitely be capable of solving all of their own problems, and there were latent dangers in the belief that the relative remoteness of government was itself an indispensable attribute of the American form of republican liberty.

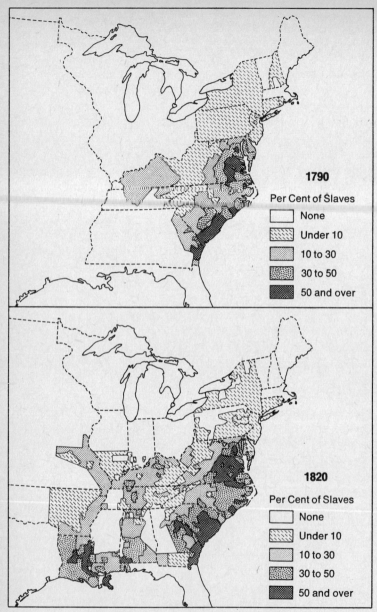

1790

Per Cent of Slaves

- None
- Under 10
- 10 to 30
- 30 to 50
- 50 and over

1820

Per Cent of Slaves

- None
- Under 10
- 10 to 30
- 30 to 50
- 50 and over

The Slave Population in 1790 and 1820

9

Deference, Social Responsibility, and Slavery

In 1788 George Washington told the French visitor Jacques Pierre Brissot de Warville, later, and briefly, a leader in the French government during the Revolution, of certain improvements that he had noticed in American society. Drunkenness was diminishing; court sessions were ceasing to be theaters of sport, drinking, and bloodshed; and class distinctions were beginning to disappear. Class distinctions had often seemed more artificial in America than in Europe. England could have shown Brissot a surprising number of examples of social familiarity, of tradesmen treading on the toes of duchesses at the pump rooms of Bath, of London society dominated by men who had nothing to commend them but their abilities. But America did not inherit the ducal covering that magnetized English society into a hierarchical formation. The deferential order that had struggled into existence in the American colonies was at best a weak imitation of the English original, and when it was placed under stress, it had much less natural tendency to recover its stability. Washington might take an indulgent view from the heights of Mount Vernon about social coalescence, but many of the traditional gentry, in almost all parts of the country, felt uneasily that the decline of deference, the overthrow of dignity and formality, would carry political repercussions.

As long ago as the 1760s, a lady of high social standing, living in the upper Hudson Valley, was half shocked and half amused at the way the local farmers, with names like "Obadiah and Zephaniah, from Hampshire or Connecticut, came in [and] sat down without invitation; and lighted their pipe without ceremony; then talked of buying land; and finally, began a discourse on politics which would have done honour to Praise God Barebones." * Yet in spite of these incidents, which became more common as the times became more turbulent, the mass of Americans acquiesced without protest in constitutional arrangements that evinced the idea of a social and propertied order, and they continued in most instances to accept leadership rather than to give it. The Marquis de Chastellux heard directly of a striking example of this attitude from Benjamin Harrison in Virginia: "Mr. Harrison told me that when he [and other delegates] left to attend the first Congress in Philadelphia [actually in 1776, not the first] certain inhabitants considerable in number but not well informed, sought them out and said to them: 'You claim that our rights and privileges are threatened; we don't see how, but nevertheless, we believe you because you tell us so. We are about to take a dangerous step; but we trust you and we will live up to your fullest expectations of us.' " Chastellux was also impressed by the deference and consideration shown by the lower classes to the small number of old Virginia families, and believed that even if the government became democratic its spirit would remain aristocratic.

In New England, which had long had a reputation for "leveling" principles, and where perhaps the upper gentry had to work hardest to maintain its standing, John Adams noted that the townsmen usually elected and re-elected the men with traditionally respected names. This, however, was not invariably true. The smaller towns of the interior, which lived relatively uncomplicated social and economic lives, also spread the burden of civic duties so widely that no group or class could be said to dominate. Even so, in the Connecticut River Valley, where the great farmers were known as "the River Gods," a steeper social order translated itself into politics. On the seaboard, the larger and wealthier communities, notably Boston, had developed a correspondingly complex hierarchy, which was reflected not only in the politics of the towns but, most significantly, in the committee structure of the assembly, where their influence was dominant after about 1760. In Connecticut Jedidiah Morse was correct in his observation that

* Praise-God Barebones was a member of the English Parliament after the execution of Charles I; this Parliament came to be known as the "Barebones Parliament," though he spelled his name Barbon.

the clergy formed a sort of aristocracy; and almost everywhere the lawyers, not loved but needed by a litigious populace, became a political fraternity of conservative interests.

The most deliberate and self-conscious attempt to form a hereditary society in America was made soon after the end of the war. Certain officers of the army formed the Society of the Cincinnati, an exclusive nationwide officers' club in which the rights of membership would be handed down in the male line. The society caused the most violent offense in a country of avowed republican principles, especially to the men who had served in the ranks. "The Order of the Cincinnati is to be the institution of an hereditary patriciate" declared one pamphleteer, speaking for many. "The idea of a man born magistrate, legislator, or judge, is absurd and unnatural. So is that of a man born as protector of his country"—a reference to Cromwell, but possibly an aside aimed at Washington, who had agreed to become president of the order. The storm of protest caused the national organization to drop the hereditary principle, although some state groups retained it. The society did continue to meet and to form in some places a nucleus for Federalist politics when the nation began to divide on party lines.

Both the founding of the Cincinnati and the opposition it aroused were signs of a growing awareness that social distinctions might be of continuing significance even for a republican people. They had no king and only the fragments of an aristocracy; when the social fabric was threatened with imminent dissolution, deference to a well-born, propertied, and educated gentry seemed the only remaining protection for order, property, and religion. Yet the relentless crumbling of the outward marks of deference was perceptible. Many travelers in the generation after American independence was established made similar reports on the informality of American social relations. For example, it was customary on farms and plantations for the whole family, including the laborers, to sit at the same table with the owner; only the Negroes were excluded. This often-repeated observation gives an important clue to the structure of social organization: "family" meant the estate—all those dependent on the productivity and order of the farm, plantation, or business as an economic and social unit. Thus, when George Mason advocated conferring the suffrage on heads of families, he was thinking of the state as made up of family units, each under the paternal authority of one man. North of Virginia and Maryland, and especially in New England, both farms and family units tended (except in the Hudson River Valley) to be narrower, the structure more distinctly "nuclear"; but the social informality was even more pronounced.

The upheavals caused by westward migrations, however, challenged the durability of this social structure. It did not collapse, for many families migrated together. But social changes took place more rapidly in the new territories where land could be had more easily by the sons as they grew up. People lost track of their former neighbors, family ties loosened, and friendships were formed and broken with a frequency that disturbed the traditional view that one took one's identity from a fixed point in place, society, and church. The new life offered much in compensation for these losses, but the suspicion endured that the compensations were mainly material while the losses were psychological or spiritual. These losses make it easier to appreciate the intensity of the appeal of religious revivals, which offered to uprooted and morally isolated individuals the rewards both of a communal experience and of a belief that God was still there.

The greatest gain attending the decline of class distinctions was what men called "liberty." Every man asserted that in America, as nowhere else, he was free. Foreign visitors found this assertion tiresome, amusing, or legitimate, according to their own tastes. Some found Americans insufferably rude, others accepted them in good part; but no European visitor could fail to notice the blunt, sometimes crude informality that seemed everywhere to appear as the personal expression of this intense conviction of personal liberty. Informal encounters constantly took place on the road, and at night at the inn; during these breaks in the journey, the driver of the stagecoach often took his meal at the same table as the passengers. He was doing his job, they were doing theirs. Whether visitors approved of or were discountenanced by this breaking of ranks, the frequency with which they commented on the custom was marked evidence of how different

America was from Europe, which was also evidence, to some extent, of how different America was from its past.

Perhaps no institution was more American in these years than the American inn, which brought together the community of the road with a compulsive intimacy. Attitudes toward diet, hygiene, and privacy followed no consistent principles. Social customs afforded little or no opportunity for personal choice; whoever wished to travel was obliged to accept the fare and the accommodations provided. La Rochefoucauld-Liancourt seems to have been more amused than dismayed by conditions that repelled many Europeans when he observed:

> There is a contrast of cleanliness with its opposite which to a stranger is very remarkable. The people of the country are as astonished that one should object to sleeping two or three in the same bed and in dirty sheets, or to drink from the same dirty glass after half a score of others, as to see one neglect to wash one's face and hands in the morning. Whiskey diluted with water is the ordinary country drink. There is no settler, however poor, whose family does not take coffee or chocolate for breakfast, and always a little salt meat; at dinner, salt meat, or salt fish, and eggs; at supper again salt meat and coffee. This is also the common regimen of the taverns.

A great deal of traveling was also done on packet boats along the coast and across the bays and broad river mouths. On the packet from Philadelphia to Charleston, La Rochefoucauld-Liancourt, usually a sympathetic observer, was genuinely shocked by one example of informality carried to extremes. One of his fellow passengers was no less a person than Oliver Ellsworth, recently appointed chief justice of the Supreme Court; yet he was treated with no more regard than was shown the Negro headwaiter. Even if allowance is made for a certain vagueness about the exact role of the Supreme Court in its early years, this lack of deference can perhaps best be interpreted as a refusal to be impressed by high judicial office.

It would be a little too facile to read into this informality a total democratization of the underlying basis of social relationships, for in politics the ordinary voter retained a traditional preference for known and respected names. The great men might have to put up more of a fight at election time, but their records of authority and their social connections gave them an inestimable advantage. In western Massachusetts, the reverberations of Shays's Rebellion failed to shake the standing of Theodore Sedgwick, one of the stiffest of social and political conservatives. His constituents continued to elect him as their representative because their habitual deference accepted his habitual authority. Even in the new states, especially in Tennessee, the large landowners kept control of the important developments in the advancing economy. The merchant houses, and above all the banks, were the property and enterprise of powerful men like William Blount, whose speculations had opened the region. In the backcountry the common people, for the time being at least, traded the substance of economic and political control for the shadow of social informality.

Farmers, especially those in the newest and westernmost clearings, often found it difficult to understand how heavily the success of their operations depended on the cities, the growing populations of which increasingly provided them with their market. The merchants who distributed their produce, the banks to whom they applied for credit, the warehouses and the expanding insurance companies were all city institutions. It was also in the cities, particularly in the large seaports, that political and social leaders began to assume certain social responsibilities that fell outside the realm of formal city government.

The marks of government, of planning, of civic responsibility were present, but were not easy to see at first glance. Philadelphia presented a typical example of basic town planning beneath uncontrolled growth. Although its physical pattern conformed to a predetermined grid plan, the traveler who approached by water would be struck by the chaos of private buildings, each erected solely in the interest of the owner of the business, and with complete disregard for civil design or convenience. The same feature was characteristic of Baltimore's burgeoning waterfront. Yet the economic life of the cities, especially those engaged in exports, was far more closely regulated than these visual observations would suggest. In New York, for example, the Common Council, made up of one alderman and one assistant from each of nine wards, sitting with the mayor and recorder, exercised extensive and detailed powers; the council authorized ferries and received the fees and profits; laid out streets and water-courses; established markets where and when they chose; and appointed assessors to measure and mark the merchandise that passed through the port and markets. Only freemen of the corporation were allowed to sell at the markets (but not on Sundays), and the council retained the power to confer this freedom.

The headlong growth and crowding of the cities, without any improvement in hygiene, made them extremely unhealthy. New York and Philadelphia had sunken "necessaries" (a euphemism for lavatories, or toilets) that collected the filth and gave off a pernicious odor, thought to be a dangerous gas. Evil-smelling gases and vapors were held to be a cause of infectious disease —a view shared by Jefferson, who believed that the swamps around the Potomac endangered the health of the new federal city when he was president. The persistent stench in the streets of New York was sharply commented on by Moreau de Saint-Méry in the 1790s. He had also to report that the streets were infested with almost every description of animals, cows and pigs in particular; the sidewalks and corridors were washed on Saturdays, but no one removed the dead dogs, cats, and rats.

The introduction of piped water made a great difference in the domestic life and public health of the cities. A pure water supply was introduced into New York City by a chartered company in 1799; before that time, most families had used the pump in Queen Street. In Philadelphia a contracting company was able by about 1806 to supply three million gallons a day, if the need arose. The water was drafted from the Schuylkill River by a forty horsepower steam engine; every householder could have a hydrant in his own home, if necessary in the attic. "This water is a great luxury," John Melish commented, "and is of incalculable advantage to the health and comfort of the community." He hoped other cities would copy the example of Philadelphia. There remained a need for filtering, for which Melish offered the plans of a Scottish mechanic. He thought Philadelphia the best-regulated city on the continent, much better than New York. The streets were broad and well paved and supplied with common sewers to carry away the filth; the gutters ran with water and the streets were cleaned every morning. One health precaution adopted during the summers was that of putting damp cloths over the food standing out in the markets. But people could do little to free themselves, their houses, their provisions, or their animals from the plagues of flies, insects, and bedbugs; they were virtually a part of the climate.

Despite all their problems, particularly of health, the cities were visibly expanding and becoming more livable through these years. The beauty of Broadway, the fine quality of many of the houses and public buildings in New York and Philadelphia, and the improvements in such amenities as garbage removal, street lighting, and fire protection impressed observers from year to year. Melish, who had been in Philadelphia as recently as 1806, was struck by its increased size and splendor in 1810. A Society of Artists had been formed with the aim of advancing the fine arts, establishing schools, and holding exhibitions to improve the public taste and remove existing prejudices, and, as he said, "to give a character to the fine arts in the United States." Its first exhibition opened in May 1811, with some five hundred objects on show, of which more than half were the work of American artists.

American culture, as the early strivings only too clearly proved, was still profoundly dependent on Britain. The fine arts were considered to be merely ornamental and in no sense as expressions of the depths and passions of the human spirit. The best American painters, such as John Singleton Copley, Gilbert Stuart, and Benjamin West, had made the better part of their careers in England, where their talents brought them a wealth, fame, and social distinction that would have been out of all question in America. John Adams entertained an earnest suspicion that painting was an effete and aristocratic art, tending to flatter the rich and corrupt the morals of the Republic, a view which happily did not prevent him from having his portrait painted. Jefferson explained the absence of a native literature in America in 1813 by saying:

> We have no distinct class of literati in our country. Every man is engaged in some industrious pursuit, and science is

but a secondary occupation, always subordinate to the main business of life. Few therefore of those who are qualified, have leisure to write.

Justice Joseph Story made a similar point in 1819, writing that "so great is the call for talents of all sorts in the active pursuits of professional and other business in America, that few of our ablest men have leisure to devote exclusively to literature, or the fine arts. . . ." It was true, as Timothy Dwight, president of Yale, explained:

> Books of almost every kind, on almost every subject, are already written to our hands. . . . As we speak the same language with the people of Great Britain . . . our commerce with it brings to us, regularly[,] not a small part of the books with which it is deluged. In every art, science, and path of literature, we obtain those, which to a great extent supply our wants . . . and this is the reason, powerfully operative, why comparatively few books are written.   •

Yet these explanations are incomplete. In Britain, the writing of books was not reserved to persons who had nothing else to do. Such active politicians as Edmund Burke and Richard Brinsley Sheridan found time to write essays on philosophy and plays; other men devoted all their professional energies to writing and made a living by it. The intellectual efforts of Americans, however, bore the same kind of practical purposes that they applied to their economic activities. One of the finest products of American thought in this period was *The Federalist,* a series of essays composed with the direct object of aiding in the adoption of the new federal Constitution. The considerable scholarship of Madison and John Adams was turned repeatedly to political aims. The ethos created by the constant American preoccupation with self-advancement and productive activity was one that discouraged literary or artistic enterprise. In addition to having to compete with the extraordinary riches of European culture, the aspiring American writer or artist was confronted with a discouraging social skepticism about the value of his work. Some overcame it and made names for themselves, and their numbers and quality climbed sharply with the advance of a more self-sufficient American culture in the nineteenth century. But the struggle was long and the lack of appreciation must have dissuaded many of genuine talent. These difficulties were compounded for American writers and artists by the related problem of critical evaluation; in the absence of a native literature, American society could not nurture an independent school of criticism.

The most fearful problem confronting city populations was caused by epidemic disease. The notorious plague of yellow fever in Philadelphia in 1793 was in fact only one of a series of epidemics that periodically struck panic into the people, and drove tens of thousands to seek refuge in the country. Francis Asbury with typical courage visited Philadelphia during the sickness of 1793 but found that he needed a pass for the ferry out; and on his way to Baltimore he encountered a guard stationed one hundred miles from that city to check possible carriers of infection from Philadelphia. Twenty thousand people left the city again when the disease struck in 1797, and the authorities required red flags to be shown on afflicted houses; Moreau de Saint-Méry, who stayed there, could count twenty from his own house. A few years later, after twenty-six thousand people had fled from New York because of the "malignant fever," city authorities imposed quarantine and health inspections on ships entering the harbor from the tropics or from the Mississippi River.

These plagues gave an overwhelming urgency to the problems of medicine, research, and hospitals. Dr. Benjamin Rush, the celebrated physician and former Philadelphia politician, worked furiously to relieve suffering and to instruct his students in the cure of disease. But Rush, prompted by this urgency, worked out a general theory that not only attributed all fevers to the same generic cause but maintained that by draining four-fifths of the blood from the body the sickness could be carried away. The lives of his patients would also have been carried away had Rush possessed accurate information about the actual quantity of blood in the body. Others were growing skeptical of the benefits of bleeding. A nasty controversy about these doctrines, carried into pamphlet war, inflamed the feelings of a public already susceptible to panic from the dread of disease. Civic hygiene and sanitation in the South were even worse, but the gentry of Charleston quieted its fears by escaping from the city to the North every sum-mer. The poor and the Negroes were left behind in large numbers, and the whites seem to have believed that Negroes were not sub-ject to yellow fever.

The need for medical education made it a matter of public con-cern. The medical school in Philadelphia was one of the oldest of civic educational institutions, having been founded before the Revolution. Harvard inaugurated its medical department in 1781, when a Massachusetts Medical Society was also established.

As for general education, Northern communities regarded it as a public responsibility, and the increase of cities carried with it a marked increase in schools. Philadelphia made school attend-ance compulsory at the age of seven. Much schooling and tuition remained in private hands, but both private and public schools gave a standardized education that ensured that the normally reared American child, especially in the cities and in most parts of the northern and middle states, could read and write; in the South, where the upper classes still preferred to educate their children in Europe, little attention was paid to the needs of poor children. Throughout the nation, small colleges increased greatly in numbers, if not perhaps in the quality of their instruction; by the end of the eighteenth century, twenty-five colleges were oper-ating on the continent, as compared with only nine at the time of the Revolution. Enrollments, even so, were small. Only some four hundred students graduated each year from all these institutions.

Medicine, hygiene, the dangers of fire, and the rigors of the climate, as well as the ambitions of the citizens, all stimulated an emerging consciousness on the part of professional and business men of the importance of pooling their abilities. Many of the dangers and discomforts, both public and private, that were endemic to their age began to yield to the combined forces of their intelligence, determination, and capital. Soon after the end of the war, the merchants and professional men of Philadelphia, for example, began to see themselves as civic and social benefactors —men interested in relieving social distress and improving the quality of life. Benjamin Franklin, by his sponsorship of im-proved organization for fire companies and by his interest in the founding of insurance associations, had been one of the first private citizens to exercise a broad public responsibility. Before the War of Independence Franklin had been a founder of the famous American Philosophical Society, whose full title included a dedication to "useful knowledge"; he was also instrumental in establishing the college that later became the University of Pennsylvania. Such civic improvements were typical of their time, for the growth of the city had earlier called similar institutions into being in Europe. Fortunately for Philadelphia, Franklin's extraordinary combination of energy and shrewd, practical insight, together with the strong Quaker tradition of service, placed it ahead of other cities in America.

Societies for all sorts of promotion and improvement, some disinterested and some frankly commercial, became extremely popular. The professional bodies formally incorporated themselves through acts of the legislature. The Philadelphia Medical Society (which imposed a fine of twenty-five to fifty cents on members who failed to remove their hats during meetings) listed 210 members in its Act of Incorporation in 1800; the Society of Victuallers, instituted in 1793 and incorporated five years later, was a charitable association for the relief of members of that trade; the printers and booksellers of Philadelphia formed a company in 1793. The city's leading men also recognized their obligation to make concerted attempts to improve the condition of the sick, the needy, and the slaves. Some 350 members associated together in 1786 as the Philadelphia Dispensary for the Medical Relief of the Poor, and engaged six physicians and surgeons to attend for an hour on three days a week. Money was raised by individual subscriptions, each subscriber having the right to place patients in the care of the dispensary. These patients were presumably the servants or dependents of the wealthier families, or those whose needs were brought to their attention; if this cannot be called socialized medicine, it can at least be seen as a responsible attempt at a kind of paternalistic medical system. A Pennsylvania Society for Promoting the Abolition of Slavery had been formed as early as 1774, and was enlarged in 1787. Various other civic groups were formed for such diverse purposes as resuscitating people believed to have drowned, promoting agriculture, promoting manufactures, and advancing political inquiries.

One of the more interesting foundations was the Society of the Sons of Saint George, whose aim was to offer advice and assistance to Englishmen in distress. The president of this society was the Honorable Richard Penn and the vice president was Robert Morris, who was to appear within a few years as an American in distress. The introduction to the rules and constitution of the society throw some light on the growth of social divisions in Philadelphia. The group disclaimed the purpose of "keeping alive any invidious national distinctions, which ought to be particularly avoided between the different nations which compose the United States of America, where all the freemen (from wheresoever they originally migrated) are brethren, friends and countrymen. . . ." After these disavowals, which reveal an acute consciousness of the possibility of conflicts between national or ethnic groups, the society explained that its object was to offer relief to Englishmen, some of whom might not have fallen to "the lowest ebb of distress" had they had some knowledge of where to look for relief. Only natives or the sons of natives of England (and possibly Wales, but presumably not Scotland or Ireland) were eligible for membership.

The libraries and museums that brought books and art into public notice and circulation were also the work of private groups, men and women of substance who recognized the duties attached to their social positions. Philadelphia led in these innovations, but was not alone; by the turn of the century New York probably had an equal number of organizations based on associated and benevolent private enterprise and including a free school, a hospital, a German Society (for the relief of distressed Germans), and that most celebrated of foundations for the relief of the poor and indigent, the Society of Tammany.

City life also afforded opportunities for the evolution of new distinctions of social class. Moreau de Saint-Méry, who for three days had been president of the Paris City government, found to his indignation in 1795 that he could not get a ticket for the ball to celebrate Washington's birthday because his occupation in Philadelphia was that of shopkeeper. Some ten years later, the Englishman John Lambert gave an account of the class structure of New York City. The first class was composed, he said, of the constituted authorities, divines, lawyers, physicians, principal merchants, and people of property; the second, of small merchants, retail dealers, clerks, subordinate officers of government, and members of the professions; the rest were "the inferior orders of people." Members of the highest class lived in a style little below that of similar Europeans; servants were usually Negroes or mulattoes, some free, others slave, but there were many white servants of both sexes. "They who expected to see a *pure republican equality* existing in America will find themselves greatly deceived," Lambert added. He also noted that the several families of rich and respectable Jews in New York enjoyed equal rights and suffered under no invidious distinctions.

City families resembled those of the country in a permissiveness toward children and young people that contrasted sharply with the practice of older countries, and possibly with earlier American customs. Young women in the cities, like their country cousins, were plainly in a hurry to get married, and few were left single by the age of twenty or twenty-one. The easy promiscuities of the back country were also reproduced in the cities, only in much more conventional styles; prostitution was extremely common, and in New York brothels were familiarly known as "holy ground." In Philadelphia girls of respected families would prostitute themselves of their own will, but would preserve their dignity by refusing to recognize in any normal social meeting a man they had entertained. Moreau de Saint-Méry thought them cold and noted that they made a point of pretending not to enjoy their sexual encounters, a matter in which he appears to have spoken from experience.

Practically all the travelers, whose observations bring out the distinctiveness of American life, were men, and therefore inclined to comment on women. Most of them thought American girls were attractive, though bad teeth were observed by some, if denied by others. The girls of South Carolina impressed visitors by their vivacity, poise, and willingness to take full part in conversation. It was often observed, however, that these bright charms were extremely liable to deterioration. American women, according to Moreau de Saint-Méry, were faded at twenty-three, old at thirty-five, and decrepit at forty-five; he also remarked that many were subject to nervous illnesses. The taking of sexual risks, which ran as a countercurrent to the public protestations of modesty, resulted in the usual accidents, especially as the known means of contraception were primitive. However, immigrants from the French colonies in the 1790s brought with them the syringe; it at first caused horror among the Americans, but was soon taken over by the Quakers. When apothecaries began to put syringes on sale, they were accepted. Cases of bastardy were frequent, and abortion was rare.

Poor sanitation, humid summers, and waves of disease left their imprint on the city populations. Half the children of Philadelphia died before reaching two years of age, according to Morse, writing shortly before the introduction of systematic water supplies. Yet widespread drinking of hard liquors killed more people than any disease. Drinking was heavy in the South, too, and in the backcountry; whiskey was sometimes used in lieu of currency in western Pennsylvania, where Alexander Hamilton's attempt to impose an excise on it provoked a minor insurrection in 1794. People suffering from excessive heat quite often unintentionally killed themselves by drinking huge quantities of ice-cold water, despite official warnings of the danger. This wild improvidence had other projections in the aggressive haste, coupled with absence of forethought, that caused innumerable, easily avoidable accidents on the highways, on ferryboats, and on bridges, which were extraordinarily poorly maintained in all parts of the country.

The modicum of privacy afforded by city life did not conceal the fact that the individual, increasingly released from the unifying influence of the family, was bound to others by a market relationship. American commentators themselves observed that the dominating spirit of the country was overwhelmingly commercial, and no doubt in response to this corrosive tendency the upper classes of the cities began to unite for public purposes. While political institutions were also increasingly responsive to public needs and popular feeling, the morals of public life were chaotic, and a formal inspection of laws and regulations would not have been enough to disclose the violent social disparities that persisted. It was still to be observed in the early years of the nineteenth century that though people boasted of freedom, indentured servants from Europe, unloaded by sea captains who got £10 a body, were traded off at markets with no more consideration than was shown to Negro slaves. And the slaves themselves remained as the most glaring contradiction to the principles that Americans publicly professed.

Slavery had long been concentrated in the southern colonies. The Continental Congress in 1774 dramatized this regional division, and by the time of the Constitutional Convention of 1787, the separation of interests between slaveholding and nonslaveholding states was already beginning to threaten the future harmony of the Union; by comparison, the conflict between small and large states, as Madison pointed out, was relatively trivial. The decline of slavery in the northern and middle states was gradual, except in Massachusetts, where the state supreme court ruled in 1783 that the declaration of rights in the state constitution, which affirmed that all men were equal, constituted a declaratory abolition of slavery. At that time, other New England states did not concur. But one by one, in a piecemeal and stumbling way, they, together with New York and Pennsylvania, eventually adopted statutes for emancipation. No part of the economy of these states was heavily dependent on slavery, and the comparatively small numbers of blacks did not present the whites with that sense of inescapable social crisis upon which discussion of emancipation repeatedly foundered further south. The farmers and workers of northern and middle states had themselves strong reasons for opposing slavery, which had a degrading effect on the dignity as well as the economic value of free labor. New England consciences moreover were disturbed by its moral implications. It is probably no coincidence that the Reverend Manasseh Cutler, the promoter and lobbyist of the Ohio Company, should have had a hand in the ordinance that excluded slavery from the Northwest.

By the early nineteenth century, less than 10 per cent of the entire slave population lay north and east of the Chesapeake Bay. The distribution of slavery was uneven in the southern and southwestern states, concentrated as it was in the Tidewater and Piedmont and thinning out with the more recent and less prosperous settlements in the valleys and across the mountains. Southern planters had become almost completely reliant on slave labor for their export produce of rice, which grew in the damp lowlands of Georgia and South Carolina, indigo, tobacco, and cotton. The dangers and difficulties arising from the presence of a large subject population were patent enough to have induced the Virginia legislature to pass an act banning further slave importations as early as 1772—a measure that met with the veto of the crown. Before the end of the eighteenth century, the problem already seemed insurmountable in parts of the South, where, for example, the Charleston district population was 85 per cent slave.

Slavery provoked one of the most acrimonious and divisive conflicts in the Constitutional Convention. While delegates from states with such diverse interests as Massachusetts, New York, and Virginia, and including such men as Gouverneur Morris and George Mason, tried to seize the opportunity to forbid the African slave trade, those from South Carolina and Georgia fought back against any attack on slavery and made clear that their states' interest in it was fixed and permanent. It is quite wrong to suppose that these Southerners saw themselves as painfully acquiescing in a temporary and unavoidable evil; they regarded slavery as the mainstay of their economy and the best device for the growth of the Southwest.

Slavery in fact served an economy that extended far beyond the South. Southern export crops made an indispensable contribution to the balance of trade of the United States as a whole. In 1793, Eli Whitney, a Northerner then living in Georgia, made one of the many technological advances that served the progress of the Industrial Revolution when he invented a simple cotton gin, a mechanical contrivance for separating cotton fiber from the seed. This invention made it possible to cultivate short staple cotton on a large scale and so to advance cotton—the growing of which was everywhere accompanied by slave labor—as an inland crop in the Southwest. The mounting city populations both in Europe and in North America formed a ready market for cheap cotton manufactures, and Whitney's invention, with subsequent refinements, multiplied many times the quantities of cotton that could be supplied to that market. Within a few years, planters who had raised a variety of crops—some of whom were seeking a substitute for indigo, which foreign competition was supplanting—were beginning to concentrate their resources on cotton. Before long, cotton became the southern staple. The invention of the cotton gin did not, as is often said, reverse the decline of slavery as an institution, for slavery was not declining; it would have remained and would have been carried into the Southwest no matter what crops had been raised there. What the gin did was to ensure that the agriculture of the South would be devoted to cotton, until the time, in 1858, when James Hammond of South Carolina, swept away by delusions of economic grandeur, could cry out: "You dare not make war on cotton—no power on earth dares make war upon it. Cotton is king!"

The work of slaves might have been performed by a wage-earning, free labor force. But few people confronted this possibility partly for economic reasons but largely because even those who deplored slavery, and told one another it would one day disappear, were unable to separate it from the problem of race. The antipathy Americans of European descent felt toward Negroes was ancient, and had been manifested in early colonial statutes against marriage or sexual relations between the races. But it was also complex and ambiguous. White men were attracted to African women, whose accessibility and defenselessness they took advantage of wherever conditions permitted. This attraction may have been stimulated in part by the excitement of crossing a social taboo, but it can hardly be described as the product of a natural antipathy. What the whites did in order to free themselves, both socially and psychologically, from the consequences of this interracial licentiousness, was to renounce its consequences by classifying all offspring of such liaisons as belonging to the Negro rather than to the white race.

In the slaveholding states this practice had economic advantages. Slavery was held to descend from the mother, so that children of mixed liaisons were slaves; it also resolved, by a shortcut that required neither intelligence nor humanity, the problem of how to describe and relate oneself to persons of mixed race. On some plantations it was possible to find slave men and slave women who were almost indistinguishable in color and feature from the families who owned them. Some white men allowed considerable freedom and favor to their black or mulatto mistresses, but similar liberties were seldom extended to the men. The black man was instinctively felt to be a threat, a fact that goes far to explain the interest some southern states developed in checking the importation of slaves from Africa even before the trade was banned by Congress in 1808. The threat was easy to believe in, for the Negroes had every reason to rebel against the power of the white. Moreover, the great rising of the slaves of the French island of Santo Domingo, which persisted through most of the 1790s and resulted in the establishment of a Negro republic, hurled tens of thousands of white French refugees onto the American continent with horrific stories of war and terror.

The Americans received the French refugees with warmth and hospitality, often voting large sums for their relief. These events appeared to confirm the instinctive fears of American whites and undoubtedly helped to stiffen their latent hostility toward Negroes and convinced them that their feelings were reciprocated. Yet for the most part the behavior of American Negroes gave surprisingly little ground for such anxieties.

The economic advantages of slavery for the southern whites were offset by its destructive moral and social effects. The traveler had only to pass below the Chesapeake or the Ohio River to notice at once the striking differences between the slave and the free societies, differences that had generated in a system that was federal in its Constitution but disunited and divergent in its social norms. Wherever slavery prevailed the women were indolent and the children vicious little tyrants who had discovered they were free to bully and torment not only the Negro children but even the adult slaves. Beneath the high living of the great planters, beneath the righteous tone of the leaders and the thinkers who had helped make the Constitution, who now administered the state governments and saw the moral gravity of their dilemma, there grew among the people of the southern states a curious, unlovely mixture of arrogant, self-centered pride and slovenliness in their ways of life.

Slavery was both a symptom and a further cause of a peculiar, sweet degeneracy of which examples abounded in town and country. Charleston society lived well, but its civic arrangements were far below those of other American cities. Apart from its Library

Society, it had little culture, its fire precautions were absurd (whole blocks of houses were destroyed by preventable fires), and no leadership stepped forth to accept the responsibilities that were then being assumed in the cities of the North. Outside the cities, roads and bridges were in worse condition than elsewhere, and the pace of life was laggard. Families were often warm, charming, and kind, but public services and standards were never a matter of social or civil pride, only of individual preference. The sense of justice was another victim; southern laws forbade Negroes to give evidence where whites were parties to a case; all these laws were severe, and those of South Carolina were savage.

In his *Notes on the State of Virginia,* composed in 1782, Jefferson indulged in severe, though private, strictures on the moral and social consequences of slavery for the white race. (He did not intend these notes for publication and asked that his remarks on slavery be suppressed.)

> There must [he said] doubtless be an unhappy influence on the manners of our people produced by the existence of slavery among us. The whole commerce between master and slave is a perpetual exercise of the most boisterous passions, the most unremitting despotism on the one part, and degrading submissions on the other. Our children see this, and learn to imitate it; for man is an imitative animal. This quality is the germ of all education in him. . . . The parent storms, the child looks on, catches the lineaments of wrath, puts on the same airs in the circle of smaller slaves, gives a loose to the worst of passions, and thus nursed, educated, and daily exercised in tyranny, cannot but be stamped by it with odious peculiarities. The man must be a prodigy who can retain his manners and morals undepraved in such circumstances. . . .

Similar effects were observed again and again by later commentators. A population surrounded by slaves not only lost much of its incentive to work, it came to despise the work slaves performed. These evils, however, were not confined to the South. The "colored" people, whether nearly black or nearly white, whether slave or free, were everywhere treated with a disdain and hostility that either eroded or bitterly hurt that quality of self-valuation on which personal vigor and enterprise must to some extent depend. In Philadelphia the religious Negro leadership attempted to remedy this malaise by establishing the Church of Saint Thomas, the first black church in the city; the move was prompted by the incivility of the white Episcopalians, who objected to sharing the floor of their own church with Negroes and tried to banish them to the gallery. The Negroes indignantly refused, withdrew, and formed their existing benevolent society into a church. The church did not fully succeed in reaching out into the black community as had been hoped; but its first minister, the Reverend Absalom Jones, a former slave who had bought his own and his wife's freedom, proved himself a man of exceptional energy and devotion. At an earlier date, the African Benevolent Society had rejected a suggestion from the Africans in Newport that they should all aim at repatriation to Africa. The Philadelphia group—whose members continually referred to themselves as "blacks"—retorted that they were citizens of America and would remain in America; they believed in peace and liberation as promised in the biblical prophecies.

Self-respect was difficult to maintain amidst a white majority that set the standards of political and social life and refused to look on Negroes as equals. Yet the cost of this treatment was also experienced, if imperfectly comprehended, by white society. When Moreau de Saint-Méry was once crossing the Chesapeake, a violent and terrifying storm tore at the ship and drove the passengers to seek shelter below; two Negro women with small children tried to get into the room, but were contemptuously thrown out by the whites, and had to endure the storm on deck. Moreau de Saint-Méry also noted a little Negro in New York with an iron chain around his neck, fastened there because he had taken leave of his master. Melish expressed his horror at being shown the spot where two Negroes had been burnt alive in Georgia, a practice which, it was reassuringly explained to him, was necessary to complete the effectiveness of death as a deterrent; otherwise, the Negroes might see it as a salvation, because they believed that their souls would return to Africa.

The ill treatment of Negroes ranged from hostile indifference to the extremities that the Protestant conscience has usually attributed to the Spanish Inquisition. This conscience was assuaged by the fact that in some places Negro slaves were better fed, clothed, and housed than the peasantry in parts of Great Britain, a point noticed by Melish in Kentucky. But the vague feeling that something ought to be done to abolish slavery was accompanied by resignation: the problem was too big, too complex, too intractable. Movements for abolition gathered no momentum south of the Chesapeake and the Ohio Valley.

This growing sectional division had a symbolic as well as a political importance. The truth was that southern society was conscious of its malaise. A healthy tradition of open debate, the avowed opinions of its foremost statesmen, and the dehumanizing effects of constantly treating people as inhuman all formed a lesion in the mind. It would not yet, at this period, be true to say that southern leadership depended on slavery as a means of maintaining its own ascendancy over the mass of the white population; the time would come, however, when Jefferson Davis would assert that "slavery elevates every white man at the South"—not to an appreciable altitude, perhaps, although the concept of white unity had its significance for white leadership. But the conflicts that people could all too clearly perceive were conflicts within themselves. They do not entirely explain all the increasing burdens of the South, but they added, like hot irons, to those burdens. Side by side with exuberant good humor, excessive hard drinking, and cordial hospitality lived a sudden violence often out of all rational proportion to whatever dispute was at issue. Equally ominous as time went on was the narrowing of the area on which rational minds could focus their inquiries.

In the diversity of America lay its riches but also its pitfalls. Unities could be discerned, but their historical foundations were frail; politically, American unity was itself an artifact, achieved and expressed through the exigencies of political action. As the compelling needs of war began to recede, as new sectors of the continent began to open, New England, New York, and parts of the South, which took some pride in their historical self-sufficiency, again began to concentrate the loyalties of their citizens. Only through a continental political system could the Americans reaffirm their national identity, and save the Republic.

10

The Politics of Unity and Dissension: The Constitution, Policy, and Parties

In the crisis of revolution and war, the American colonies achieved the unity that was the requisite condition of success. Soldiers, political leaders, and many who aspired to benefit from independence had come through it all with a toughened sense of the needs, and possibilities, of making a new nation. Little of the internal dissension, in state legislatures or in Congress, arose from opposition to the main aims of the war; the men who made the new governments ran into many difficulties over internal policy but carried most of the people with them in the War for American Independence.

Their eventual military success was not enough to make safe the political structure that had cost such labor. Everything depended on the political and geographical level at which the possibilities for unity were perceived. It was one thing for the leadership of individual states to establish control within their own communities; it was a much more complex task to knit these communities together. Neither the history nor the political geography of the colonies had given much ground for assuming that they could by nature form a permanent political whole. What was needed, from the continental point of view, was a system of interlocking state leaderships that would eventually prompt the establishment of a stronger central constitution than the Articles of Confederation.

Outstanding among the men who could think in terms of the possibility of national unity were those who had steered the Congress through the war and had kept the disparate colonies together through many dark hours filled with the equal possibility of defeat. It was they, and their associates holding positions of leadership and influence in most of the states, who succeeded in remaking the constitutional structure. By this achievement, they held the gains of the Revolution and made the United States into a nation that could later conquer the continent and become a world power. This outcome was by no means inevitable during the precarious years that followed the end of the war; and it was an outcome to which, in any case, many Americans spread through wide reaches of the country had little desire to subscribe. To them, the Union would become too politically centralized, too subject to the domination of wealthy and aristocratic leadership, too like the Europe from which they had escaped.

Proponents of state sovereignty believed that the loose system of confederation was closer to the people because the electors could exert a direct influence over their state assemblies; in this way the existing system was more "democratic"—a word that was beginning to be used in a favorable sense. Conversely, they feared that the people of the states would never be able to control a central legislature, endowed with powers of taxation and law making throughout the land. This profound distrust of power, especially when exercised by a central authority remote from its subjects, was a characteristic of American thought, inculcated largely from British experience; it appeared both in Antifederalist opposition to the Constitution and later in the Jeffersonian Republican party. But state government was not by definition the same thing as popular or democratic government, and the states differed widely in the extent and directness of popular participation, and also, as experience showed, in its results. Considered as a continental constitution, moreover, the Articles of Confederation were hardly democratic, for the will of the majority could be blocked by a single state.

This power to veto, which contemporary critics likened to the *liberum veto* of the Polish Diet, where any nobleman could prevent the assembly from acting, almost brought the operations of the Congress to a standstill. The concluding phases of the war were accompanied by a decline in its effectiveness; under the rule by which individual members could not succeed themselves after a three-year turn, many of the ablest men retired and put their energies back into their own states. Congress's inability to raise adequate supplies in response to its requisitions on the states reduced its power, kept the army in arrears of pay, and weakened the confidence of the public. The creditors holding various continental promissory notes began to realize that they could look for payment only from a new and stronger central government, or, alternatively, from their own states.

Robert Morris, the superintendent of finance and known as "the Financier," made the first moves to check this fiscal disintegration before the end of the war. As noted previously, he was influential, at the close of 1781, in founding the Bank of North America, which gave the Congress a well-funded and flexible financial instrument that was supported by many persons of economic substance. He also promoted two plans for strengthening the Congress's powers of taxation. Under the first, the Impost of 1781, Congress could levy a 5 per cent duty on all imports into the country, the proceeds to be used to discharge both principal and interest on war debts. The need was urgent and twelve states quickly agreed to the impost. Rhode Island, however, refused to ratify it and the entire plan collapsed.

Morris himself had reservations about the second measure, which was brought forward in 1783 by the new group of nationalists in Congress. This impost would have been limited to an operation of twenty-five years—a provision Hamilton opposed because he did not believe the debt could be paid off in that time, and, moreover, he wanted the Congress to have a permanent power of taxation. The tax revenues would be allocated to discharge the debt within the states where they were raised and would be collected by officers appointed to those states. All the states had to agree to the proposals, but once they concurred the compact was to be irrevocable.

The finance plan was meant to meet some of the sensitivities over sovereignty of the more intransigent states. It was not, however, a piece of mere contingency legislation designed for a particular crisis; Morris and Hamilton in particular were determined to create a continuing public interest in the congressional debt, which would resemble the national debt in European countries and have the same effect of binding the wealthiest and most influential men to the central government. "A national debt if it is not excessive," wrote Hamilton, "will be to us a national blessing; it will be a powerfull cement of our union." The emergency had grown more serious since the defeat of Morris's first plan. The inability of the Congress to pay its burden of debts and the consequent slump in creditors' confidence in its future performance had already, as early as 1782, led some of them to urge their state governments to assume the responsibility. In November 1782 Maryland provided that her own citizens who held certificates of the national debt could exchange them for state securities, which meant that the Maryland government was taking the place of Congress as the bearer of the public debt. The New Jersey legislature followed with similar action in 1783. But much the most significant measures were those of Pennsylvania, if only because of the high proportion of the congressional debt held there.

Morris and his allies fought the Pennsylvania proposal with all their powers, and for the best of reasons. Nothing could pose a greater menace to the future of the Confederation than the assumption by state governments of the congressional debt. If Congress were forced to relinquish the obligation of paying its own creditors, then it would quickly lose all claim to govern. The struggle in Pennsylvania cut across existing party lines because so many creditors, normally allies of Morris and the state's Republican party, wanted their money more than they wanted anything else, and they doubted the future of the Congress. The end of the war and the disappearance of the British enemy had the usual slackening effect on the feeling of political or fiscal urgency in all the states, which could, without difficulty, be regarded as allied states rather than as a new nation. (When people abbreviated the name of the United States, they always wrote "The u. States," "united" being an adjective rather than a substantive part of the name.) After a prolonged struggle, the Pennsylvania legislature in 1785 enacted assumption of the state's share of the congressional debt. Meanwhile, the sheer recalcitrance of other states in meeting their legitimate financial obligations to the Congress began to arouse antagonisms and threats of coercion. New Jersey legislators were bluntly warned by a member of a congressional delegation that "a new confederation will put you in your proper place."

The nationalists had reason for alarm. The United States had signed a treaty of peace with Great Britain that involved the obligation of American citizens to pay debts owed before the war, an obligation that the Congress had no power to enforce. Meanwhile, British troops remained in possession of certain northern border forts, some of them inside American territory. Simultaneously, individual states began setting up customs barriers against each other and entering into boundary controversies that, in the absence of some superior, central force, could one day mean war. Nor could westward expansion continue unabated without involving risks of conflict. The nationalists knew that if the Confederation failed, new formations could be expected: the New England states would probably form a unit; the central Atlantic states might form another, with or without Virginia; and the southern states would most likely join in a confederation with designs on the Southwest. So manifest was the likelihood of the disintegration of the United States that the authors of *The Federalist Papers,* urging the adoption of the federal Constitution, devoted much of the first six numbers to the dangers and consequences of a split into at least three new confederations.

Congressional leaders were keenly aware of these problems. But not all their policies were satisfactory to all the major interests, and when in 1786 John Jay, secretary for foreign affairs, reached an agreement with the Spanish minister, Don Diego de Gardoqui, he aroused the resentment of the South. The South had been displeased because its ambitions in the Southwest had been thwarted by Spain's control of the Mississippi and Congress's inability to do anything about it. Spain was in a powerful position to bid for the support of settlers seeking land and protection; it was probably the Roman Catholic religious requirements imposed by Spanish authorities, however, rather than any basic loyalty to the United States, that brought many of these restless migrants back into the American fold. The Jay-Gardoqui agreement, initialed but never ratified, would have secured commercial privileges of great value in direct trade with Spain, thus gratifying powerful northeastern and seaboard-merchant interests; the price, however, was to be the closure of the mouth of the Mississippi for twenty or thirty years. Nothing could have more forcibly demonstrated the strength of merchant influence in Congress and on its officers. The treaty, nevertheless, had to be scrapped in the face of protests from southern delegations. This episode resulted directly in the constitutional clause by which treaties, negotiated by the executive, must be ratified by two-thirds of the voting members of the Senate.

The nationalists were not confined to any one section. On the contrary, the years of war had brought forward many men of ability whose vision, seasoned by experience, took in the prospects of a greater and stronger union, able to defend American interests on a level with the powers of Europe. The principal business houses had developed a ramifying network of interstate connections that had everything to lose by the breakup of the Confederation, unless it was replaced by a stronger government, and much to gain from a unified economic policy. Moreover, men who had served at a continental level—men such as Washington, John Adams, Hamilton, Madison, Jefferson, and Jay—had acquired a continental point of view, although some of them, notably Jefferson, retained a close sense of affinity with their home states. The former army officers, the businessmen, and the political leaders who had come to believe in a union transcending the states in many cases had practical interests that a union would serve; and these interests were not without a share in imparting a continental breadth to their vision.

Washington had a direct and personal concern for the improvement of navigation in the upper reaches of the Potomac, where he owned land whose value would rise with development. A meeting in 1786 between delegations from Virginia and Maryland was promoted by this interest; its sequel was a wider meeting held that same September at Annapolis of delegations from five states. By the time of the Annapolis Convention, the nationalists had begun to formulate more advanced plans looking toward a new and more centralized government. Despite years of negotiation, remonstration, and warnings, the Congress had been unable to persuade all the states to ratify the finance plan of 1783. Rhode Island, surprisingly, agreed to cooperate, under terms of its own, only to find that New York had imposed new conditions. Shays's Rebellion, in the late summer of 1786, suddenly shook the leisured pace of these motions and played into the hands of the nationalist leadership.

Hamilton drafted a report representing the views of the five delegations that had come to Annapolis, and Congress was called on to summon the next spring in Philadelphia a general convention of all states to amend the Articles. State legislatures began to answer this call even before the Congress formally endorsed it in February 1787. Even as the state representatives began to trickle into the city, which had seen the first meetings of the Continental Congress, the strong delegation from Virginia, with support from the forceful nationalists who lived in Philadelphia and would represent their state, had already drawn up a plan that reached far beyond the Articles of Confederation to a new Union.

In making the Constitution and in securing its ratification, members of the nationalist group, who soon won a marked propaganda advantage by styling themselves "Federalists"—the name that properly belonged to supporters of the Confederation —had immense obstacles to overcome. But they had certain advantages, of which perhaps the most important in the convention itself was the initiative. The plan presented by the Virginia delegation proposed nothing less than a revolutionary reordering of the entire system of government; and because no other delegation had come prepared, the Virginia Plan became the agenda for discussion. Before the debates began, Washington was elected president; the next step was to agree that the convention should meet in secret, about which there was little difficulty; members fully appreciated that public discussions would expose them to incessant pressures, and would limit both their frankness and flexibility in debate. The next and bigger problem was to supersede the instructions by which the delegations were empowered to act. The convention had been called to strengthen the Articles, and some delegates protested that they had no authority to proceed with a new plan of government. The majority agreed, however, that a constitutional convention could propose whatever it liked, for no plan could bind the states without their own agreement.

The Virginia Plan proposed to replace the old Congress, which was in effect a meeting of state delegations, with a new, bicameral national legislature. This transformation represented the change from a confederation of sovereign states to a national, if federated, union. Both houses were to be based on numerical representation; members of the lower house would be elected directly by the people and those of the upper house by the lower house itself. The executive, a single office, was to be elected by a joint session of the upper and lower houses. The plan also called for a separate federal judiciary, the absence of which had badly impaired the legal authority of the old Congress. The new Congress would exercise powers over all those matters of legislation that fell within the compass of parliamentary competence in older countries—and thereby become an effective legislature. No longer would the states stand between their citizens and the central government: the Congress would tax individuals, its laws would bind all equally, the states would be restrained from embarking on private economic policies, and recalcitrant states could be coerced by a federal force.

The scope of these proposals took many members by surprise. As the convention took them up, examining them one by one in a practical way, their novelty wore off, however, and when, two weeks later, William Paterson of New Jersey asked for an adjournment, the Virginia Plan had gained strategically important ground. Its opponents made counterproposals when Paterson presented the New Jersey Plan, but they were never completely able to recover from the Virginian initiative. The New Jersey Plan, essentially, was merely a revision of the Articles. States, not individuals, would be represented in Congress, and all would have an equal vote; the plan did, however, envisage a separate executive and a general judiciary, and it did give the Congress more extensive economic powers than the old one possessed.

The small states were terrified of the consequences of the Virginia Plan. Yet at times they appeared willing to abandon the existing state boundaries and go into a completely redrawn union. The spokesmen from the big states, notably Virginia, Pennsylvania, and Massachusetts, in their turn found it hard to understand what their neighbors were afraid of, and sometimes became openly exasperated by the violence of their opposition. A generation later, after the acquisition of the huge Louisiana Territory had altered the balance of American geography, it became difficult to see the exigencies of these discussions; the worries of little eastern states like New Jersey and Maryland about the structure of the Union had lost their significance. Moreover, it was more pertinent to argue at the time, as Madison and Rufus King did, that the really divisive element was slavery, not small-state representation.

In one sense, the small-state men did represent, though perhaps not intentionally, an underlying opposition that was to appear when the convention had done its work and the new Constitution was brought before the several state conventions that were summoned to ratify it. They feared an overpowering government. What they thought they discerned was a new power that would take the place of the British system they had fought to overthrow—an American central government in the hands of an aristocracy of wealth, with power to remake both the political policy of and the social structure within the states themselves. They lost the fight to defeat the Virginia Plan outright, but they forced a crisis over the crucial issue of representation. And here they secured their point. "The great difficulty," said Madison, "lies in the affair of representation," a view he had held since before the convention began.

It was central to the Virginia Plan that both houses were to be based on numbers. The nationalists believed that the theoretical principles of majority rule should be converted into a practical system of government, because that system was the only one that could safeguard the fundamental interests they considered to be at stake. Madison was firm on the central point of majority rule, but he was unduly optimistic about the states' response to it. "The change in the principle of representation," he wrote to Edmund Randolph, "will be relished by a majority of the States, and those too of the most influence. The Northern States will be reconciled to it by the actual superiority of their populousness: the Southern by their *expected* superiority in this point." The big states embodied both the major concentrations of wealth and the larger masses of population; some, not yet large, could expect to

gain by their own increase. The nationalists, experienced politicians of standing in their states, appointed by their state legislatures to act as delegates in this convention, had grasped the
principle involved in the question of representation. It was, in
effect, a re-enactment on a continental scale of the issues that
had been resolved earlier in Massachusetts. There might be occasional setbacks due to adverse majorities, but, in general, so
long as the leaders of the large states retained their political
grip, they had nothing much to fear from a proportional or
numerical basis of representation. The alternative was not the
representation of a variety of valid interests, but merely the ob-
structive power of individual states, which as political entities
could be expected in the course of time to become less and less
relevant to the practical problems of the Union.

The specific need to build the interests of property into the
system was catered for in the Senate, which was expected to be
a sort of nonhereditary counterpart of the House of Lords. But
this element of the system got lost in the counterattack of the
small states. The convention had reached a deadlock when a new
committee, from which the nationalists were deliberately excluded,
proposed the compromise that had earlier been put forward by
Connecticut. The Senate ceased to represent property and became
the chamber in which the states, by equal and individual representation, would preserve their sovereignty; the House, in accordance with the Virginia Plan, would be based on proportional
representation. It was a blow to the nationalists, but their only
alternative to rejecting it was the breakup of the convention,
which their opponents appeared ready to bring about.

The remainder of a hot Philadelphia summer was spent in
hammering out agreements over the character and election of the
executive, over taxation, western lands, and the slave trade. The
executive caused a new and dangerous controversy. The nationalists wanted to keep it out of the hands of the states, but many
delegates feared that election by the national legislature would
make him unduly dependent on that branch. The electoral-college
system, adopted late in the proceedings, had advantages built into
its clumsiness. The majority principle was retained by giving each
state an electoral-college membership equal to its full congres-

sional representation, and the colleges themselves, meeting in
each state and elected either by the people or by the legislature,
according to local choice, could be expected to include the same
leadership that would normally find its way into state legislatures.
The electoral college, then, would conform to and safeguard
prevailing American Whig views on the responsibilities of republican government. The grosser matter of popular will would
be strained out through the fine mesh of leadership. "To entrust
the selection of leaders to the people," explained Mason, "would
be like giving the choice of colours to a blind man." He meant
not that the people were naturally blind but that they could not
be trusted to judge between men whom they literally did not
know. It was a protection against heated impulse, against sudden
popular upsurges, and against demagogues, of whom responsible
American leaders were much afraid.

Several delegates openly feared the results of giving too much
power to the people. "We have suffered from an excess of
democracy," said both Randolph of Virginia and Elbridge Gerry
of Massachusetts in similar words at the beginning of the convention. But this hostility diminished as the debates went on, and
the proposal of certain conservatives, notably Gouverneur Morris,
to place a property qualification on the suffrage was wisely rejected; qualifications for voting were to be left in each state on the
same footing as for the lower house in that state. Through a compromise engineered by Morris, who spoke for those eastern conservatives who feared the prospective power of a poor but
numerous population in the West, federal taxation was to be
apportioned according to numbers, a move intended to balance
their voting power. Slavery, however, was a more critical issue,
and the attempts to ban the African slave trade caused renewed
dissension.

The debates in the convention were accompanied by private
meetings at which some of these issues were sorted into deals
between the interested parties. One of these arrangements brought
about Connecticut's support for continuation of the slave trade
in exchange for support over certain land interests that Connecticut claimed from Pennsylvania. As a result of further, and
more public, bargaining, the Congress was to be deprived of

power to place a duty on agricultural exports except by a two-thirds vote (which the South could prevent) and the African slave trade was to be allowed to continue for twenty years, after which Congress might impose a ban. The convention adopted from a Maryland precedent (where it had a somewhat different application) a plan under which three-fifths of the slaves would be counted as persons for the purpose of allocating representatives; in exchange, direct taxation would also be determined on the same basis as representation.

These arrangements gave the South a great prospective advantage. Southern exports were already catching up with those of the North, and the southern population was expected by many to race ahead; with a permanent over-representation grafted into the Constitution, southern states could look forward to a prolonged period of dominance in American government. When that period came to an end, eleven southern states decided to secede from the Union.

The new Constitution gave the United States a much stronger central government, and the new bicameral Congress, despite its intricate electoral basis, was given those substantive powers on matters of general and economic policy that the individual states had exercised under the Confederation. It was to take the masterful initiative of a great chief justice, John Marshall, to establish the ascendancy of Congress over interstate commerce; much, as yet, remained in an outline that could be filled in with different colors according to taste and purpose. The new system did possess, however, what men called "energy." The new executive, whom Jefferson aptly styled an "elective monarch," had extensive influence over home policy as well as foreign; heads of government departments possessed room for initiatives; Congress gained extensive and flexible powers of legislation; its members henceforth could make policy for the whole Union. The convention wisely recognized that a Constitution, in order to be permanent, must be adaptable, and they included provisions for amendment. This step, which seems obvious in retrospect, was farsighted in its time, when people tended to think of constitutions as fixed; in most contemporary thought, when a constitution changed, it degenerated, and needed to be restored to its original form.

The idea that change might be improvement, and that changing conditions might require corresponding alterations in the frame of government, was an example of that combination of confidence and practical wisdom that helped to stabilize English and American political institutions.

In the belief that a separation of powers was mandatory as a safeguard of liberty, the main departments of government—legislative, executive, and judicial—were sorted by the convention into separate branches. In practical politics, of course, the powers exercised by these branches could never be kept entirely separate; it was not really so much the power as the functions of government that were entrusted to the three coordinate branches. The convention never intended the separation to be so rigid as to paralyze the government. Congress was made supreme over legislation, but the president would always need to have a line of communications to Congress, and was given the right to make recommendations on policy. If the Supreme Court were ever to exercise the power to review congressional statutes, an authority that was not specifically defined but seemed to many people to be implied by the express terms of the Constitution, then by doing so it would be entering into the process of legislation. The superiority of the federal Constitution over the states was manifested by the power of the Court to pass judgment on state laws that appeared to contravene the Constitution itself; the Constitution was defined as "the supreme law of the land."

The new Congress received important powers that had been denied its predecessor. The state governments lost the authority to issue currency—though, in fact, they later recovered a large part of it by chartering banks that could issue their own notes. The Congress, however, assumed the power "to lay and collect Taxes, Duties, Imposts, and Excises, to pay the Debts and provide for the common Defense and general Welfare of the United States" —all of which taxes and duties were to be uniform. The Congress would also regulate commerce with foreign nations and among the states. In sum, its power would extend "to make all Laws which shall be necessary and proper for carrying into Execution the foregoing Powers"—a stipulation capable of indefinite interpretation, as the constitutional history of the United States was to prove. These were extensive as well as new powers, and everything would depend on how, and by whom, they were used.

The new Constitution was intended to be a practical instrument. It was not concerned with rights, but with functions and interests, with obtaining a judicious balance between the effectiveness of political power exercised by a central system and the distribution of that power that would forever prevent the system from becoming tyrannical. The omission of a bill of rights, nonetheless, was a tactical error. The many opponents of stronger government believed that their suspicions were justified when they found themselves faced with a document giving the central authorities far greater powers than before and remaining silent about those very rights they had fought the War of Independence to protect. In some state conventions, including Virginia's and New York's, the Federalists virtually had to agree to amend the Constitution by adopting a bill of rights in order to secure even a small majority for ratification. The first ten amendments, passed and ratified in the first new Congress of 1791, embodied these affirmations of the rights of American citizens; the rights that the British had secured partly by statute and partly through judicial decisions were thus taken over by Americans as fundamental law. These rights were susceptible to a variety of interpretations that could come into collision with governmental policies. It is significant that most of the questions on which the Supreme Court subsequently invalidated congressional legislation arose in connection with amendments rather than with the original substance of the Constitution.

Anti-Federalist opposition, however, took its roots in sectors of American life—the small farmers, for example, and debtors—that had been only feebly represented at the Philadelphia convention. All the main provisions of the Constitution—on presidential and congressional powers; on the authority to make foreign policy, to collect taxes, and to provide for defense—represented the country's main sources and centers of economic strength. Many of the delegates were slave owners and landowners, others were merchants, a few had professional qualifications, and many overlapped these distinctions; the bargaining over freedom of exports, over settlement of land disputes, the slave trade, and the bases for representation and taxation was fought out between men who represented intrinsically reconcilable interests. America would benefit from a division of labor among its geographical regions of economic expertise, from its potentialities for investment, and from the exploitation of resources. The Constitution would permit those interests to develop without interfering radically with the private arrangements of different sections of the nation. The word "slavery" was carefully excluded, but the institution was implicitly recognized by a clause that permitted the passage of laws requiring the return of fugitives, including not only criminals but "persons held to service."

The convention had thus reached a compromise on the issue that was, in principle, the most irreconcilable of all. The alternative would have been to let South Carolina and Georgia set themselves up as independent nations—which is exactly what they tried to do, in conjunction with nine other slave states, a lifetime later.

The compromise on slavery turned a critical corner, after which most of the great property owners in America were able to give their support to the Constitution. The numerous holders of congressional securities, widespread in Pennsylvania and the Northeast, could now expect the funding of the debt and a real repayment of the interest on their certificates; these certificates, most of which had changed hands many times since their original issue, naturally began to appreciate in value, and many members of the convention itself took the trouble to acquire them. But many people in different walks of life distrusted these trends and feared the consequences. Small farmers, small businessmen, often in debt to their more influential neighbors, believed that the mighty had deliberately wrought a Constitution that would open avenues for a moneyed aristocracy.

The numerous statements of this feeling give to much of the Anti-Federalist argument a decided note of what would later be called class consciousness. Anti-federalism was most rampant among debtors and those who had supported action for the relief of debtors by state governments. They frequently expressed resentment against the pretensions of their social superiors, and discerned, with some accuracy, that a government under the control of the masters of commerce, law, and money would be made to work for those interests. Amos Singletary, a small farmer, movingly stated the case in the Massachusetts ratifying convention:

> These lawyers, and men of learning, and moneyed men, that talk so finely, and gloss over matters so smoothly, to make us poor illiterate people swallow down the pill, expect to get into Congress themselves; they expect to be the managers of this Constitution, and get all the power and all the money into their own hands, and then they will swallow up all us little folks like the great *Leviathan*, Mr. President; yes, just as the whale swallowed up *Jonah*.

Much of the force of this line of opposition derived from the tacit admission that the Federalists were able to make the better of the argument. By definition, or by inference, they were the lawyers, the traditional political managers (whose hard-money policies had caused so much resentment in Massachusetts), the leading merchants, and the aspiring aristocrats of the new system. In New York the lawyer and merchant Melancton Smith observed in a powerful speech:

> The great consider themselves above the common people, entitled to more respect, do not associate with them; they fancy themselves to have a right of preëminence in everything. In short, they possess the same feelings, and are under the influence of the same motives, as an hereditary nobility.

Anti-federalism was extremely potent in New York, where the controlling party of Governor Clinton saw little advantage in handing over its prerogatives to a central government. The only center of Federalist sentiment was in New York City, and it was partly by veiled threats that the city might secede from the state that Hamilton succeeded in squeezing a small Federalist majority out of a reluctant ratifying convention.

A correlation existed between the anti-federalism of Clinton and his supporters and that of Mason and some of the more powerful opponents of ratification in Virginia. Mason, who had been a member of the Virginia delegation, opposed the Constitution on the ground that it would help create a new aristocracy and would undermine the agrarian and republican basis of the nation. Mason, an owner of a good deal of land and a large number of slaves, shared the smaller farmer's fear of a financial aristocracy subverting the agrarian foundations of American virtue. But men like Clinton and Mason expected to dominate their own patrimonies as they had done in previous years. They not only felt no need of the assistance of a stronger federal government, they suspected that such a government would encroach on local powers.

The "class" aspect of anti-federalism was thus authentic and yet deceptive. Some of the Anti-Federalist speeches would have been equally valid as criticisms of great landowners who, as it happened, were also Anti-Federalists. What they shared was a rhetoric rather than a social identity, though their case was different in different places. They were able to enlist the support of numerous small farmers living on subsistence farms, on or beyond the margins of the market network that radiated from the cities— one reason being that the cities themselves were bastions of federalism. Charleston elected an unopposed Federalist delegation to South Carolina's ratifying convention, while in Philadelphia the Federalists appear to have outnumbered their opponents by eight to one. Federalists gained more than 90 per cent of the votes cast in New York City. Boston was held under supple but firm Federalist leadership. The preponderance of Federalist power lay in the unity of interests among the merchants, the artisans, the laborers, and the traders, all of whose efforts were economically interdependent. The old politics of deference, ably sustained by Federalist control of the press and considerable pressure on individual leaders, gave the city vote to the Constitution. This Federalist strength in the cities was abetted by large numbers of farmers whose economic welfare hinged on the city and the international markets. Thomas Tredwell, a member of the ratifying convention in New York, observed with much accuracy that the contest over ratification was "between navigating and non-navigating individuals."

Social deference had a silent but important relation to political indifference. Considering the excitement of recent years, the voting throughout the country for the ratifying conventions was surprisingly light. Cities could always be counted on to respond to political calls; but it has been estimated that as few as 4 or 5 per cent of the adult male population, which means perhaps 8 or 10 per cent of the qualified voters, turned out at the polls through the country as a whole. In some instances, rural voters had so little knowledge of the issues that they confided their votes to men of opposite views, on the old principle that it was the job of the leaders to take the responsibility for such decisions. The success of the Federalists was thus in large measure a manifestation of their superior position in American life. Their influence over the press made an appreciable difference in the flow of information about the meaning of the Constitution. The closely reasoned, if sometimes tendentious, arguments that Madison, Hamilton, and Jay published in the New York papers, under the joint name of "Publius," were circulated while the ratifying debates proceeded. The authority of the men of more learning, of former military rank, of greater social standing carried many people who would undoubtedly have voted the other way if the same leadership had urged them to do so. It was of no small weight that George Washington was known to favor the Constitution.

The debates had divided the country, and in some conventions, notably in New York and Virginia, the outcome was perilously close. Nevertheless, the launching of the new Constitution was celebrated by great processions, banquets, and revelry by practically all classes in Boston, New York, and Philadelphia. However severe the fight may have been, the new administration, with Washington as the first president of the United States, began its regime with a general disposition for its success.

ᴇ⚔11⚔ᴐ

Personifications of the American Future: Hamilton and Jefferson

The goodwill toward Washington's administration was powerfully reinforced throughout the country by the feeling of gratitude and respect for Washington himself. His character did not, perhaps, arouse emotions of warmth, but no man in the nation—possibly in the world—was more implicitly trusted for his record of physical courage and patriotic integrity. Washington had been head of the army, but he had never before been head of a government. He soon discovered—as he no doubt suspected, for he had no particular relish for his new role—that it was impossible to govern without making decisions, and that it was impossible to make decisions without making enemies. Before the end of his second administration, the Father of His Country had become the victim of political vituperation.

The divisions in the new nation had been of the sort that could be readily reawakened when events took a turn that reminded people of their former doubts and antagonisms. A strong line of continuity ran through the economic interests and political philosophy of the former supporters of the Articles of Confederation, the opponents of the Constitution, and, later, the adherents of the Jeffersonian-Republican party. There were also discontinuities, and important ones. It was one thing to believe, as many men of differing views did, that authority ought usually to be exercised by persons of acknowledged social distinction and wealth. But it was quite another matter to use the powers of initiation that the new Constitution conferred on the administration in order to carry out a specific program of political and economic policy. When Alexander Hamilton, the new secretary of the treasury, began to use his powers for these purposes, he set in motion the processes that were to induce a formed opposition, both in Congress and throughout the states.

In his five years of office, Hamilton left an indelible imprint on American history. Charming, quick-witted, and intensely persuasive, Hamilton was as assured of his own abilities as he was of his aims. He wanted to secure to the central administration the first loyalties and interests of the foremost families in the nation; he had no doubts of the need for energetic leadership, for long-range planning, and for the inauguration of steps that would ultimately convert the United States into a mighty economic power. He had no fears of an aristocracy; his reservations about the Constitution were entirely due to the weaknesses that encumbered the national administration. He wanted a stronger presidency and a stronger army—of which, in case of necessity, he was perfectly willing to take command.

Hamilton fully appreciated that America was an agricultural nation, and his measures could do little more than give an initial push to the possibilities of industrial development. In a private capacity, he took a close interest in the attempt to found a great manufacturing center at Paterson, New Jersey; the enterprise proved to be premature and resulted in a total failure, though within a few years a small group of Massachusetts businessmen, led by Francis Lowell, did succeed in founding a textile industry on similar principles of concentration of labor and plant and the large-scale production of a simple product. Hamilton, who admired England and had grasped the importance of the role of the Bank of England in the development of the British economy, was the principal figure in persuading Congress to charter the first Bank of the United States. This institution, partly under public control and partly a private corporation, provided a flexible financial instrument for the Treasury Department, a source of financial stability, and an attraction for investors. He went on in a series of cogent state papers to argue the importance of promoting commerce and manufactures, and he successfully implemented, over varying degrees of opposition, his critically important plans by which the new government assumed, first, the debts of the old Continental Congress (which it was morally obliged to do) and, secondly, those of the individual states.

This latter assumption policy caused sharp controversy. It was seen as a move to do just what Hamilton intended: to attract to the federal government the loyalties, along with the economic interests, of the public creditors of the states. Only gradually, however, did men who distrusted these measures move toward a counterpolicy of united opposition. Jefferson, who as secretary of state had been consulted on the founding of the bank, opposed it on the ground that it was unconstitutional for the Congress to charter a private corporation, and, indeed, the clauses of the Constitution could be searched in vain for such a grant of power. Hamilton overcame these doubts, which Washington shared, by advancing the constitutional doctrine of implied powers; and in this matter, as in the assumption of state debts, Hamilton's extraordinary persuasive abilities carried the argument with Washington and with the members of Congress.

Hamilton's policies, as their implications became more and more apparent, divided first Washington's administration, then Congress, and finally the country. While both were still holding office, Jefferson and Hamilton engaged in virulent pamphlet warfare with one another, each, of course, using an assumed name. Jefferson and Madison, who was now a member of the House of Representatives, brought the poet Philip Freneau to Washington to run a newspaper on the political side that was beginning to be called "Republican," as opposed to "Federalist." Madison also worked with John Beckley, clerk of the House, in organizing the nucleus of a party in the Congress. It was slow work, for only a few local elections were fought on the still inchoate national issues, and it was usually after an election rather than before that the views of the successful candidates could be assessed. By the time Hamilton retired, in 1795, to repair his private fortunes, a political cleavage, extending beyond the little knots of Federalists and Republicans in Congress, had begun to divide the nation and embroil its people in a new wave of passionate party warfare. This division was made more dramatic and intense by the furious hatreds and attachments that arose from the most world-shaking event of the era—the French Revolution.

Sympathy for the Revolution seemed a natural sentiment in

republican America, though the fact that some of the very people who had helped the American cause were now the victims somewhat obscured the issues. When the Reign of Terror broke out, much of the American sympathy with the revolutionaries palled. But the Americans were divided once again by the new war in Europe when Britain took sides against France. The Federalists, whose strength was in the centers of commerce and among the farms producing for export, were led by men whose business ties were mainly with Britain. Most American trade was still with Britain, and most import duties were levied on British goods. Hamilton was keenly aware that the war with Britain would "cut up credit by the roots" and destroy the financial foundations he had tried to build. Most of the Jeffersonians continued to dislike Britain and retained a residue of sympathy for France.

It was impossible for the administration to ignore the conflict, which deranged the quiet life of the countryside and the busy commerce of the ports. Washington quickly took charge of American foreign policy. He began in 1793 by proclaiming the neutrality of the United States, thus disappointing the many ardent supporters of France. Then, to protect American interests at sea, he authorized Jay to negotiate a treaty with Britain. Jay was obliged to negotiate from a weak position, in no way improved by Hamilton's secret liaisons with the British. The effect of the treaty that he brought home was to place the maritime commerce of the United States virtually under the patronage of the Royal Navy.

Each side had outstanding grievances from the unfulfilled terms of the Peace of 1783, which Jay's Treaty now attempted to resolve. The British agreed to give up their fortified posts on the Canadian border by 1796 on condition that the United States guarantee the payment of the pre-1776 war debts. Britain secured her fur-trading interests south and west of the Great Lakes, and in turn agreed to a commercial treaty. But Britain insisted on conducting the war at sea in accordance with her own arbitrary Rule of 1756, by which she intervened against trade with the enemy's colonies, to the detriment of Americans. Britain also garnered other naval advantages and port and refueling facilities of importance in wartime, but yielded on certain points mainly connected with the Canadian frontiers. By securing a guarantee that British merchandise would be freed from discrimination, Britain succeeded in neutralizing at one stroke the effects of the American navigation laws of 1789 and 1790. The conditions attached to any American trade with the British West Indies were so humiliating that the Senate struck out the clause in question. The United States also failed to block British naval impressment of British deserters claiming American citizenship—or even, in some cases, of Americans wrongly seized.

The treaty was the main topic of conversation in taverns, newspapers, and public meetings for months during the debate over its ratification by the Senate. It was extremely unpopular and was sorely resented. By accepting it, Washington showed that he recognized a harsh principle of international politics: where isolation is impossible, it is necessary for the weak to seek protection, which is given by the strong; ideological sympathies are secondary. The administration's best argument was that without the treaty the conflicts at sea could quickly mean a new war with Britain. Fear of another war turned the argument where both national pride and national sympathies cut the other way. Washington was fortunately able to present the treaty to the Senate along with a much more attractive agreement, negotiated by Thomas Pinckney with Spain, which opened up the mouth of the Mississippi for American commerce. The Senate ratified both, but that did not end the matter; the Republicans in the House for some time contemplated further obstruction by refusing the appropriations necessary to put Jay's Treaty into effect. This maneuver failed, albeit narrowly, and Washington remained master of his own foreign policy.

Hamilton's domestic policies had also opened divisions that involved questions of principle. Was the new Republic to become a front-rank commercial nation, controlled by a politically powerful new aristocracy, and looking for credit and commercial expansion to the industrial and financial system of Britain? And, if so, was its government to amass the powers, the energy, of European governments? The Bank of the United States, the assumption of state debts, and the advocacy of long-range, public-credit policies had raised these issues, and all of them had implied a flexible construction of the Constitution. The importance of Jay's Treaty was that it brought foreign policy squarely into the home ground of American politics, and forced people to identify themselves according to sympathies and interests attached to the giant contestants of Europe.

America could never have escaped these forces, whatever its form of government, and a weaker form might have been torn to shreds in the struggle. The Constitution had been designed by men who believed that political parties were made up by narrow, self-interested factions; the complex of balances in the Constitution was expected to thwart the growth of party politics. It was, therefore, a harsh comment on the hopes of the framers when they found themselves actually engaged in party organization. As they took sides, they handled the moral problem by explaining that it was the other side that was engaged in divisive, factional activities. Washington himself believed that the Republic was a fabric of many strands, but without fundamental divisions; all the strands met in the presidency, which must always remain above party. This view caused him to denounce the Democratic (or Republican) societies, more than thirty of which had sprung up in different parts of the country in the wake of the French Revolution. These clubs, with their pro-French sympathies, helped to stimulate an interest in politics, though they do not seem to have been in touch with the incipient Republican party in Congress. Washington blamed one of them for the Whiskey Rebellion, which occurred in western Pennsylvania in 1794, and was, in effect, a farm-area taxpayers' revolt against Hamilton's excise law. An army of some thirteen thousand was summoned to crush the disturbance, which had alarmed Washington, though it offered Hamilton a welcome opportunity for military parade.

The burden of Washington's denunciation was that these thirty groups were "self-created societies." In theory the Republic offered a proper system of representation; he seemed to think that such formations lay outside the constitutional system and were therefore subversive. Washington's *Farewell Address* included passages, drafted by Hamilton, attacking parties. The Federalists, of course, were not under attack because they were not admitted to be a party; the blame for the rise of party warfare was directed solely against the opposition.

Despite these disavowals, the political formations that had surfaced would go far toward altering the structure of American politics. In the process, they undermined existing social relationships. By 1797, Jefferson himself could observe in Philadelphia that "men who have been intimate all their lives, cross the streets to avoid meeting, and turn their heads another way, lest they should be obliged to touch their hats." Deborah Logan, the wife of a Philadelphia Republican, reported that "friendships were dissolved, tradesmen dismissed, and custom withdrawn from the Republican party." The opposing parties were identified by their foreign attachments, which in the process were magnified and distorted. Federalists became "Anglomen'" and "Monocrats"; they were widely believed to be planning the introduction of monarchy into the United States. The Republicans became Jacobins, "Gallomen," levelers, and, of course, atheists. Instead of being a local or temporary aberration from a harmonious norm, party identification itself defined all social relationships. The more men were dismayed and horrified by these developments, the more fiercely they denounced their political enemies for having brought them about.

Under the presidency of John Adams, who had earlier remarked, during the controversy over the Democratic Clubs, that "political clubs must and ought to be lawful in every free country," the Federalist administration became repressive. Under the Sedition Act, editors went to jail for criticizing the administration; and under the closely linked Alien Acts, Frenchmen, recently the friendliest of aliens, found themselves persecuted for suspected allegiance to France. The effect of Jay's Treaty was to place the United States in a position akin to hostility toward France, and French depredations on American shipping resulted in an open though undeclared state of maritime war. The prospect of war once again roused Hamilton, who conceived of himself as the commander of an invincible American army whose sphere might eventually include the Latin-American colonies, once these were liberated from Spain and Portugal.

Adams, however, wanted peace. At the risk of a fatal split in the Federalist party, and despite vexations and provocations from the French, he eventually succeeded in negotiating a settlement that averted full-scale war with France. The Federalists became, in effect, two parties, with President Adams and Alexander Hamilton, now a private citizen of New York, directing the opposing wings. In time, the president became aware that three members of his cabinet were taking their instructions from Hamilton, and in due course he dismissed them. His authority, nonetheless, was damaged, and as he faced the election of 1800, masses of his earlier supporters began to drift into the ranks of the Jeffersonian Republicans.

The opposition under Adams became more vigorous, more sustained, and more strident than it had been under Washington. In reply to the Sedition and Alien acts, Jefferson and Madison drafted resolutions that, with some modifications, were adopted respectively by the legislatures of Kentucky and Virginia. These famous resolves interposed the rights of individual states against the abuse of power by the federal government, and declared that the states could nullify federal acts that impaired the states' own fundamental interests. It was an astonishing reversal for Madison, the nationalist of the Constitutional Convention and of *The Federalist*. Yet there was an underlying consistency throughout Madison's concern for the protection of minority interests, whether of property or of states, for he had not envisaged that federal power would be used to oppress the interests of a minority or that his colleagues of earlier years would turn into the oppressors.

Adams, too, had changed. His early faith in the virtue of the American people had slowly given way to a pessimistic conviction that they could too easily be corrupted and misled. He had always had a certain fascination with the glitter of aristocracy, and events both at home and in France convinced him that a forceful executive and an independent upper house were necessary to make a republic safe against democratic agitations. In earlier years, when he advocated a mixed or balanced government, he referred primarily to the separate branches of government and the avoidance of concentrated power; by the 1790s, however, he was thinking of the antagonism between aristocracy and democracy. "The great art of lawgiving," he explained in 1789, "consists in balancing the poor against the rich in the legislature." These views and a belief that the magnificence of high offices of state must be seen and felt by the people, added to an acute touchiness about his personal dignity, made him a vulnerable target for Republican ridicule. He was accused of monarchical leanings, which he hotly denied. As a candidate for re-election, however, he carried decreasing conviction, despite the fact that his policy of peace with France was both politically courageous and nationally correct.

It was precisely because all the variegated strands of American society came together in the presidency—as Washington rightly held—that the political opposition made that high office its target. Jefferson had been reluctant, on personal grounds, to oppose Adams in 1796, and had fallen into place as vice president. But in 1800 he contested the presidency with conviction. His partisans everywhere mobilized their constituencies, where they developed techniques, such as house-to-house canvassing, that were to become part of the permanent equipment of democratic politics.

Adams was not, and had never been, the representative leader of the High Federalist faction dominated by Hamilton. He never liked the Bank of the United States, and he did not want to be a pawn in converting the nation to commercial, still less industrial, capitalism. In later and calmer years, reflection would reveal that his views were not as far from Jefferson's as they looked at the time. The Federalists depended not alone on the seaports but on a mass of commercially oriented agriculture; now, however, the farmers and planters who had been willing to give their allegiance to Washington were able to give that allegiance back to the Virginian leadership of Jefferson without any profound change in their own sentiments. The main difficulties were sectional rather than ideological. This was the importance of the alliance between Virginia and New York, which Jefferson and Madison molded during the 1790s.

Jefferson gained steadily, especially after 1798, and election returns in individual states disclosed a deep shift away from Federalist government. Yet this shift was caused by a feeling that it was the Federalists who had changed, by ceasing to represent the fundamental agrarian interests of the nation. The Jeffersonian opposition, therefore, was able to tap a natural reservoir of sympathy and support; the agrarian mass of America had little liking for a policy that seemed to be placing all the advantages in the hands of the moneyed interests—the merchants and bankers—rather than the agricultural producers of the nation's wealth. Jefferson did not aim at a transformation but rather at a restoration of the pacific norm by which he wanted to see the nation live and grow.

Jefferson also won effective support from a quarter that was not formally political—the enthusiastic religious revivalists. In Kentucky, according to a participant who also recorded local history, the spirit of the revival combined "zeal for liberty" with "indignation against the old aristocracy." Thomas Allen, a New England evangelist, declared that federalism "consists in the love of arbitrary power. . . . It is hostile to the character of Jehovah, and the love of our Neighbour. . . ." Revivalists everywhere saw the Federalists as standing for a social order and a religious discipline that was antipathetic to freedom of religion and to the social democracy of which religious freedom was one of the expressions.

Jefferson's victory in 1800 could reasonably be foreseen. But it was more difficult to be confident of the eventual outcome. Vociferous Federalists, especially in New England, predicted horrendous consequences and seemed to anticipate the doom of the Republic. Some of them gave the impression that it would be safer to quit the Union than to hand over their liberties to Jefferson. The transfer of power was indeed fraught with uncertainty that the passage of later elections has made difficult to understand.

The world of 1800 could show few, if any, examples of a peaceful and orderly change of government resulting from a general election. In Britain, elections did affect the composition of Parliament and the strength of governments; but the modern party system had not developed, and no administration had yet resigned as the result of losing an election. In America, when John Adams rode away from Washington before the inauguration to avoid the sight of his successor, he yielded power with a heavy heart, but with a civil tranquillity that would have accompanied few, if any, such transactions in Europe at that time. The High Federalists had no recourse but to accept their defeat. If they had attempted either rebellion or secession, they would have discredited themselves forever, and this they instinctively, if reluctantly, appreciated. Their only recourse was that of remaining within the system, with the hope, however thin, of fighting back and winning at the next election. America had demonstrated to itself, and to the world, that representative government could be made to support the continuity of institutions.

Jefferson later became fond of referring to his election as "the great revolution of 1800," but his intentions were not revolutionary. He sincerely believed that he had prevented, not instigated, a great and alarming transformation of the nation. He at once addressed himself to the task of restoring the shaken harmony of the Republic. "We are all Republicans, we are all Federalists," he stated mildly in his Inaugural Address. Jefferson saw his role in a light remarkably similar to Washington's: he wanted to preside over an undivided republic in which political opposition would dwindle away. He had helped to instigate the party system, but he had no wish to perpetuate it. In order to remain in power, and to pursue a policy, however, he was obliged to work through the most effective channels available, and his own Republican party was certainly the most important of these.

He would have wished that his party might eventually encompass the entire political system. But future elections now beckoned his opponents, and even erstwhile allies who began to become disenchanted with his policies. The development of the politics of a democracy could not be stopped merely because one's own side had won. He was soon to face other difficulties. A deliberate philosopher of limited government was now confronted with the problems of governing in a period of threatening international turmoil. For more than twelve years, America had been led from the top. Jefferson was inclined to let it take its own shape, its own direction—managed perhaps, but not driven. But history would not leave him, or his country, in peace.

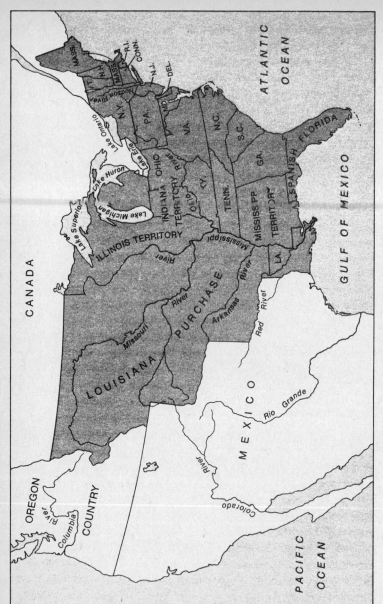

America in 1815

12

Growth of Population,
War, and the
New Balance of Sections

The new nation owed its existence in large measure to a firm, supple, and relatively stable leadership. That leadership, however, had never been exclusively central in its point of view, and the impulsively growing sections that constantly redrew the geography of the United States began, soon after the War of Independence, to speak with an increasingly imperative voice. Jefferson, more than Washington or Adams, was in tune with this voice. When, acting without constitutional sanction, he acquired the Louisiana Territory from France in 1803, he enacted a masterstroke of executive policy that doubled the size of the country. This vast aggrandizement of physical space was itself symbolic of the mood of the people.

Both physically and figuratively, the people were extraordinarily remote from their national leaders. Politicians eagerly sought election to Congress, but once arrived there, they found themselves singularly isolated not only from their constituents but also from most of their colleagues. The topography of Washington was in some ways representative of the centrifugal character of the nation. The capital was not a city but a loose cluster of separate villages. "One might take a ride of several hours within the precincts," reported one surprised visitor, "without meeting with a single individual to disturb one's meditation." "In the very heart of the city," said another, "not a sound is to be heard. . . ." Legislators, members of the executive, and the permanent bureaucracy were separated not only by the Constitution but by copses, creeks, and swamps. One congressman fell from his horse, somewhere between the White House and the Capitol, and half comically described his plight: "Figure to yourself a man almost bruised to death, on a dark, cold night, in the heart of the capital of the United States, out of sight or hearing of human habitation, and you will have a tolerably exact idea of my situation."

Party politics certainly had some influence on elections, but it took all the persuasive social skill of President Jefferson to coax from the representatives of the far-flung districts anything like a coherent attachment to either party or policy. When Jefferson was gone, the central impulse disappeared. No successor until Andrew Jackson could impose a sense of will or purpose on Congress. The legislators grouped themselves in their boardinghouses, and it was there rather than in the legislative chambers that loyalties were forged and attitudes formulated. Members of Congress remained basically susceptible to the dictates of local and usually distant communities. Yet the series of crises that confronted federal authorities from the beginning of Washington's administration to the end of Madison's made it imperative for them to formulate policies, which in turn had to be communicated to both the legislators and the people.

The country, however, was becoming more extensive and amorphous. The geographical advance of the United States was not intrinsically nationalistic in character. When the settlers in Kentucky, still at that time lying within the bounds of Virginia, heard about the Jay-Gardoqui agreement of 1786, their fury drove many of them to consider a Spanish allegiance; General James Wilkinson, a Kentucky speculator who was for many years the senior United States officer in the Southwest, judged the moment opportune for entering secretly into the service of Spain, in which he remained for the rest of his professional life. In 1793 George Rogers Clark, embittered by what he felt to be a lack of recognition for military services, offered to raise a western army to deliver Louisiana to France; he received a commission for the purpose from the flamboyant French emissary "Citizen" Edmond Genêt, although the French government later vetoed the campaign. Wilkinson and Clark were only two examples of ambitious western leaders who would not hesitate to place the fortunes of their entire section under the protection of European nations. The Americans who migrated into Texas did separate themselves, to become nominal subjects of Mexico after its rupture with Spain. They declared themselves independent in 1836, and it was not until 1845 that Texas was incorporated into the United States.

By 1793 France was at war with Prussia, Hapsburg Austria, Spain, Sardinia, the Netherlands, and Britain. With a lurking threat that the wars in Europe might embroil the United States, and with Indian nations more united and more hostile than at any time since Pontiac's rising, Washington during his presidency had little freedom from anxiety about the future of his country. The people of the frontier settlements lived in a state of wariness interrupted only by terror. In 1791 an expedition under Arthur St. Clair, sent by Washington to pacify the northwestern Indians, was routed near the Wabash; the administration had to face the prospect of a full-scale and extremely costly war, made all the more dangerous by the uneasy state of relations with Britain and the closeness of British ties with the Indian nations.

Washington had the satisfaction of presiding over the settlement of the most urgent of these dangers. Anthony Wayne's devastating defeat of the Indians at Fallen Timbers resulted in the Treaty of Greenville in 1795 and the clearing of the Northwest for effective settlement. Jay's Treaty, humiliating though it must have been to Washington himself, eased the danger of renewed war with Britain, which in view of British naval supremacy might well have been a total disaster for the United States; an American defeat could easily have reopened the continent for European exploitation. But Britain did not want to see her European rivals renewing their challenge in America, and so long as the United States offered no threat, Britain was prepared to use her navy to shield the United States. Jefferson, never a friend to Britain, understood the relationship; in his view the key was New Orleans, and he observed that whoever held that city was America's natural enemy. If it fell to France, "We must marry ourselves to the British fleet and nation." It would decidedly have been a marriage of necessity, not of love.

In 1800 Bonaparte, then first consul of France, persuaded Spain to relinquish Louisiana, in defiance of the Treaty of Paris made in 1783. American military power consisted of a small army, the state militia forces, and a few gunboats; if Bonaparte had determined on a military occupation of the French territories, the history of North America might have taken a very different course. Napoleon's purpose, however, was deflected, partly because of the dire situation in Santo Domingo. In 1803 the first consul offered to sell the Louisiana Territory for $15 million, a proposal that President Jefferson quickly endorsed. His scruples about this arbitrary stroke of executive power proved to be a luxury that time did not permit him to indulge. Bonaparte, the most powerful ruler in the world, might change his mind while the Senate debated; Jefferson, therefore, acted as the executive representative of the nation and was left to meditate later on the philosophy of constitutional power.

Jefferson's curiosity about the interior combined with his intense nationalism to induce him in 1803 to authorize the western expedition of Meriwether Lewis and William Clark. The two spent two years exploring the passes and river courses of the continent, as far as the Columbia River, coming within sight of the Pacific. Their findings gave Americans ample indication of the immense scale, and geographical variety, of the continent that seemed open to them for an indefinite future of expansion; traders and trappers began at once to pursue the paths they had opened.

Geographical movement was not the only kind of expansion in which Americans were engaged. The Revolution, which in a sense was a product of American self-confidence, released tremendous energy, partly channeled, partly dispersed. Movement of population was accompanied by growth of population, by the clearing of forests, the laying out and planting of farms, by new enterprises in city and country and new expressions in speech and manners. The growth of the population itself was a manifestation of this exuberant, self-assured national dynamism. The assumption of Franklin and others that the colonial population doubled itself every twenty-five years was not much wide of the mark. Differences in population growth between regions were so pronounced that general conclusions tend to give an impression of consistency that the continent did not possess. Nevertheless, during the second half of the eighteenth century, an overall growth rate of 26 to 30 per cent each decade seems to have taken place. This percentage is slightly lower than would be required for Franklin's (and later Malthus's) estimate, but it is appreciably higher than that of Britain or any other country in Europe at any time in the eighteenth or nineteenth centuries.

The high rate of infant mortality in the cities was offset by much better prospects for survival in the country, and Americans were to an overwhelming extent a people of farmers. In 1800, 72.8 per cent of persons gainfully employed were making their livings on the land; even a decade later the increase of cities had reduced this figure a mere 1 per cent. William Currie, a Philadelphia physician, commented in a book published in 1792 on "the disparity between the healthiness of a large town and the country which surrounds it. . . . Nearly one half of the children born in Philadelphia, die under two years of age, and chiefly with a disease in the stomach and bowels. Very few die at this age in the country." Once an American country dweller had reached maturity, he stood a good chance of living to or beyond what would now be called middle age. It was a young population, however, of which as much as 50 per cent were probably under twenty-one, a figure that varies slightly in place and time but remains fairly constant. This age structure, incidentally, throws additional light on the age restrictions imposed by state laws not for voting but for holding office; their tendency was to require experience as a qualification even where economic considerations were placed at a minimum.

The most important single explanation for the American expectation of life was food. European travelers in the American countryside often noticed the healthiness and attractive vitality of the people. In Europe most peasants could produce barely enough for the survival of their families; they lived on the edge of hunger. In America, however, where the first fact about the food supply was its abundance, hunger was rare. Tables, if they did not groan, were often loaded in summer and autumn with a wholesome assortment of fruits, vegetables, bread and corn loaves of differing shapes and contents, meat, game, and fish. These foods were not necessarily signs of luxury or wealth but of an ordinary farm's produce, supplemented from the market or from hunting expeditions in nearby woods. The importation by western Europe of vegetables, previously unknown, from America was probably partly responsible for the improvement in health and longevity, with a concomitant rise of population, that took place gradually in Britain and on the Continent during the eighteenth century. In America the effects from fresh vegetables were more dramatic, more immediate, and more extensive. The disappearance of rickets in children, "this scourge of infants" as Dr. Currie called it, was undoubtedly a result of nutrition.

The American population multiplied so fast after independence that the 1780s still stand as the decade of the most rapid percentage increase of any in the span of American history. Without serious inflation or fluctuation in monetary values subsequent to the financial crises following the War of Independence, the economy was able to absorb and supply this continuing increase. A new generation of merchants, who became rich during the recovery from the troubles of the 1780s and then made huge profits from the risky but rewarding maritime commerce during the Wars of the French Revolution, gained considerable influence in New England and accumulated the resources for what would later be industrial investments. The merchants were among the many individuals and their families who made advances in their own style and standards of life. But this was not the common picture; economic growth in the cities left the farmers of the countryside largely untouched.

Even by the end of the War of 1812, a survey would have revealed that most people were living much as they and their forebears had lived thirty years earlier. Most farms not only produced their own food, but their own clothes; the women and often the children were occupied in weaving, which they did for their families and on commission in a widespread version of the old "putting-out" system of manufactures. The new mills of Lowell, near Boston, were beginning to draw farm girls into a concentrated industry, a process sharply stimulated by the exigencies of war and by the prolonged periods of stringency resulting from Jefferson's attempt to impose an economic embargo on Britain. The Lowell venture and similar developments in Charleston were an augury. But on the whole, country life continued to be subject to many of the same limitations as in earlier generations. There was little innovation in the equipment used in farming, chemical agriculture was known only to men with large estates and scientific interests, and most farm families produced not only their own food but their own soap, candles, and furniture; often they built their own houses.

Heating (in spite of the invention of Franklin's famous central stove) was still usually supplied by a wood fire that left much of the house, in city or country, almost unbearably cold in winter. Piped water and public waste-disposal systems existed only in the cities. Even most manufacturing workshops continued to use the same tools and the same methods of production that had been in use since before the Revolution. Evidence of any appreciable rise in the standard of living is scant. Despite individual variations, the level of the average per capita income does not appear to have risen between 1799 and 1819 (for which an estimate has been made). The standard of living of the average American already compared favorably with that of European peasants and workers, but it was a standard diffused over a widening geography and over an increasing population; the standard spread rather than rose in the decades following the Revolution.

The expansion of the nation could be looked on as progress or it could be seen to threaten disintegration. Before the beginning of the nineteenth century, the advances in ship design and the novelty of hardening the surfaces of highways were practically the only improvements that made travel any faster than it had been for the previous two thousand years, when the Romans extended their empire over western Europe. With such lines of communication, it was difficult to conceive of a single nation's boundaries stretching to the far side of the Mississippi Valley and embracing New Orleans and the shores of the Great Lakes. Albert Gallatin, Jefferson's farsighted secretary of the treasury, drew up a plan for the federal sponsorship of an extensive network of highways, canals, and river improvements that showed an awareness of the dimension of the problem; Jefferson was duly impressed, but daunted by what he believed to be constitutional obstacles to interstate action by the federal government. No legislation followed, and the states remained as the exclusive sponsors of their own internal improvements.

In these same years a few engineers and inventors were experimenting with steam as a motive power for propelling boats. The development of steam transport may be credited with creating,

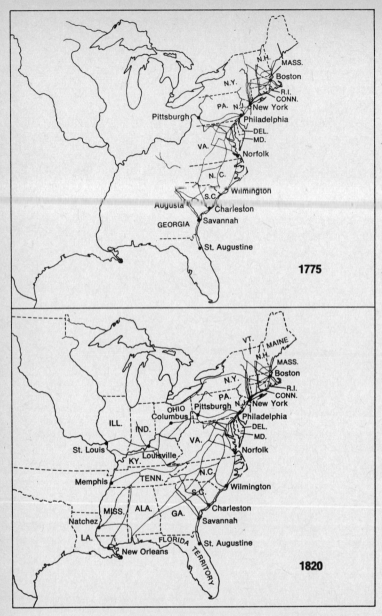

1775

1820

Principal Roads: 1775–1820

among other things, the communications system that enabled the Union to surmount the problems of its own geography. The first steamboat churned through a short stretch of the River Saône in France in 1783 but got no further. An American, John Fitch, built the first steam vessel that operated effectively, but he could raise neither capital nor encouragement, and died in poverty in 1798. American engineers were poorly informed about technological progress in Europe, while much of the public was scornfully incredulous. It was only when Robert Fulton obtained substantial patronage that the engineering problems could be solved. In August 1807 his ship of long and narrow design, later called the Clermont, completed the up-and-down-stream voyage between New York and Albany in sixty-two hours. This demonstration had a dramatic effect on public opinion, which was quickly convinced that a new age of enterprise had been opened. Within a few years steamboats were pushing their way up the Mississippi (an impossibility for flatboats and a struggle for more sophisticated vessels) and plying most of the major inland waterways. Enterprising companies sprang up to take advantage of the vast, new opportunities offered by the steam vessel. As in Europe, canals were constructed to connect rivers, and the stimulus of steam helped to create a network of inland waterways. The increase in water traffic, itself a spur to technological invention, also brought the chartering and laying out of new highways, many of which were operated by private corporations that paid for their ventures by collecting tolls.

One of the most distinctively American features to develop as a consequence of this system of communications was a new type of hotel. The American inn, which accommodated practically all comers, was little more than an enlarged family home, run on a family basis. But the cities, bidding against each other for custom, investment, and immigrants, soon became the centers of a new institution, the quasi-public building, often established with civic support. It was not long before the hotel began to concentrate the life of the community; young couples lived there, public lounges and amusements were provided, and the variety of services reflected the means and tastes of a nascent upper class of merchants and lawyers. The first of the great American hotels was the Boston

Exchange Hotel, opened to the public in 1809. Its eight stories, three hundred rooms, and numerous facilities gave it the reputation of being the largest building in America and "the most elegant hotel in the United States." Its ground floor contained offices and shops, and some of Boston's leading merchants had offices there. The Exchange burned down in 1818 and the economic crisis of that year prevented rebuilding. Its example, however, was quickly copied in other cities, where the existence of a "first-class hotel" became a symbol of civic pride and a substantial investment in the city's economic advancement.

Americans adopted the French word "hotel" during the 1790s, substituting it for "tavern." But only Americans who had traveled in Europe, or who had talked with visiting Britons, were likely to recognize that their own speech had begun to develop independent characteristics. Such expressions as "I guess" and "I reckon" were already popular in America though unknown in England. The American use of the verb "to fix" had also appeared by the early nineteenth century—to the amused astonishment of visitors; one of them concluded that the Americans would end up murdering the English language. Southern speech was particularly different—its most marked characteristic attributable to the penetration of Negro accents and dialects into the ordinary language of whites.

The spread of population into the Mississippi Valley soon fulfilled the conditions for the admission of new states. Ohio was formally incorporated into the Union as early as 1803, Indiana in 1816, Illinois in 1818; and the Southwest, whose territory had been catered for by an enabling act in 1790, produced the new states of Mississippi in 1817 and Alabama in 1819. A new population balance of sections was coming into existence; already it was possible to foresee the Midwest as a heartland rather than a series of thinly manned outposts. Yet shortly after the acquisition of Louisiana, the national leadership in Washington was abruptly forced to revert its attention to problems that arose primarily from the wars in Europe.

During his second administration, Jefferson was destined to preside over the shattering of some of his favorite dreams. He had sought a regime that would so far reunite the disparate segments and factions that the newborn party system would disappear, leaving in its place a single Republican party, led, naturally enough, by himself and his disciples. Instead, his own party began to develop those fissures that are the almost inevitable consequences of success. Furthermore, Jefferson's policies had driven the commercial centers of the nation into active opposition; the Federalists, now under the direction of a new and tough generation of political fighters, regrouped after his retirement for a valiant challenge to the Republican ascendancy in national politics.

The chief remaining Federalist stronghold in the constitutional structure was the Supreme Court, to which Jefferson's fellow Virginian John Marshall had been appointed by John Adams as the last gasp of his administration. During the thirty-five years that followed, Marshall, in a series of forcefully argued decisions, determined the superior authority both of the federal courts and of the federal government. In taking the first step toward this determination, he risked a collision with the executive. In *Marbury* v. *Madison* (1803) Marshall asserted the right of the Supreme Court to overrule an executive department, in this case the State Department. By a devious piece of technical reasoning, however, he carefully avoided battle by refraining from implementing that right in the case in point. He also, almost incidentally, affirmed the power of the Court to review and, if necessary, to void congressional legislation. This point, fraught as it was with long-term significance, was not especially controversial, as most Republicans agreed with him. Jefferson regarded Marshall as a dangerous partisan and enemy, and he would have liked to get rid of him. That, however, was not altogether practicable; the only means of driving a federal judge from the bench was the clumsy procedure of impeachment—which was badly mismanaged in the trial of Justice Samuel Chase, from which Jefferson stood personally aloof. In Marshall's case the Republicans had no hope of success; the result was that Marshall was to outlast Jefferson in public office by a quarter of a century.

There were other difficulties. Within Jefferson's party the stinging, high-pitched voice of another Virginian, the eccentric and virulent John Randolph of Roanoke, questioned the integrity of the administration. Randolph began attacking the administration in 1805 when it recommended a compromise settlement of claims arising from the scandal of the Yazoo land companies, a massive sale perpetrated in Georgia in 1795 by bribed legislators. The sales had been invalidated, but many innocent second purchasers lived in New England, where the Republicans badly needed political support: the compromise, therefore, was expedient as well as reasonable. Randolph's attack split the party and instigated the formation of an informal, thorny group known as the Tertium Quids. Answerable only to his own constituents, Randolph was free to attack on any issue to which his bright but morbid and vindictive mind was attracted, and Jefferson found him an acute embarrassment. Randolph, however, eventually became his own worst enemy, and damaged himself irreparably by his handling of the Chase impeachment.

The severest test for Jefferson and his friend and successor James Madison was to come from abroad. The United States might have seemed an enviably situated nation for so pacifically minded a president as Jefferson. The Atlantic Ocean was certainly a formidable bulwark for nurturing feelings of national superiority to the causes that drove Europe into its repeated wars. Yet if the United States was to treat that ocean as a highway rather than a barrier, it could not indefinitely enjoy the luxury of being without a foreign policy. In its monumental conflict with Napoleonic France, Britain was fighting for its life, and its navy was its greatest arm of war. Controversy with the United States arose over two issues: impressment and Britain's seizure of ships declared in violation of conditions acceptable to its courts for wartime commerce with the enemy.

Impressment concerned men; seizures of cargoes and ships concerned property. The American merchants, who were the chief victims of the capture of ships and their cargoes, were also the chief beneficiaries of the risky but enormously profitable wartime commerce. Much as they would have welcomed some adequate protection, they did not believe that national honor could be safeguarded, or the British coerced into concessions, by so radical a measure as the cessation of American commerce. Yet that was the course that Jefferson and Madison, who as secretary of state was primarily responsible for the formulation of policy, deliberately pursued.

Impressment raised the question of whether the United States could protect its own citizens. The problem was by no means new, for British naval recruitment was carried on in emergencies by press gangs who rounded up eligible men and carried them off to service on his majesty's ships. Finding British naval service unattractive, many sailors escaped to the United States, where British ships frequently docked for supplies and repairs. Most of them enlisted in the American merchant marine, which, according to an estimate made in 1812 by the American secretary of the treasury, recruited about twenty-five hundred Britons each year. This drain of British manpower had eased a little after 1807, but continued on a scale that could not be ignored by a nation engaged in a life-and-death struggle, whose only security was its superiority at sea. The best estimates suggested that, even by American definition, in 1809 and 1810 as many as ten thousand British subjects were serving on American ships, a number equal to the recruitment needed to maintain the existing strength of the Royal Navy.

The American grievance arose from the British practice of stopping American ships at sea and commandeering British deserters. Even when questions of law were set aside, an American and an English mariner did not obviously differ, and many innocent Americans were also taken captive. No responsible administration could have failed to protest against this abuse. The outrage that might have given the most immediate justification for war occurred in 1807, when a British man-of-war, H.M.S. *Leopard,* after a brief engagement, sent a party aboard the U.S.S. *Chesapeake* and seized four alleged British deserters. Three of the men were Americans who had served in the British navy, but their nationality was of small consequence in comparison with the fact that the action violated American sovereignty: the *Chesapeake* was a naval vessel. For the first time since the end of the War of Independence, Americans in all sections, and of all economic interests, were swept by something resembling a national emotion. The question at issue seemed little less than the recognition, by Britain, of American independence, for the episode infuriatingly reminded Americans of their former colonial status, which George Berkeley, the British admiral commanding from headquarters in Halifax, seemed to feel was still in force.

It was Jefferson who in this crisis avoided war. He refused to recall Congress, accepted British apologies, and allowed the tumult to subside. His philosophy was sincerely pacific, and he did not believe that the United States could obtain by war any advantages that would be worth the costs. The acceptance of British apologies did not mean that Jefferson and Madison were indifferent to their country's interests or its honor. Nevertheless, they might have secured their objectives more effectively in the long run as well as the short if their reactions had been based on a sounder appraisal of America's true sources of strength in relation to the powers of Europe.

Unfortunately, Jefferson's conception of foreign relations was not merely pacific, it was also unrealistic. For reasons of economy, and because of his dislike of armies and navies, he developed the view that all America needed for its own seaboard defense was a strategic deployment of gunboats—not a very formidable challenge to the naval power of Britain after Trafalgar. American economic pressures were therefore unsupported by the least threat of developing a superior force, which in part accounts for the long period of British indifference to the American mixture of expostulation and self-wounding restraints.

Jefferson and Madison could have had a treaty in 1806, when their emissaries, James Monroe and William Pinkney, reached an unexpected measure of agreement with the British government in London. The British would not abandon impressment, but they would confine it to British ports, which was itself a major concession, if the Americans would agree, on their side, to return genuine deserters. The British also agreed to some concessions in the rules by which cargoes that had been unloaded in the United States could be seized after being re-exported. But the American leaders, on reading the terms, took high ground; for one thing they knew the value of British desertions to their own merchant marine, and, for another, they rejected on principle the proposed compromise over impressment.

Of all the measures of Jefferson's regime, the Embargo Act was by far the most stringent. The act was signed at the close of 1807 and was in force until March 1809, during which time it prohibited vessels of nearly every kind from sailing for foreign ports and even required bonds for those in the coastal trade. The damage caused to the American economy was serious, and was endurable chiefly because business had been favorable in previous years and some financial reserves had been accumulated. During the embargo's fourteen months of operation, some 100,000 workers in the maritime industries and 30,000 seamen were put out of work. Business activity dropped by more than 75 per cent from that of the year 1807. In New York 120 businesses crashed and 1,200 debtors were imprisoned. All seaports, except Philadelphia, suffered, but Boston was much the worst victim; grass literally grew between the flagstones on the deserted wharves while idle ships crowded the harbor.

One of the most dangerous aspects of the embargo, dangerous, that is, to the unity of the Republic, was in the uneven distribution of its consequences. Most farmers were able to maintain prices by withholding supplies, and many businessmen managed to survive adequately enough on the import trade. But New Englanders, above all the powerful Federalist merchants of Massachusetts, became convinced that the policy in Washington sprang from the diabolical machinations of the southern leadership, bent on ruining New England. The political result was to add a sectional connotation to the rancor between Federalists and Republicans. Bostonians recalled their plight under the Boston Port Act of George III and cursed the federal administration as an equally malignant tyranny. The Federalists, who were now receiving impetus from a group of younger men such as Robert Goodloe Harper and Harrison Gray Otis, renewed their determination to recapture national power.

They had persuasive reasons for lamenting not only the embargo, which satirists reversed to read "Ograbme," but the whole drift of national affairs. Underlying Federalist criticisms was the conviction that the American people had at one time accepted a social order that was more stratified and more harmonious than what they saw when they looked around them under Republican rule. They believed that it was this social order that had been fought for and saved in the Revolution, and that without order, rank, and deference, the Republic would fall apart. Their reading of history—which was chiefly in ancient history—taught them that democracy always degenerated into tyranny. A republican form of government could be saved only by a profound respect for the laws, and principally those that protected property, by the maintenance of a hierarchical social order, and by a socially influential system of religion. They were equally certain that Jefferson and his followers were the enemies of all these values. A few years earlier, the Federalists had allowed themselves to be handicapped by their own feelings of social superiority. Many of them were unwilling to contest elections for a pre-eminence that they held to be theirs by right; they appreciated the point that dignity is not always enhanced by having to fight for it. But the storm of opposition to the embargo swiftly changed the climate and gave Federalists hope of regaining power. The storm reached such a pitch and aroused so much resentment that the Congress repealed the embargo in 1809, just before Jefferson retired from his last public office—vexed, hurt, and disappointed. His presidency was not among the public services he chose to record on his tombstone. But the problems that had perturbed his term of office did not abate, nor did the Federalist challenge to Republican hegemony.

Madison presided over new moves to bring pressure on Britain and France. One such move was the Non-Intercourse Act, which, in effect, offered either belligerent the choice of being the first to comply with American demands and thus to be relieved of the weight of American sanctions. In the meantime, however, the shifting geographical balance in population of the nation brought new forces to the national counsels.

In the Northwest, the settlers experienced a fresh wave of fear when they learned that the Indian nations were regrouping under the formidable leadership of the Shawnee chief Tecumseh. Hardly anyone in the Ohio Valley doubted that the British behind the Canadian borders were in league with the Indians, so that in spite of their terrors, the farmers were aroused to further hatred against Britain. Tecumseh remained on the defensive after the battle near Tippecanoe in 1811, a battle in which many Americans believed he had been killed. The victory over the Indians increased the courage of the Americans of the Northwest; its people were now ready to stiffen the sinews of the hesitant Madison administration for a further encounter with Britain.

Some of the younger men in Congress, among them John C. Calhoun of South Carolina and Henry Clay of Kentucky, breathed a confident and impetuous nationalism. Clay called imperiously for the conquest of Canada, which indeed offered the line along which Britain was most vulnerable to attack. After the collapse of the Indians, the Northwest became excited over the possibilities of invasion, although once again the military prospects of such a campaign were overestimated. At the same time the extreme South looked eagerly for a chance to seize Florida from the Spanish.

The new West, north and south, gave nerve and impetus to the administration in its foreign dealings. Yet it was not on the continental frontiers but on the Atlantic that the issue of sovereignty was joined. The points of dispute between America and Great Britain had not changed radically since the unsuccessful but promising negotiations six years earlier. British orders-in-council, imposing a comprehensive blockade on ports under French control, had come to constitute a new American grievance—which, however, was equalized by Napoleon's unilateral blockade of the British Isles. Impressment still continued as a grievance, provoking yet hardly intolerable. But Madison, buttressed by men like Calhoun, could not forever countenance the impotence and humiliation of the United States. The self-declared "War Hawks" argued that the British challenge must be accepted, not primarily as a matter of protecting commerce, but of vindicating the national honor. "If we submit to the pretensions of England, now openly avowed," exclaimed Calhoun, "the independence of this nation is lost." Preparation for hostilities began in April 1812, and on June 18 Congress responded to a message from Madison with a declaration of war on Britain. To the British, the war was seen as a kind of frontier brush fire; to Americans, it was considered a second struggle for the assertion of independence.

The war began and ended in historical ironies. The British cabinet agreed, under heavy pressure from merchants, to rescind the objectionable orders-in-council just before Congress declared war but too late for the news to cross the Atlantic in time to affect the American decision. At the end, after two and a half years of inconclusive and sporadic fighting, the Americans under General

Andrew Jackson won their only important land victory in the battle of New Orleans, just after the terms of peace had been concluded at Ghent by the British and American negotiators.

The war, however, was not without action, and its conclusion was not without legend. A British raiding party attacked Washington, burned most of its public buildings, and drove President Madison and his administration to seek refuge in the countryside. American naval ships achieved some successes on the Great Lakes, and their depredations in British home waters caused more damage than the British thought it comfortable to admit. In Kentucky, a legend was peacefully allowed to develop that Kentucky marksmen had won the battle of New Orleans, although in fact they never arrived on the scene; the confidence of the West in its unconquerable prowess was one of the lasting and uncontested psychological consequences of the war. Another, with more specific political implications, was the reputation of Andrew Jackson.

The terms of the peace were almost as inconclusive as the fighting itself. The dispute over impressment was not solved, it simply died away with the ending of the Napoleonic Wars. The Americans and British did establish a formula for the exercise of common sense in foreign matters when they agreed to the appointment of a joint commission to determine disputed boundaries between Canada and the United States.

For political philosophers of the Jeffersonian persuasion, the war and the events surrounding it had produced certain necessary but unwelcome lessons. Embargo, non-intercourse, and blockade had emphasized once more, as they had done in the days of the American Revolution, that America must invest in its own resources and make at least some of its own goods. Jefferson, who had always hated cities, which he regarded as sores on the body of the Republic, reluctantly admitted that manufactures were a necessity and that the cities in which they were made had some service to offer society. The Republicans also had lessons to learn about finance. In 1812, on the casting vote of Vice President George Clinton, the Senate had declined to renew the charter of the Bank of the United States. Nothing could have been more expressive of the ferment of economic ambition that drove the people of all sections into new enterprises—in farming, land speculation, and business—than the hectic demand for banks. So important was bank credit to economic expansion that an eminent historian of the subject has compared it to "a new form of energy, like steam." Banking, however, was a complex and perilous operation, requiring restraints, safeguards, and forms of accountability. The vacuum created by the disappearance of the national bank was quickly filled by a plethora of badly run and inadequately funded local banks set up in many parts of the country; the rejection of the national bank also left the federal administration without the services of a central financial instrument. For the Federalists, still coveting office and hoping for favor, it was an ironic experience to witness James Madison signing, at the close of his presidency, the charter of the Second Bank of the United States—a measure of Republican policy and a result of the ability to learn from experience.

In 1814 the Federalist opposition, failing to foresee the end of the war, organized a convention at Hartford, Connecticut, to consolidate the opposition. Feeling against the war in New England was intense, and some of the more extreme Federalists had begun to talk of secession by the New England states to avoid the consequences of southern domination of the national government. These views did not control the Hartford Convention, but they did contribute to its reputation. The news of peace, and of Jackson's victory, suddenly rendered this protest irrelevant, and made it look offensively unpatriotic. As a result, the Federalists' national prestige received a blow from which it never recovered, although for several years the party remained influential in some states. It was a portent for the future that the Hartford Convention's public declaration of grievances began by listing the over-representation given to the South by the federal ratio—the enumeration of three-fifths of the slaves for purposes of representation. To the Hartford delegates, the policy of embargo and war had been a southern conspiracy, embarked on without regard to the losses and sufferings of New England and the seaports; and these events had raised the question of what was in store for their section if the South and slavery continued indefinitely to dominate the policies of the Union.

New England was visibly losing its influence. The new distribution of population was beginning to alter the balance of forces in

Congress, and it was from Congress rather than from the executive that policies increasingly emanated. Ardent nationalism, coupled with a rising interest in manufactures among some of the neophyte representatives, produced the beginnings of a more sophisticated tariff policy in 1816. But this was only one among the several issues that presaged division rather than unity as the nation grew in mass and wealth.

Since the beginnings of the dispute with Britain in 1763, Americans, first as colonists and then as citizens of their own Republic, had used politics as an instrument not only of action but of national identity. Their political institutions became to them a source of immense pride. Some were worried about the deterioration of the old and simple republican virtues, and others disliked the social implications of the mass democracy that seemed on the verge of taking hold, where it had not already done so. Few, however, could be found to compare the American Republic unfavorably with any of the existing constitutions of Europe. The economic advantages that attracted immigrants and enthralled Americans were supported by the political foundations of a free press, free choice of religion, and an electoral system from which economic restrictions, where they survived, were being removed. Because Americans had secured these gains largely by their own efforts, and because they knew that the liberals of Europe were still far from achieving them, they came to regard their Republic with a pride that sometimes amounted to arrogance. To be disrespectful of other people's institutions, social preferences, or vital interests was to court dangerous ambitions; the original inhabitants of the continent were to be the first but not the last to feel the brute force of American nationalism.

In America, however, nationalism did not effect the political unities that it produced elsewhere. The Congress had about it little of the sense of urgent national purpose that had often prevailed in earlier years. Americans looked to the immense continent to receive their abounding energies, but these energies pressed in differing and sometimes conflicting directions. For nearly half a century, the continent would yet offer them space to absorb, rather than to resolve, the deep, incipient, sectional conflict. With space, it also offered them time. In the end, both would run out.

Conclusion

The unity that can be attributed, both in a chronological and in a political sense, to the period that began with the first disputes between Britain and her American colonies and ended with the close of the second Anglo-American war in 1815 was an artificial creation, a product of the controlled efforts of men. It did not result from drift, or merely from the shape that social and economic life were taking of their own impulses in different regions of the continent. The work of achieving at least enough social cohesion to bring a federal republic into existence and to make it strong enough to survive war, party strife, and sectional dissension was by its nature political work. American society cannot be said to have lived by or for politics in this era, for Americans of all classes were content to leave politics alone; but society did, perhaps to an unusual extent, define itself politically. Without a series of sustained, determined, and highly intelligent efforts, the regional societies of the mainland colonies could never have secured their independence or made a new nation.

The keenest and best-informed political minds were at their best in political action rather than in theory. The era produced little of profound speculative importance, but it did produce pragmatic works of such power and brilliance as to contribute permanently to the literature of political analysis. The sustained quality of the outpouring on social problems is one of the most remarkable features of the American achievement. It would be difficult to study the period without becoming genuinely interested in the quality of the minds that were being consistently applied to social, economic, and political problems; and these problems, whether urgent or distant, were seen to be acutely relevant to the aims and ideals of contemporaries.

The rhetoric of American social and political discourse was itself one of the unifying elements of an exceptionally diverse social order. The structural similarity between the political institutions of the states was another. These unifying factors, which were partly

233

the natural result of a conscious and cultivated inheritance and partly the discovered consequence of answering the necessities of constantly recurring crises, did much to make a federal order into a practical possibility. The Constitution, with its specific guarantee that every state was to have a "republican form of government," spoke the language of these well-recognized political institutions. These affinities were a necessary minimum for some degree of unity, but it did not follow that their existence necessarily meant that Americans had molded themselves into a single society. The Constitution as it emerged from Philadelphia and from the first ten amendments was certainly not the only document that would have been capable, at that time, of expressing the degree of political unity most desired by a probable majority of politically intelligent people. If a well-wrought plan to strengthen the old Congress had been put forward at the very beginning of the Philadelphia convention, the United States might have acquired a more responsible, or parliamentary, form of government, rather than one that held the executive at an artificial distance from the legislative body.

History does not record whether such a form of American government would have withstood the stresses of the European wars of the years between 1792 and 1815 and all the tension and division they carried to the American continent. Still less does it suggest an ultimate resolution of the gigantic problem of slavery. However, it is doubtful whether any of the men whose labors brought the great Republic into existence, and who subscribed so eloquently to the rhetoric of America's common language of politics, allowed themselves to be deceived about the perfection of their achievements. The perils of the future, of which they were fully aware, arose not alone from the chances and contingencies of unpredictable events. Whatever their own particular affinity or interest, the Founding Fathers well knew that the federal structure contained and represented regional, social, and economic differences that would continue to pull in diverging directions. Slavery and freedom, social equality and class divisions, commercial and industrial development and agricultural solidity—these distinctions could live together and serve each other, but they could also come to embody fundamental differences over ultimate aims.

If the makers of the system had reason enough to be anxious

about the distant outcome, and differed as to what kind of nation they wanted the United States to become, they still had good reason for immense satisfaction with the amount of unity that they had brought about. Yet many of those who had exerted themselves most tirelessly in making a success of the struggle with Britain, and in creating the Constitution itself, would have been dismayed by the state to which both economic and political life had sunk by the time of the portentous advent of Andrew Jackson in 1828— if they had not been some years earlier. Momentous changes had come about, and many of those changes would have been classified by the founders of the Republic as precisely the kind of degeneration that fulfilled some of their worst fears, the one important exception being that of a military dictatorship, which was expected to arise from the collapse of democracy. Some of their successors did even convince themselves that Jackson's reign was a new form of tyranny. Most of the nation's founders would also have deplored the almost obsessive spirit of commerce and economic ambition as they would have deplored the division of the nation into organized parties.

Yet, ironically, both in politics and economic activity, they presided over the inauguration of these changes, in certain cases labored to introduce them. These practical departures from the principles so passionately embraced in the past proved something rather different from the classical theory of the degeneration of democratic republics; and a perspective taken a lifetime after the opening of the period would have revealed consistencies that were perhaps more important than the corruption and decay that were so often deplored.

The truth is that the organization of social and economic aims into the institutional forms of political parties did represent a continuity with earlier aims. The liberties of person and property, of representative government and legal rights that were proclaimed by the makers of the Revolution were at least defensibly consistent in principle with such marked changes as the development of a party system, and with such specific policies under the new government as the creation of a national bank and the introduction of a limited measure of a central economic policy. Most Americans also continued to enjoy a degree of continuity in their ways of life.

The leaders who forged American society, and whose language did so much to give it a nationally conceived identity, had summoned up the remote powers of government and installed them as a permanent phenomenon, touching every individual, and drawing from every individual a nominal consent that was sometimes required to become active participation. Americans needed government, but resented and attempted to thwart its operations; they had called an intensely acquisitive and increasingly capitalistic society into being, while frequently denying and disclaiming its moral consequences. Whether these ambiguities were to be mere differences of emphasis or violent and intolerable contradictions, they were the stuff of the American politics of the future, and that politics would be charged with all the turbulent ambitions of American society.

Further Readings

The following bibliographical essay is intended as an outline of the ways in which historians, from the time of the struggle for American independence, have written about the late colonial and early national periods. The literature is immense, and much that would be important to a more complete study is necessarily omitted here. An attempt has been made to select works that indicate trends or points of view as well as those that are of intrinsic importance. For fuller bibliographical information, the student may consult the guides in the New American Nation series, in the Economic History of the United States series, and in *The Harvard Guide to American History,* edited by Oscar Handlin and others. The two books of Daniel J. Boorstin on *The Americans* also contain valuable bibliographical information.

The earliest histories of the American Revolution were written by contemporaries, whose records and opinions may be considered as part of the Revolution itself. Those emanating from the winning side represented its intellectual fulfillment and justification. The losers attempted to vindicate British policy and their own allegiance to Britain; they were inclined to see the revolutionary leaders as unscrupulous schemers in charge of mobs. These works concern themselves with social history, not as an immediate object of understanding but as a means of explaining the movement for independence.

Contemporary accounts began with William Gordon, *The History of the Rise, Progress, and Establishment of the Independence of the United States of America* (London, 1788; New York, 1789); next came the work of the South Carolina physician David Ramsay, *History of the American Revolution* (Philadelphia, 1789); Mrs. Mercy Otis Warren's *History of the Rise, Progress, and Termination of the American Revolution* (3 vols., Boston) was published in 1805. These works extol the achievements of the makers of American independence. This perspective, which is in a sense the American continuation of the Whig historical tradition, received its most expansive treatment from the Democratic politician and diplomatist George Bancroft, who, when he turned to history, had no difficulty in seeing the Revolution as the divinely inspired completion of the democratic cause in America. Bancroft's *History of the United States from the Discovery of the American Continent* ran eventually to ten volumes, appearing in Boston between 1836 and 1874; he later revised it. Notwithstanding its democratic theme, the story is told largely in conventional terms and is concerned more with leadership, great men, and great themes than with the condition of the common people.

Differences of opinion about purpose and policy soon appeared as reasons for writing history as one believed posterity ought to review it; in this spirit, John Marshall wrote his five-volume *Life of George Washington* (London, 1804–1807; revised in many editions) with a pronounced Federalist bias. Not all contemporaries saw so much to celebrate. Thomas Hutchinson, chief justice, lieutenant governor, and governor of Massachusetts, who ended his life in English exile, wrote his three-volume *History of the Colony and Province of Massachusetts Bay* (Boston, 1764 and 1828; London, 1765; new ed., Cambridge, 1936) as a vindication of both his own and the crown's government and as an explanation of their overthrow—caused by the machinations of a small band of determined revolutionaries that was manipulating dangerous mobs. Not, however, until the mid-nineteenth century did the United States produce in Richard Hildreth a historian of substantial quality whose disenchantment with the Revolution was impersonal. Hildreth's *History of the United States* (6 vols., 1849–1856; revised several times) is the first important work written with skepticism about the motives of the Founding Fathers. Hildreth, however, made little impression on his contemporaries and has never been widely read.

Social changes in the later nineteenth century caused a malaise among some gentlemen of conservative temperament that reflected the way in which they looked at the past. Their attitude helped to inspire studies that were no longer unsympathetic to the Loyalists, who seemed until then to have suffered one of history's most complete eclipses. Among these studies are A. E. Ryerson's *The*

Loyalists of America and their Times from 1620 to 1816 (2 vols., Toronto, 1880) and C. H. Van Tyne's *The Loyalists in the American Revolution* (New York, 1902). Later Loyalist studies include Lewis Einstein's *Divided Loyalties* (Boston and New York, 1933), Wilbur H. Siebert's *The Flight of the American Loyalists to the British Isles* (Columbus, 1911), William H. Nelson's *The American Tory* (Oxford, 1961), and Wallace Brown's *The King's Friends: the Composition and Motives of the American Loyalist Claimants* (Providence, 1965).

Early in the twentieth century, the English historian Sir George Otto Trevelyan revived the Whig tradition with a finely written, three-volume work, *The American Revolution* (London, 1899–1907). At about the same time, Moses Coit Tyler dug up numerous forgotten writers and thus made an advance toward a more popular approach to the period; his work, *The Literary History of the American Revolution, 1763–1783* (2 vols., New York, 1897), in which leadership figures less prominently, stimulated interest in the contribution of the common man, whom American historians had rather depreciated in spite of their democratic avowals. The same years gave rise to somewhat divergent views of the American Revolution and its social consequences. George Louis Beer looked with unaccustomed sympathy at the British connection, and in two influential works, *The Commercial Policy of England toward the American Colonies* (New York, 1893) and *British Colonial Policy* (New York, 1907), he began a trend toward a more detached, analytical view of the economics of the empire and the motives of the Americans. Henry Cabot Lodge's *Alexander Hamilton* (Boston and New York, 1882) was written to rescue Hamilton's then diminished reputation in the cause of honoring the forces of industrial growth and social conservatism.

The same method, however, could serve different social purposes, and the Progressive movement yielded, in its intellectual manifestations, a more significant stream of historical revision. There is no simple explanation of the impulses behind American historical thought in this period. A sense of social crisis seems to have arisen from the awareness that no more free land was to be had in the West; this knowledge was the immediate stimulus to the most influential of all single-track interpretations of American history, Frederick Jackson Turner's *The Frontier in American History* (New York, 1920), which first appeared as a paper in 1893. Since Turner attributed American democracy to the frontier, he did not leave much room for the Revolution, except in the secondary sense of opening more frontiers. He and his disciples examined the processes of settlement and local government in different sections and territories. By the time of Turner's death in 1932, his theory was beginning to come under attack—vulnerable because it ignored the history of institutions, failed to take account of class conflicts and other interest clashes, and did not clearly or consistently define the frontier itself. The most interesting attempt to retrieve something from Turner's ideas has been that of Stanley Elkins and Eric McKitrick, whose long essay "A Meaning for Turner's Frontier: I. Democracy and the Old Northwest; II. The Southwest Frontier and New England" appeared in the *Political Science Quarterly* 69 (September and December 1954).

The retrospective social conscience of the Progressives turned them to a new and instrumental attitude: the social uses of history. The rise of corporate business, combined with the closing of the frontier, prompted fears that the era of opportunity had come to an end. Social and economic anxieties were in the air and lent greater urgency to questions asked by social and economic history. This "New History," as it called itself, had been spurred by similar developments in Europe. Its most spectacular product was Charles A. Beard's *An Economic Interpretation of the Constitution of the United States* (New York, 1913), which rather crudely analyzes the economic interests of the delegates to the Constitutional Convention and strongly implies that they were actuated by private motives. Beard dissolved the aura of sanctity that had protected the founders of the Constitution from intrusive questions, and helped to institute a realistic interest in the economic aspects of American life. He followed with *The Economic Origins of Jeffersonian Democracy* (New York, 1915), which takes a significant step toward the analysis of social structure as an object of research. Soon afterward Arthur M. Schlesinger, in *Colonial Merchants and the American Revolution, 1763–1776* (New York, 1918), developed a case for viewing economic interests as prime movers in revolutionary politics; in the same spirit was Charles M. Andrews'

The Boston Merchants and the Non-Importation Movement (Cambridge, 1917). A few years earlier, Carl L. Becker had argued persuasively that revolutionary politics were influenced by domestic conflict; his important monograph *A History of Political Parties in the Province of New York, 1760–1776* (Madison, 1909) has been touched up but never superseded. Later, Becker wrote a subtle textual and literary analysis of *The Declaration of Independence: A Study in the History of Political Ideas* (New York, 1922), placing the document in its context of natural-rights philosophy. Less directly under Progressive influence, T. P. Abernethy embarked on studies of early Southwestern settlement and politics; his skeptical findings about the traditional claims for the "democracy" of the West make an interesting comparison with Beard's skepticism about the disinterestedness of the founders. Abernethy's contributions, *From Frontier to Plantation in Tennessee* (Chapel Hill, 1932), *Three Virginia Frontiers* (Baton Rouge, 1940), and *Western Lands and the American Revolution* (New York, 1937), all showed how greatly the course of revolutionary politics and settlement was dominated by big speculators and powerful leaders.

The Progressive inspiration was present in one massive enterprise in literary history, Vernon Louis Parrington's *Main Currents in American Thought: An Interpretation of American Literature from the Beginning to 1920* (3 vols., New York, 1927–1930), of which the first two volumes deal with our period. Parrington was disposed to resolve complexities into a series of repeated encounters between the forces of progress (democracy) and reaction (social conservatism, economic privilege), but he wrote well and with extensive learning. The deepening interest in ordinary life and ordinary people that characterized the writing of this "New History" led to the publication of the twelve-volume series *History of American Life* (New York, 1927–1948), edited by Schlesinger and Dixon Ryan Fox. Fox had earlier written an elegant monograph, *The Decline of Aristocracy in the Politics of New York* (New York, 1919). In the new series, the volume appropriate to our period was written by John A. Krout and Fox, *The Completion of Independence* (New York, 1944). Concepts of sharp internal conflict are at work in attempts to explain the movement for independence in Pennsylvania in J. Paul Selsam's *The Pennsylvania*

Constitution of 1776: A Study in Revolutionary Democracy (Phila-delphia, 1936) and Robert L. Brunhouse's *Counter-Revolution in Pennsylvania, 1776–1790* (Harrisburg, 1942). David Hawke's *In the Midst of a Revolution* (Philadelphia, 1961) clarifies the part played by domestic radicalism in the general crisis as it affected Pennsylvania.

Meanwhile, two historians—Edward Channing and Samuel Eliot Morison—stood aside from the more obvious pressures of social change and produced a large body of independent work. Channing's *History of the United States* (6 vols., New York, 1905–1925) describes many aspects of life. Morison, who, by the range, bulk, and scholarship of his vast corpus of work, has some claim to be considered the master of early American history, began by editing *The Life and Letters of Harrison Gray Otis, Federalist, 1765–1848* (2 vols., Boston and New York, 1913), now revised as *Harrison Gray Otis, 1765–1848, the Urbane Federalist* (Boston, 1969). Morison contributed to the social, religious, economic, and educational history of early America, with special reference to New England, in *The Maritime History of Massachusetts, 1783–1860* (Boston and New York, 1921) and in his official history, *Three Centuries of Harvard* (Cambridge, 1936). John Franklin Jame-son, a founder of the American Historical Association and of its *Review,* in *The American Revolution Considered as a Social Move-ment* (Princeton, 1926) discussed many of the internal conse-quences of the struggle for independence and reopened the question of the "revolutionary" character of the Revolution. This problem of ambivalence in the Revolution has also been discussed by R. R. Palmer in the first volume, *The Challenge,* of his *Age of the Demo-cratic Revolution* (2 vols., Princeton, 1959–1964).

Marxists taught, and the "New History" school agreed, that politics usually reflects economic interests; the Progressive interpre-tation of the past had a tendency to assume that if class distinction was invisible, it must have been present, though submerged, be-cause it eventually surfaced as class conflict. These assumptions implied the necessity for careful research into the social and eco-nomic structure of local areas such as states, cities, and towns—research which members of that generation, for the most part, did not undertake. Their point of view, which was suspicious of the businessmen to whom they attributed much of the responsibility for the Constitution, was sympathetic to the Articles of Confederation, as embodying the basic aims of the Declaration of Independence. The most important studies reflecting these views have been those of Merrill Jensen, in *The Articles of Confederation: An Interpretation of the Social-Constitutional History of the American Revolution, 1774–1781* (Madison, 1940) and in *The New Nation* (New York, 1953). It may here be added that Jensen's *The Founding of a Nation: A History of the American Revolution, 1763–1776* (New York, 1968) is a mature and rounded study of the events leading to the Revolution in both England and America. In principle, the Whiggism of the American patriots could be held to lead either to more consolidated government or to loose confederation. John C. Miller's *Origins of the American Revolution* (Boston, 1943; rev. ed., Stanford, 1967) is a thoroughly researched account of the development of American opposition and its political principles. An important study, whose implications are broader than its title at first suggests, is E. James Ferguson's *The Power of the Purse, a History of American Public Finance, 1776–1790* (Chapel Hill, 1961), a clear and significant appraisal of the connections between public finance and politics through state and continental government.

One important consequence of problems raised by the previous generation's interest in economic conflict was that a much closer look at state and local history was in order. Some of the most valuable work of the past twenty or more years has resulted from the proposition that only local history could yield fundamental information. Thus Robert E. Brown's *Middle Class Democracy and the American Revolution in Massachusetts, 1691–1780* (Ithaca, 1955), followed by his and B. Katherine Brown's *Virginia, 1705–1766: Aristocracy or Democracy?* (East Lansing, 1964) are the resuts of prolonged attention to tax rolls, town and country records, voting statistics, and other sources of local history; the books also represent a strong commitment to the view that colonial American society satisfied the criteria of "democracy." This stand was questioned by J. R. Pole in an article, "Historians and the Problem of Early American Democracy," *American Historical Review* (April 1962), wherein the "democratic" aspects of American life are set in the framework of a "deferential" society. The conceptual problems raised by the Browns' devotion to a single thesis were ably discussed by Richard Buel, Jr., in "Democracy and the American Revolution: a Frame of Reference," *William and Mary Quarterly* (April 1964). Before the Browns' work appeared, Leonard W. Labaree's *Conservatism in Early American History* (New York, 1948) had capably focused attention on the complexity and staying power of the forces making for stability and privilege in late colonial America. Another work that by its subject matter tends to dwell on social order is the continuation of *Sibley's Harvard Graduates*, edited by Clifford K. Shipton (Cambridge, 1873—in continuation); these biographies are still a mine of information.

The value of local studies has been demonstrated in such works as Benjamin W. Labaree's *Patriots and Partisans: The Merchants of Newburyport, 1764–1815* (Cambridge, 1962) and Charles S. Grant's *Democracy in the Connecticut Frontier Town of Kent* (New York, 1961). Manning J. Dauer's *The Adams Federalists* (Baltimore, 1953) is based on much research into social and economic structures, and follows and sustains the basic assumptions of Beard. The work of Harry B. Yoshpe in *The Disposition of Loyalist Estates in the Southern District of the State of New York* (New York, 1939) provides important information about the social consequences of independence, and has yet to be followed up in other states.

Refinements in research methods and the availability of increased resources of documents, such as those on suffrage, have in themselves influenced the definitions of problems. A. E. McKinley's *The Suffrage Franchise in the Thirteen English Colonies in America* (Philadelphia, 1905) remains a useful survey of the election laws, but assumes that laws were translated into facts. Chilton Williamson's *American Suffrage: From Property to Democracy, 1760–1860* (Princeton, 1960) deals realistically with the history of voting and the relation of suffrage to politics and society. Fletcher M. Green, *Constitutional Development in the South Atlantic States, 1776–1860: A Study in the Evolution of Democracy* (Chapel Hill, 1930) is still a useful guide to the nominal advance of democracy. But more detailed work in social structure and its political implications has thrown these developments into clearer relief. In this connection, see, for the earlier period, Jackson Turner Main's *The Social Structure of Revolutionary America* (Princeton, 1965); his "Government by the People: The American Revolution and the Democratization of the Legislatures," *William and Mary Quarterly* (July 1966); and his *Upper House in Revolutionary America, 1763–1788* (Madison, 1967). These works reveal tremendous amounts of relevant information; they suggest the sort of research that must precede another wave of general formulations. Similarly, for the colonial period, Jack P. Greene's *The Quest for Power: The Lower Houses of Assembly in the Southern Royal Colonies, 1689–1766* (Chapel Hill, 1963) draws its strength from research in legislative records, demonstrating both the rise of the assembly and the internal organization that made the assemblies competent agencies of self-government. Statistical methods have usefully contributed to New England history in Michael Zuckerman's *Peaceable Kingdoms: New England Towns in the Eighteenth Century* (New York, 1970) and Robert M. Zemsky's *Merchants, Farmers and River Gods* (New York, 1971).

Urban history has become a recognized "field," a development pioneered by Carl Bridenbaugh. His and Jessica Bridenbaugh's *Rebels and Gentlemen: Philadelphia in the Age of Franklin* (New York, 1942) and *Cities in Revolt: Urban Life in America, 1743–1776* (New York, 1955, reprint 1968) show the texture of the growing town populations and the distinctiveness of their problems compared with those of the country. Richard C. Wade's *The Urban Frontier: The Rise of Western Cities, 1790–1830* (Cambridge, 1959) explains the role of the city in western development. A brilliant combination of the urban and the political, of great importance for the study of federal government, is James S. Young's *The Washington Community 1800–1828* (New York, 1966).

The fashion set by Beard continued to dominate the analysis of the making of the Constitution, down to Forrest McDonald's *We the People: The Economic Origins of the Constitution* (Chicago, 1958), a critique also based on exhaustive, person-by-person research; in *E Pluribus Unum: The Formation of the American Republic, 1776–1790* (Boston, 1965), he attempted a general interpretation, relying substantially on material interests and private

deals rather than on professed beliefs and public debates. Robert
E. Brown's *Charles Beard and the Constitution: A Critical Analysis
of "An Economic Interpretation of the Constitution"* (Princeton,
1956) is a relentless attack on Beard's historical and logical
methods. Opponents of the Constitution have also been subjected
to analysis in both their ideologies and their social origins. The
most penetrating critique is Cecelia M. Kenyon's essay "Men of
Little Faith: The Anti-Federalists on the Nature of Representative
Government," *William and Mary Quarterly* (January 1955); see
also her edited collection of tracts, with its long introductory essay,
The Antifederalists (Indianapolis, 1966). Jackson T. Main's *The
Antifederalists: Critics of the Constitution, 1781–1788* (Chapel
Hill, 1961) draws distinctions between amounts of wealth and the
economic interests of different regions, thus deepening the older
kind of economic analysis, but not satisfying McDonald, whose
"The Anti-Federalists, 1781–1789," *Wisconsin Magazine of His-
tory* (Spring 1963), emphasizes the hyphen (because there was no
single philosophy); it is reprinted in Jack P. Greene, ed., *The
Reinterpretation of the American Revolution 1763–1789* (New
York, 1968). A skeptical view of the making of the Constitution
appears in W. W. Crosskey, *Politics and the Constitution in the
History of the United States* (Chicago, 1953).

Parallel with the greater attention given to social structure and
the distribution of wealth, a new interest in ideology has marked a
swing away from the Beardian preoccupation with the clash of
economic interests. Much of its impetus has been provided by
Bernard Bailyn, first with his edition, *Pamphlets of the American
Revolution, 1750–1776* (Cambridge, 1965), the introduction to
which appeared in revised form as *The Ideological Origins of the
American Revolution* (Cambridge, 1967). The view that ideas
make—indeed, that they *are*—events, sustains Gordon S. Wood's
spacious interpretation, *The Creation of the American Republic,
1776–1787* (Chapel Hill, 1969). The connections between ideology and institutions, and their relationship to the central problems of political authority, are explored in a comparative study,
J. R. Pole's *Political Representation in England and the Origins of
the American Republic* (London and New York, 1966), which

explains the development of the principle of majority rule. At an earlier date, however, Louis Hartz's *The Liberal Tradition in America: An Interpretation of American Political Thought Since the Revolution* (New York, 1955) argued that the controlling conditions in the development of American democracy were a basic "liberal" thrust meeting an absence of resistance from any feudal aristocracy; later, in *The Founding of New Societies: Studies in the History of the United States, Latin America, South Africa, Canada, and Australia* (New York, 1964), Hartz developed the thesis that colonial institutions were derived from "fragments" of their parent societies. These views represent an extreme departure from those of the Turner school. A skillful interpretation giving prominence to ideological assumptions is Yehoshua Arieli's *Individualism and Nationalism in American Ideology* (Cambridge, 1964).

American political ideas could never be completely separated from their religious antecedents, as shown by Edmund S. Morgan in "The Puritan Ethic and the Coming of the American Revolution," *William and Mary Quarterly* (January 1967). Perry Miller's works, notably *The New England Mind: From Colony to Province* (Cambridge, 1953), have inspired much thinking about the Puritan legacy, and influenced Alan Heimert's *Religion and the American Mind, from the Great Awakening to the Revolution* (Cambridge, 1966), which discusses the political implications of extreme religious dissent; Heimert's argument is somewhat to the left of Carl Bridenbaugh's *Mitre and Sceptre: Transatlantic Faiths, Ideas, Personalities, and Politics, 1689–1775* (New York, 1962), which points out the political relationships between American anti-Episcopalianism and the English Dissenters. The social as well as the theological background to religious development has always claimed the attention of historians of religion, whose themes have often affected a larger proportion of the feelings of the American people than the politics that gains so much more consideration. See, for example, Alice M. Baldwin, *The New England Clergy and the American Revolution* (Durham, 1928); Herbert M. Morais, *Deism in Eighteenth Century America* (New York, 1934); W. W. Sweet, *Religion in the Development of American Culture, 1765–*

1860 (New York, 1952); Wade C. Barclay, *History of Methodist Missions,* which is the first volume of *Early American Methodism, 1769–1844* (2 vols., New York, 1949).

Political historians have been tempted to divide early national history by its obvious periods, which means that the era of the Revolution is followed by that of the Constitution, leading in turn to the Federalist era; the election of Jefferson opens yet another phase, one that is ended by the War of 1812. It has often been assumed that the rise of the "common man" to political prominence belonged to the Jacksonian era. But the kind of political history that investigates local sources has been finding the common man at earlier dates. This discovery was not made, however, by the first great historian of the Jeffersonian period, Henry Adams, whose *History of the United States during the Administrations of Thomas Jefferson and James Madison* (9 vols., New York, 1889–1891) is largely concerned with high policy; it also contains a sensitive sketch of the country in 1800. More recent works, however, have explored the local sources of national parties as well as their central organization. John C. Miller's *The Federalist Era, 1789–1801* (New York, 1960) is a general work. Noble E. Cunningham's *The Jeffersonian Republicans: The Formation of Party Organization, 1789–1801* (Chapel Hill, 1957) and his *The Jeffersonian Republicans in Power: Party Operations, 1801–1809* (Chapel Hill, 1963) stress the central organization as the originating force; Alfred F. Young's *The Democratic Republicans of New York: The Origins, 1763–1797* (Chapel Hill, 1967) is a detailed study of the relationship between party power and social structure that successfully breaks with conventional periodization. Richard P. McCormick's *Experiment in Independence: New Jersey in the Critical Period, 1781–1789* (New Brunswick, 1950) is perhaps the best example of a state history; and his *History of Voting in New Jersey: A Study of the Development of Election Machinery, 1664–1911* (New Brunswick, 1953) is a model of what such studies should be. A compact synthesis and interpretation of early parties is William N. Chambers' *Political Parties in a New Nation, 1776–1809* (New York, 1963). Richard Hofstadter's *The Idea of a Party System: The Rise of Legitimate Opposition in the United States, 1740–1840* (Berkeley and Los Angeles, 1969) combines historical survey with subtle reflections on the nature of the problem. Paul Goodman's *The Democratic Republicans of Massachusetts: Politics in a Young Republic* (Cambridge, 1964); David Hackett Fischer, *The Revolution of American Conservatism: The Federalist Party in the Era of Jeffersonian Democracy* (New York, 1965); and James M. Banner, *To the Hartford Convention: The Federalists and the Origins of Party Politics in Massachusetts, 1789–1815* (New York, 1969) do much to illuminate the history of Jeffersonianism and Federalism in Massachusetts.

American diplomacy was closely tied to domestic issues in the early years. See in particular Samuel Flagg Bemis, *The Diplomacy of the American Revolution* (New York and London, 1935); Alexander DeConde, *Entangling Alliance: Politics and Diplomacy under George Washington* (Durham, 1958); Bradford Perkins, *Prologue to War: England and the United States, 1805–1812* (Berkeley and Los Angeles, 1961); Reginald Horsman, *The Causes of the War of 1812* (Philadelphia, 1962). An interpretation of the American national interest in the War of 1812 has been offered by Roger H. Brown in *The Republic in Peril: 1812* (New York, 1964). Important studies in central administration, linking it with political attitudes, have been written by Leonard D. White: *The Federalists* (New York, 1948) and *The Jeffersonians: A Study in Administrative History* (New York, 1956).

Two significant analyses of public economic policy in specific states have done much to undermine the idea that Americans of the early period believed in an ungoverned, "free enterprise" economy. Louis Hartz's *Economic Policy and Democratic Thought: Pennsylvania, 1776–1860* (Cambridge, 1948) and Oscar and Mary F. Handlin's *Commonwealth: A Study of the Role of Government in the American Economy: Massachusetts, 1774–1861* (New York, 1947) have influenced subsequent thinking about the role of the state in early economic life. The writing of economic history has been less influenced by conventional periodization than that of political history. Much information is in Victor S. Clark's *History of Manufactures in the United States, 1607–1860* (2 vols., New York, 1916–1928) and in Lewis C. Gray's *History of Agriculture in the Southern United States to 1860* (Washington, 1933); consult also Percy W. Bidwell and John I. Falconer, *History of*

Agriculture in the Northern United States, 1620–1860 (Washington, 1925). Valuable studies of great business houses are: Ralph W. Hidy, *The House of Baring in Anglo-American Trade and Finance: English Merchant Bankers at Work, 1763–1861* (Cambridge, 1949); W. T. Baxter, *The House of Hancock: Business in Boston, 1724–1775* (Cambridge, 1945); James B. Hedges, *The Browns of Providence Plantations* (Cambridge, 1952). Business and continental politics have been explored by Robert A. East in *Business Enterprise in the American Revolutionary Era* (New York, 1938) and in his "The Massachusetts Conservatives in the Critical Period" in Richard B. Morris, ed., *The Era of the American Revolution* (New York, 1939; reprint 1965). Oscar and Mary F. Handlin's "Revolutionary Economic Policy in Massachusetts," *William and Mary Quarterly* (January 1947), is also pertinent. Curtis P. Nettels's *The Emergence of a National Economy, 1775–1815* (New York, 1962) synthesizes a vast literature and has a copious bibliography. Special studies of value are: Clarence L. Ver Steeg, *Robert Morris, Revolutionary Financier* (Philadelphia, 1954); Jeannette Mirsky and Allan Nevins, *The World of Eli Whitney* (New York, 1952); Constance McL. Green, *Eli Whitney and the Birth of American Technology* (Boston, 1956); and Louis C. Hunter, *Steamboats on the Western Rivers: An Economic and Technological History* (Cambridge, 1949). The second volume of Joseph Dorfman's *The Economic Mind in American Civilization* (5 vols., New York, 1946–1959) reviews economic thought in this period.

Demographic studies in America begin with the fundamental fact of immigration, for which the basic work remains Marcus Lee Hansen's *The Atlantic Migration, 1607–1860: A History of the Continuous Settlement of the United States* (Cambridge, 1940). Probably the most important recent contributions have been those of J. Potter in "The Growth of Population in America, 1760–1860" in D. V. Glass and D. E. C. Eversley, eds., *Population in History: Essays in Historical Demography* (London, 1965); and Potter's "American Population in the Early National Period" in Paul Deprez, ed., *Population and Economics* (Winnipeg, 1970). Generally, social and geographical studies have included demographic information rather than specialized in it. See Ralph H.

Brown, *Historical Geography of the United States* (New York, 1948); Robert E. Riegel, *America Moves West* (3d ed., New York, 1956); Ray A. Billington, *Westward Expansion: A History of the American Frontier* (New York, 1949); and Louis B. Wright, *Culture on the Moving Frontier* (Bloomington, 1955), which emphasizes the continuity of British influences. The unsettled conditions of the frontier and the dangers they posed for national security have been well depicted in Dale Van Every's *Ark of Empire: The American Frontier 1784–1803* (New York, 1963).

American thought, political and social, helped to create the new nation, and was itself influenced by new problems. The recently revived interest in political ideology does not supersede certain broader studies, mostly a little earlier in date, which include: Merle Curti, *The Growth of American Thought* (New York and London, 1943); Harvey Wish, *Society and Thought in America* (New York, 1950–1952); Clinton Rossiter, *Seedtime of the Republic* (New York, 1953); Daniel J. Boorstin, *The Lost World of Thomas Jefferson* (New York, 1948); and Adrienne Koch, *The Philosophy of Thomas Jefferson* (New York, 1943). Intellectual activity receives less than its due in the highly informative and absorbing works of Daniel J. Boorstin, *The Americans: The Colonial Experience* (New York, 1958) and *The Americans: The National Experience* (New York, 1965).

Slavery and racial problems have lately begun to receive attention as being central rather than peripheral to American life. The most important books are Winthrop D. Jordan's *White Over Black: American Attitudes toward the Negro, 1550–1812* (Chapel Hill, 1968) and David Brion Davis's *The Problem of Slavery in Western Culture* (Ithaca, 1966), which surveys the early American antislavery movement. Negro activity is described in Benjamin Quarles's *The Negro in the American Revolution* (Chapel Hill, 1961). The role of slavery has been reopened by Staughton Lynd in *Class Conflict, Slavery, and the United States Constitution: Ten Essays* (Indianapolis, 1967). Work must still be done on the differences in types of slavery and on race relations in various regions.

Cultural developments have been treated in depth by Boorstin (see above), by Bridenbaugh in his books on the cities (above) and in his *Peter Harrison: First American Architect* (Chapel Hill, 1949), and by Wright (above). See also James T. Flexner, *The Light of Distant Skies, 1760–1835* (New York, 1954), which reveals the influence of Europe on early American painting; Harry R. Warfel, *Noah Webster, Schoolmaster to America* (New York, 1936); Virgil Barker, *American Painting, History and Interpretation* (New York, 1950); and Samuel Isham, *The History of American Painting* (New York, 1905; rev. ed., 1927). A great deal about the life of the nation and its sections can be gathered from numerous biographies of individuals, most of whom are primarily remembered for political careers. Only a few can be mentioned in this space: Douglas Southall Freeman's seven-volume *George Washington: A Biography* (New York, 1948–1957); Dumas Malone's imposing series on *Jefferson and His Time* (3 vols., Boston, 1948–1962) and his *Thomas Jefferson as Political Leader* (Berkeley and Los Angeles, 1963); and Nathan Schachner's *Thomas Jefferson; A Biography* (2 vols., New York, 1951; reissued as 1 vol., 1957), which endures as a perceptive and compact work. There are many studies of Alexander Hamilton, among the best being those of Broadus Mitchell: *Alexander Hamilton* (2 vols., New York, 1957–1962) and *Alexander Hamilton: The Revolutionary Years* (New York, 1970). Irving Brant has done much to establish James Madison's place in the politics of his times in *James Madison* (6 vols., New York, 1941–1961). John Adams has received much attention both as political thinker and politician; Page Smith's *John Adams* (2 vols., Garden City, 1962) will be consulted for many years. Merrill Peterson's massive *Thomas Jefferson and the New Nation: A Biography* (New York, 1970) is not soon likely to be superseded. Publication of the papers of some of these statesmen has also provided scholars with a rich and continuing source of detailed information.

Law and the Constitution are closely related to the fabric of society. Julius Goebel and T. Raymond Naughton's *Law Enforcement in Colonial New York: A Study in Criminal Procedure (1664–1776)* (New York, 1944) is a model of scholarship that establishes the early place of the common law. Andrew C. McLaughlin's *A Constitutional History of the United States* (New York, 1935) is valuable on the early period, and much material has been unearthed by Charles Warren in a series of works that includes *Congress, the Constitution and the Supreme Court* (Boston, 1925; rev. ed., 1935), *The Making of the Constitution* (Boston, 1928), and *The Supreme Court in United States History* (3 vols., Boston, 1922–1923; rev. ed., 2 vols., Boston, 1937). See also Carl B. Swisher's *The Growth of Constitutional Power in the United States* (Chicago, 1946) and Charles Grove Haines's *The Role of the Supreme Court in American Government and Politics 1789–1835* (Berkeley and Los Angeles, 1944).

The refinement of certain recent techniques of quantification and simulation should open the possibility for more advanced studies in economic history, which has tended to be left too much to specialists, and in demographic studies, which are belatedly gaining popularity in the United States. The nature and relationships of the various communities of America, their reaction to stress and change, and the connected problems of racial and religious perceptions need much more thought and research than they have received. The interest in the sociology of the past, which has been gaining momentum, will continue to pose new questions for the historian and also for the social scientist. The careful and continued exploration of these problems could eventually bring about a map of the earlier period that might largely supersede our present conception of that society.

Index